Lecture Notes in Computer Science 9312

Commenced Publication in 1973
Founding and Former Series Editors:
Gerhard Goos, Juris Hartmanis, and Jan van Leeuwen

More information about this series at http://www.springer.com/series/7408

Achim Ebert · Shah Rukh Humayoun
Norbert Seyff · Anna Perini
Simone D.J. Barbosa (Eds.)

Usability- and Accessibility-Focused Requirements Engineering

First International Workshop, UsARE 2012, Held in Conjunction with
ICSE 2012, Zurich, Switzerland, June 4, 2012 and
Second International Workshop, UsARE 2014, Held in Conjunction with
RE 2014, Karlskrona, Sweden, August 25, 2014
Revised Selected Papers

Springer

Editors

Achim Ebert
University of Kaiserslautern
Kaiserslautern
Germany

Shah Rukh Humayoun
University of Kaiserslautern
Kaiserslautern
Germany

Norbert Seyff
University of Applied Sciences and Arts
  Northwestern Switzerland
Windisch
Switzerland

and

University of Zurich
Zurich
Switzerland

Anna Perini
FBK-CIT
Trento
Italy

Simone D.J. Barbosa
University of Rio de Janeiro
Rio de Janeiro
Brazil

ISSN 0302-9743   ISSN 1611-3349 (electronic)
Lecture Notes in Computer Science
ISBN 978-3-319-45915-8   ISBN 978-3-319-45916-5 (eBook)
DOI 10.1007/978-3-319-45916-5

Library of Congress Control Number: 2016950390

LNCS Sublibrary: SL2 – Programming and Software Engineering

Printed on acid-free paper

This Springer imprint is published by Springer Nature
The registered company is Springer International Publishing AG Switzerland

Preface

This volume is based on two workshops, Usability- and Accessibility-Focused Requirements Engineering (UsARE), which took place in 2012 and 2014. The first event, UsARE 2012, was supported by IEEE and was held on June 4, 2012, in conjunction with the IEEE 34th International Conference on Software Engineering (ICSE 2012) in Zurich, Switzerland. The second event, UsARE 2014, was supported by IEEE and IFIP and was held on August 25, 2014, in conjunction with the 22nd IEEE International Requirements Engineering Conference (RE 2014) in Karlskrona, Sweden.

The UsARE workshops provided a platform for discussions to address the proper integration of system usability and accessibility requirements into the software engineering process. UsARE focused on both Human–Computer Interaction (HCI) and Requirement Engineering (RE). Researchers and practitioners were invited to submit contributions including research papers (technical solutions and empirical studies), practice papers (experience reports and problem statements), tool demonstration papers, case studies, and best practices. Each submission was reviewed by at least three Program Committee (PC) members. For UsARE 2012, we had a total number of seven accepted papers in all categories out of 13 submissions. For UsARE 2014, we had a total number of eight accepted papers (three 8-page long and five 4-page short papers) in all categories out of 13 submissions. We are grateful for the time and effort the PC members and additional reviewers spent in the selection process.

The single UsARE workshop programs were divided into sessions for paper presentations and interactive sessions where participants got the chance to explore and share ideas and experiences about solved and unsolved problems. Our workshops had a total number of 18 participants in 2012 and 22 participants in 2014. All of them actively participated in the joint discussions to bridge the gap between HCI and RE and to go beyond existing work in these fields. Without their active participation, a book like this would not be possible!

Finally, we would also like to thank IEEE, IFIP, Interaction Design Foundation, and the organizers' institutions for supporting the events.

June 2016

Achim Ebert
Shah Rukh Humayoun
Norbert Seyff
Anna Perini
Simone Barbosa

Organization

UsARE 2012

IEEE First International Workshop on Usability and Accessibility Focused Requirements Engineering

Organizing Committee

Tiziana Catarci	Sapienza University of Rome, Italy
Anna Perini	FBK, ICT-irst, Italy
Norbert Seyff	University of Applied Sciences and Arts Northwestern Switzerland, Switzerland
	University of Zurich, Switzerland
Shah Rukh Humayoun	University of Kaiserslautern, Germany
Nauman A. Qureshi	National University of Sciences and Technology (NUST), Pakistan

Program Committee

Margherita Antona	Foundation for Research and Technology - Hellas (FORTH), Greece
Nelly Bancomo	Inria – Paris, France
Yael Dubinsky	IBM Research – Haifa Lab, Israel
Achim Ebert	University of Kaiserslautern, Germany
Silvia Gabrielli	Create-Net, Italy
Ivan Jureta	University of Namur, Belgium
Stephen Kimani	JKUAT, Kenya
Sotirios Liaskos	York University, Canada
Luisa Mich	University of Trento, Italy
Barbara Paech	University of Heidelberg, Germany
Saim Rasheed	King Abdul Aziz University, Saudi Arabia
Giuseppe Santucci	Sapeinza University of Rome, Italy
Pete Sawyer	Lancaster University, UK
Angelo Susi	FBK-IRST, Italy
Giuliana Vitiello	University of Salerno, Italy
Diana Yifan Xu	University of Central Lancashire, UK
Massimo Zancanaro	FBK-IRST, Italy

Additional Reviewer

Alexander Delater	University of Heidelberg, Germany

UsARE 2014

IEEE/IFIP Second International Workshop on Usability and Accessibility Focused Requirements Engineering

Organizing Committee

General Chair

Shah Rukh Humayoun   University of Kaiserslautern, Germany

Program Co-chairs

Norbert Seyff   University of Applied Sciences and Arts Northwestern
                       Switzerland, Switzerland
                       University of Zurich, Switzerland
Nauman A. Qureshi   National University of Sciences and Technology (NUST),
                       Pakistan
Anna Perini   FBK, ICT-irst, Italy
Achim Ebert   University of Kaiserslautern, Germany
David Callele   University of Saskatchewan, Canada
Simone D.J. Barbosa   Pontifical Catholic University of Rio de Janeiro, Brazil

Program Committee

Ragaad AlTarawneh   University of Kaiserslautern, Germany
Margherita Antona   Foundation for Research and Technology - Hellas, Greece
Tayana Conte   UFAM, Brazil
Yael Dubinsky   IBM Research - Haifa, Israel
Silvia Gabrielli   CREATE-NET, Italy
Steffen Hess   Fraunhofer IESE, Germany
Ivan Jureta   University of Namur, Belgium
Stephen Kimani   JKUAT, Kenya
Sotirios Liaskos   York University, Canada
Sabrina Marczak   PUCRS, Brazil
Luisa Mich   University of Trento, Italy
Henry Muccini   University of L'Aquila, Italy
Barbara Paech   University of Heidelberg, Germany
Pete Sawyer   Lancaster University, UK
Angelo Susi   Fondazione Bruno Kessler – IRST, Italy
Giuliana Vitiello   University of Salerno, Italy
Diana Yifan Xu   University of Central Lancashire, UK

Additional Reviewer

Thorsten Merten   University of Heidelberg, Germany

Contents

Applications

Introduction and Overview

Bridging the Gap Between Requirements Engineering and Human-Computer Interaction

Achim Ebert[1(✉)], Shah Rukh Humayoun[1], Norbert Seyff[2,3],
Anna Perini[4], and Simone D.J. Barbosa[5]

[1] Computer Graphics and HCI Group, University of Kaiserslautern, Kaiserslautern, Germany
{ebert,humayoun}@cs.uni-kl.de
[2] University of Applied Sciences and Arts Northwestern Switzerland, Windisch, Switzerland
norbert.seyff@fhnw.ch
[3] University of Zurich, Zurich, Switzerland
[4] Fondazione Bruno Kessler – ICT, Trento, Italy
perini@fbk.eu
[5] Pontifical Catholic University of Rio de Janeiro, Rio de Janeiro, Brazil
simone@inf.puc-rio.br

1 Introduction

This book is intended to discuss important issues concerning Requirements Engineering (RE) and Human-Computer Interaction (HCI), especially the ones related to usability and accessibility. It is dedicated to observations, concepts, approaches, frameworks and practices that promote understanding, facilitating, and increasing the awareness of the role of usability and accessibility requirements and their proper integration into the requirement engineering process. The book is based on the two workshops on Usability- and Accessibility-focused Requirements Engineering (UsARE), which took place in 2012 and 2014. The first event, UsARE 2012 [8], was supported by IEEE and was held on June 04, 2012 in conjunction with the IEEE 34th International Conference on Software Engineering (ICSE 2012) in Zurich, Switzerland. The second event, UsARE 2014 [9], was supported by IEEE and IFIP and was held on August 25, 2014 in conjunction with the 22nd IEEE International Requirements Engineering Conference (RE 2014) in Karlskrona, Sweden. On both occasions, each submission was reviewed by at least three program committee members. This was followed by discussions amongst the organizers which led to a total number of 7 accepted papers for UsARE 2012 and 8 accepted papers for UsARE 2014. On both occasions, the workshop proceedings were published online by the IEEE Xplore Digital Library. The workshop summary and the results of the interactive session of the first event were published as a report in the ACM Software Engineering Notes in the issue of January 2013 [2].

There were 18 participants in UsARE 2012 and 22 participants in UsARE 2014. During the events, the authors presented their work; this was followed by intense discussions, in which participants actively took part. The last session in both events was dedicated to interactive discussions through the *interactive group discussion strategy*.

The idea of publishing the book with extended versions of the papers was born during the second event. All participants agreed that the topics definitely deserved to be

A. Ebert et al. (Eds.): UsARE 2012/2014, LNCS 9312, pp. 3–7, 2016.
DOI: 10.1007/978-3-319-45916-5_1

explored further in order to give the related research communities in-depth outcomes of the research as workshop papers' lengths (4 pages for short and 7 pages for long) were not enough to present the ideas in much depth. We hope that the heavily extended papers in this book will help the readers to get a better insight on the research done by the participants of the two UsARE workshops.

2   Goals and Issues

High-level usability is acknowledged as a significant quality attribute of software products, while poor usability and inefficient design of the end product are common causes for failed software products [1, 6, 7]. Usability is defined by the International Organization for Standardization (ISO) as *"the extent to which the product can be used by specified users to achieve specified goals with effectiveness, efficiency, and satisfaction in a specified context of use"* [4]. The ISO/IEC Guidelines 71 define accessible design as *"design focused on principles of extending standard design to people with some type of performance limitation to maximize the number of potential customers who can readily use a product, building or service"* [5].

During the requirements analysis phase, software development teams may mainly focus on functional requirements. They may ignore system usability and accessibility concerns (such as effectivity, satisfaction, utility, learnability, memorability and visibility) due to multiple reasons, e.g., limited budget and resources. An early analysis of usability and accessibility requirements can guide the analysis at design-time; this results in a specification that provides more effective criteria to evaluate the software-to-be. Including system usability and accessibility requirements only at later development stages can be very costly [10]. Moreover, ignoring them in early stages could lead to delays in product development and deployment and can enhance the risks of project and software failure [3].

The focus of system usability and accessibility requirements is to ensure that the system is in compliance with the intended properties, which allows the users to use the system more efficiently and effectively in order to achieve their desired goals. Although requirements engineering has started to cope with system usability and accessibility issues along with other non-functional requirements, its efforts are still timid and systems often do not provide good usability and accessibility features. Therefore, it is important to properly integrate the system usability and accessibility requirements into the requirements engineering process and then to maintain them along other system requirements throughout the product lifecycle. This was the reason behind providing a suitable venue for discussions, which focused particularly on the integrated process and its effects on software development.

Overall, this book and the workshops previously held aim at creating awareness of the research and software development communities to focus a bit more on the following questions:

- How to incorporate system usability and accessibility requirements at early stages of RE;
- How to involve end users in the requirement phases in order to understand the usability and accessibility requirements more properly;

- How to maintain the system usability and accessibility requirements throughout the development alongside other system requirements;
- How to manage and control requirements changes by assessing system usability and accessibility at run-time;
- How usability can improve dynamic elicitation of requirements from the end-users; and
- How requirements for accessibility and usability can be analyzed and managed in case of self-adaptive systems.

3   The Articles in This Book

This book consists of 10 chapters of which 9 are extended versions of the papers presented at the two UsARE events. Amongst them, 3 are extended versions of the papers presented at UsARE 2012 and 6 are extended versions of papers presented at UsARE 2014. There is one new chapter that was not presented at any of the previous events; however, it is added as authors are doing relevant work on the same topic. Each chapter was reviewed by at least 2 reviewers and an editor; to finalize the chapter, this was followed by a discussion between the editors. The chapters are organized into three sections according to their main focus: *usability and user experience*, *accessibility* and *applications*.

In the first section, four chapters provide methods and approaches regarding usability and user experience focused requirements engineering. First, Sutcliffe provides a method for analyzing emotion and motivation in requirements engineering using theories from psychology of emotion and motivation. Further, he describes the usage of agent technology in storyboards and scenario analysis and explains it with case studies from the health informatics. Then, Cindy et al. focus on personas as a tool for defining users' attributes and later as a document to be used throughout the entire development process. Drawing from their observations of five projects where personas were used, they highlight the opportunities and challenges that we could face while integrating personas within different activities of requirements engineering. After that, Kropp and Koischwitz introduce the role of On-site User Experience Consultant (osUX consultant) to support user-centered design integration with agile requirements engineering for fixed-price software development projects. Further, they highlight methods and practices of osUX consultancy to appropriately fit it into different agile RE process phases in order to avoid any conflict with other participating roles in the process. In the last part of this section, Xu and Read try to fill the gap between the human-computer interaction and requirements engineering within the scope of children or young people as the end users. They therefore focus on challenges and issues of gathering requirements from children and young people and suggest to treat children as research partners in this process.

The second section of the book concentrates on issues and their solutions when dealing with accessibility-related requirements engineering. There are three chapters in this section by several scholars from the area of accessibility. First, Ferati et al. provide the results of three workshops conducted with various stakeholders. They found that a one-solution-fits-all model is inadequate for the visually impaired community with respect to providing web experience. Evaluation results of their prototype built with eight adaption techniques indicate better performance with non-WCAG compliant websites compared to compliant ones. Then Belani et al. target media accessibility, information mobilization and consciousness for sensitive user groups. They highlight an augmentative requirements engineering framework, experience-driven from several projects and applications in Croatia, for augmentative and alternative communication services for sensitive user groups. In the last chapter of this section, Ludi targets teaching Mathematics and Science for visually impaired students using an Apple iPad as a tool. He presents strategies and techniques that were used for teaching different groups, distributed geographically and representing diverse constituencies. The results were used to model domain knowledge and to specify the target system's requirements.

The last section of the book comprises three chapters that discuss the application of usability- and accessibility-focused requirements engineering in different domains. First, De Silva et al. target users of mobile phones in developing countries. Their case study project was built for farmers in Sri Lanka with the purpose of helping them make more informed decisions. They describe how they combined different theories and methods taken from requirements engineering and human-computer interaction for gathering the requirements in this project. They found a systematic pattern of a combined RE and HCI process. Then Matsuno et al. propose a new conscious eye blink differentiation method taking into account individual differences, which can be used for developing eye blink user interfaces. Results of their evaluation suggest the feasibility of incorporating an automatic differentiation of conscious eye blinks using a conventional video camera. In the last chapter of this section, as well as of the book, Hu et al. describe how they designed a virtual community prototype for chronic diseases healthcare. This is done through getting requirements using questionnaires from healthcare recipients and interviewing healthcare providers. They suggest that using shared community platforms where all the stakeholders can be engaged would help in moderating the interoperability problems in healthcare systems.

Overall, these chapters cover requirements engineering from different perspectives of HCI and provide a comprehensive overview of the area to the readers. We hope you will find this book a useful bridge to fill the gap between RE and HCI. Finally, we are grateful for the time and efforts the authors and reviewers spent shaping this book in its current form. We are also grateful to the PC members, authors, and attendees for their contribution to the successful execution of the past two events.

References

1. Anderson, J., Fleek, F., Garrity, K., Drake, F.: Integrating usability techniques into software development. IEEE Softw. **18**(1), 46–53 (2001)
2. Catarci, T., Perini, A., Seyff, N., Humayoun, S.R., Qureshi, N.A.: First international workshop on usability and accessibility focused requirements engineering (UsARE 2012) summary report. ACM SIGSOFT Softw. Eng. Notes **38**(1), 43–46 (2013)
3. Charette, R.N.: Why software fails. IEEE Spectr. **42**(9), 42–49 (2005). IEEE Press, Piscataway

4. ISO 9241-11: Ergonomic Requirements for Office Work with Visual Display Terminals (vdts). The International Organization for Standardization (1998)

5. ISO/IEC Guide: 71 Guidelines for Standards Developers to Address the Needs of Older Persons and Persons with Disabilities. International Organization for Standardization (ISO) (2001)

6. Landauer, T.K.: The Trouble with Computers: Usefulness, Usability, and Productivity. The MIT Press, Cambridge (1996)

7. Norman, D.: Why doing user observations first is wrong. Interactions **13**, 50 (2006)

8. Proceedings of the IEEE First International Workshop on Usability and Accessibility Focused Requirements Engineering (UsARE 2012), 04 June 2012, IEEE Catalog Number: CFP1203T-ART, ISBN: 978-1-4673-1846-4 (2012)

9. Proceedings of the IEEE 2nd International Workshop on Usability and Accessibility Focused Requirements Engineering, UsARE 2014, 25–25 August 2014, Karlskrona, Sweden, IEEE Catalog Number: CFP1403T-ART ISBN: 978-1-4799-6352-2 (2014)

10. Souza, R.: Design accessible sites now. Forrester Report, December 2001. http://www.forrester.com/ER/Research/Report/Summary/0,1338,11431,00.html

Usability and User Experience

User-Oriented Requirements Engineering

Alistair Sutcliffe[✉]

School of Computing and Communications, University of Lancaster, Bailrigg, Lancaster, UK
sutcliag@lancaster.ac.uk

Abstract. A method for analysing emotion and motivation in requirements engineering (RE) is described. The method extends personal RE where requirements are for individual users and their needs. Theories from the psychology of emotion and motivation are introduced and applied in a top-down pathway motivated by system goals to influence users, and a bottom-up scenario-based path to analyse affective situations which might be produced by user-oriented RE. Use of agent technology in storyboards and scenario analysis of affective situations is described and illustrated with case studies in health informatics for persuasive technology applications.

Keywords: Personal requirements · Emotion · Motivation · Scenarios · Interactive agents · Persuasive technology · Health informatics

1 Introduction

At first sight people's emotions may seem to have little relevance to requirements engineering (RE), since handling emotion, "a strong feeling deriving from one's circumstances, mood, or relationships with others" (OED), involves general inter-personal skills rather than RE methods *per se*. Emotions may be manifest in meetings, negotiations, and inter-personal communication aspects of requirements analysis, where sensitivity to emotional responses of stakeholders may give vital clues about the appropriateness and acceptability of goals and requirements [1]. However, emotions may be implicated in a growing class of applications where goals are personal [2, 3] since they relate to individual people. For example, achieving personal goals may evoke pleasure, while failing to achieve a personal goal may cause pain and frustration. Considering emotion as part of the requirements picture for personal goals enables designers to anticipate human emotional responses and mitigate their downsides, for example by providing sympathetic advice when goals are not achieved or relaxing goals to avoid disappointment.

Many advisory or explanatory systems have a high-level goal to influence human behaviour; for example, marketing in e-commerce aims to persuade people to buy products, while e-health systems may attempt to influence users towards improving their lifestyle. These applications, frequently described as persuasive technology or captology [4], incorporate design features which play on people's emotions. Somewhat surprisingly, people tend to react to even minimal human presence on computers by treating

© IFIP International Federation for Information Processing 2016
Published by Springer International Publishing Switzerland 2016. All Rights Reserved
A. Ebert et al. (Eds.): UsARE 2012/2014, LNCS 9312, pp. 11–33, 2016.
DOI: 10.1007/978-3-319-45916-5_2

the computer representation (i.e. virtual agent, character or even a photograph of a person) as if it were a real person. The CASA (Computer As Social Actor) effect [5] is extremely influential, hence choice of media, characters, and dialogue content can all be manipulated to evoke emotional responses. User interface technology has now progressed to enable development with character-based agents as a standard technology [6]. Embodied Conversational Agents (ECAs) are equipped with a range of features that can be used for emotive effect: facial expressions, gaze, scripted voice, and body posture. Requirements analysis therefore needs to address how people may react to character-based interfaces, to plan for productive influences of human emotion and to anticipate adverse responses. User-Oriented Requirements Engineering (UORE) may also raise ethical issues; for example, failure to anticipate possible human responses to personal or design goals may cause anger and disappointment that ethical statements and plans should avoid.

Further motivation to consider human emotion within the requirements process arises from the rapid growth of social software. Requirements for software tools to create social applications such as e-communities need to consider social emotions, such as empathy in social relationships, and efficacy (social empowerment) in collective action. Design principles for e-community sites [7] draw attention to social emotions of responsibility and encourage a sense of belonging, while inclusive design for e-communities has to encourage active participation so users do not feel annoyed at being left out or that, while they participate, others are free loaders [8].

As more applications become oriented towards entertainment and personal systems, requirements will become increasingly focused on users as individuals rather than on goals for groups of stakeholders. Personal requirements have been addressed in the context of assistive technology [2] and where individuals' behaviour needs to be monitored, so that attainment of personal goals can be assessed. However, analysis of users' affective reaction to requirements and exploration of designs has received little attention in the RE community apart from some consideration in games [9, 10]. This paper proposes a model and process for analysing the role of emotion in interactive, user-centred applications, with requirements directed towards agent-based interfaces and social software. It does not address the more general problem of handling emotion during the requirements process since this perspective concerns inter-personal skills and communication rather than RE *per se*. In the next section, previous literature in RE and related disciplines is reviewed. In Sect. 3, models and theories of motivation and emotion are briefly reviewed, with their relevance to RE. A process of analysing emotional responses by stakeholders and specifying requirements for affective applications in described in Sect. 4, followed by an illustration of the process in case studies of persuasive e-health applications. The paper concludes with a discussion of the prospects for personally oriented RE and affective applications.

2   Related Research

The role of emotion in games applications was analysed by Callele et al. [9, 10] who described a process of scripting with storyboards and scenarios for planning user interaction. Design effects to evoke emotions such as surprise and fear were annotated on to drawings of the game world; however, no particular model of emotion was proposed. Emotions formed a component of a requirements analysis process which addressed stakeholder values in RE [11]; however, in this case emotions were treated from the viewpoint of stakeholder-analyst interaction, with some guidelines for requirements management if emotional responses were detected, e.g. user frustration might indicate disagreement with goals or requirements not representing their views. Furthermore, Thew and Sutcliffe [1] did not consider the role of emotion in personalised applications.

Value-based design [12] elicits user feelings and attitudes to potential systems by presenting cue cards associated with possible emotional responses and user values. Scenarios and storyboarding techniques are used to elicit stakeholder responses, but value-based design does not focus directly on user emotions; instead, it aims to elicit users' attitudes and feelings about products and prototypes as an aid towards refining requirements with human-centred values. Values and affective responses have been investigated by Cockton et al. [13] in worth maps, which attempt to document stakeholders' views about products or prototypes. Worth maps may include emotional responses, but their main focus, similar to value-based design, is to elicit informal descriptions of potential products expressed in stakeholders' language of feelings, values and attitudes. In human-computer interaction, the concept of User Experience (UX) has emerged to describe affective aspects of products [14] and hence what might be regarded as requirements for user acceptance. UX draws attention to aesthetics and enjoyable properties of interactive applications, but no guidelines have been proposed on how to analyse UX or for designing features to deliver an enjoyable user experience.

The role of emotion in user-centred design of products was reviewed by Norman [15], who argued that good design should inspire positive emotional responses from users, such as joy, surprise and pleasure; however, Norman was less forthcoming on how to realise affect-inducing design, beyond reference to the concept of affordances, intuitively understandable user interface features. Techniques for exploring affect in requirements include use of personas, pen portraits of typical users, including their feelings and possibly emotion in their personalities [16]. Personas were developed further into extreme characters [17] as a means of eliciting stakeholders' feelings in response to provocative statements about designs, although neither of these techniques considers the role of emotion explicitly. Requirements for emotion are tacitly included in design of embodied conversational agents [18–21] as scripts for controlling facial expression, posture and gaze of virtual agents. Scripts control expression of emotions by the agent, and may be embedded in an overall plan for conversation with users to influence their mood and emotional responses. However, the ECA literature contains no techniques for eliciting or specifying desired emotional responses.

3   Theories of Emotion and Motivation

The starting point for the analysis is a focus on personal goals, i.e. goals related to an individual's needs. Two areas of psychology are relevant to personal needs: first, motivation theory, which explains deep-seated goals or drives which determine our behaviour; and secondly, emotions, which characterise our automatic reactions to events and situations. The intention is to augment personal goal analysis with knowledge from psychology about goals which are tacit (motivation] and reactions that may arise when goals or motivations are frustrated (emotions). We might anticipate rational reactions when obstacles [22] confront goals; however, not all reactions are rational, hence knowledge of human emotion might be usefully deployed in the RE process. Motivations and emotions will also play a role in amplifying understanding of RE models which include relationships between (human) agents such as trust, responsibility [19], and agent properties including capabilities, skills and preferences [23].

Psychologists distinguish between emotions, which are specific responses, and moods, which reflect more general good or bad feelings. Moods are temporary, whereas emotions are part of our cognitive response and persist as memories of responses to events, objects and people. Emotions may be either positive (pleasure and joy) or negative (fear, disgust) and may have a force, e.g. worry or anxiety is a mild form of fear. There are many theories of emotion; however, three have received more attention in the design of software systems. First, Norman's [15] model divides emotional responses into three layers: the visceral layer which produces psychosomatic responses to fear and anger; a behavioural layer that dictates actions in response to emotion, such as rejecting a product; and finally a reflective layer in which emotional responses are rationalised, e.g. disappointment in a product after a poor user experience. Norman advises that software design should encourage emotions of pleasure, joy and surprise for positive behavioural and reflective responses, but gives little advice on how to achieve such responses in a design. Second, ECA designers have favoured Ekman's [24] theory which characterises a simple set of basic emotions: anger, disgust, fear, sadness and surprise, which are communicated by facial expressions. The third more comprehensive theory is the OCC model [25] which contains a taxonomy of 22 emotions, classified into reactions to events, agents (other people) and objects which may be either positive or negative. A simplified view of the OCC taxonomy is shown in Fig. 1. Reaction to events depends on whether the consequences concern oneself (+ve hope, −ve fear) or others, and then the impact of the event (satisfaction, fears confirmed, relief, disappointment). Responses to objects may either be mild (like or dislike) or stronger (love/hate). Emotional response to agents' actions depends on who the action relates to (self, others, group) and then the perceived effect of the action and whether it was positive, such as pride as a positive response to one's own action, or reproach as a negative reaction to another person's action. Event-related emotions are responses to situations and changes in the environment and are related either to oneself or others in terms of consequences and impact. For example, joy is a positive assessment of an event (e.g. birthday party) relating to oneself with a general impact, and hope is the positive emotion in a specific response to getting a present, which may happen (satisfaction) or not (disappointment). Some emotions such as gratification, remorse, gratitude and anger are complex responses to events and agents/objects. Even though the OCC model is comprehensive it does not account for social emotions such as empathy (+ve reaction to an agent) and belonging (+ve reaction to group membership) [26]. In spite of these limitations, the OCC model is suitable for application to requirements analysis since the event/agent/object taxonomy and decision tree can be applied to analysing emotional reactions. Individual stakeholders may experience emotions in response to events, objects or agents produced by the software system, or which may be a consequence of events and objects in the system environment. Once a range of "emotion inducing" states have been identified, responses to them can be planned as requirements for software agents and their behaviour.

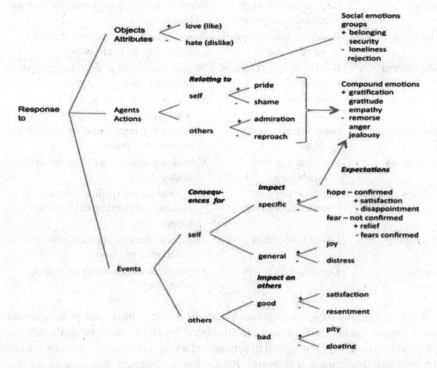

Fig. 1. OCC model decision tree for classifying emotions; augmented with social emotions

3.1 Motivation Analysis

Motivations are related to personality, and can be considered as long-lasting, high-level personal goals [2]. Motivations were classified by Maslow [27] into levels ranging from basic bodily needs such as hunger and thirst, to higher-level needs for security, comfort and safety, and finally socially related motivations of self-esteem and altruism. Table 1 summarises the more important motivations for requirements analysis, synthesised from Maslow's motivation theory [27] and other theories of human needs (e.g. [26]). Motivations are not easy to detect [28] so elicitation guidance from the description in column 2 can only provide hints to guide questions, some of which are suggested by the motivation type itself, i.e. questions about interest in learning, or willingness to help others. Column 3 suggests implications for personal goals and needs for each motivation type;

for example, self-efficacy, curiosity and learning point towards the need for opportunities to experiment which may suggest requirements for customisable or programmable systems.

Table 1. Motivations and their consequences

Motivation	Description	Implications
Safety	Self preservation, avoid injury, discomfort	Avoid danger: safety critical applications; avoid natural and artificial threats to self
Power	Need to control others, authority, command	Work organisation, responsibility, control hierarchy
Possession	Desire for material goods, wealth	Resource control, monetary incentives, ownership, products, wealth
Achievement	Need to design, construct, organise	Project & personal goals, completing tasks, lifestyle targets
Self-esteem	Need to feel satisfied with oneself	Linked personal goals, personal achievement, also perception of self
Peer-esteem	Need to feel valued by others	Inclusion in groups, teams social feedback and rewards, praise
Self-efficacy	Confidence in own capabilities	Confidence building, training, encourage responsibility
Curiosity, learning	Desire to discover, understand world	Opportunities to experiment, time to explore, self tutoring and learning support
Sociability	Desire to be part of a group	Group membership and social relationships, collaboration in work
Altruism	Desire to help others	Opportunities and rewards for helping, selfless act

Safety subsumes basic motivations to satisfy hunger, thirst, and protect oneself. Power, possession and achievement are all related directly to personal goals, although in different ways. Power is manifest in actions and social relationships, and is associated with responsibility, trust and authority. Possession is more personal, concerning goals to own resources, wealth or products. Achievement (or failure) is the end state of most goals, although in motivation theory it spans many personal goals as a lifetime ambition. Self- and peer-esteem concern personal perceptions of self and of self by others, which may indirectly be related to goals if achievement is frustrated, leading to a decline in self-esteem. Motivations of self- and peer-esteem can indicate designing systems to suit individual needs; for instance, in e-commerce, marketing tools can be customised to praise customers [4] and thereby improve their self-esteem (positive wellbeing). An example of fostering peer-esteem is giving thanks and praise for contributions within e-communities [7] and broadcasting such praise to the whole user community.

Self-efficacy is realising one's potential, hence increasing abilities and responsibility. Altruism and sociability are social motivations driving group behaviour, the need to belong to groups and undertake selfless acts, which incidentally increase peer esteem and hence the sense of belonging to the group. People with high sociability motivation will collaborate and cooperate with others in group working. Motivations can be measured by questionnaires; however, in most RE simple question checklists of motivations are sufficient to direct requirements investigation.

4   Applying Emotions and Motivations to RE

Emotions and motivations are used as tools for thought in scenario-based RE for personal RE. Motivational analysis complements goal-based requirements approaches; in contrast, emotions are reactions, and consequently these fit with scenario-based RE [29] as a means of assessing the implications of situations. The UORE process is summarised in Fig. 2.

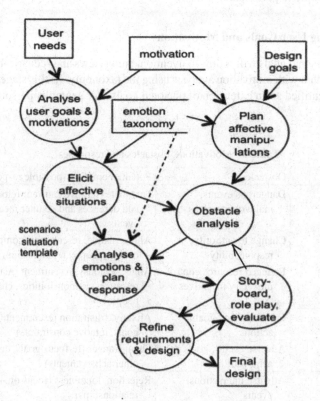

Fig. 2. Summary of the User-Oriented Requirements Engineering (UORE) process

The process follows two related pathways: first, the analysis path starts from users' needs where the motivation component in the UORE method is applied; then, affective situations are considered by identifying scenarios for the user roles and stakeholders who may experience significant emotions, followed by analysis of the situations and events that may lead to emotional experiences. Obstacle analysis contributes by investigating barriers to achieving personal goals, motivations or in problems in achieving the desired emotional reaction. The second planning path has its origins in design goals or high-level system requirements to influence users and their personal goals. System agents and actions are specified in response to anticipated situations. The two pathways interact: the system goals planning pathway suggests situations for follow-up analysis, while affective situations identified in the domain may alter plans and system goals. Analysis of affect may be stimulated by the type of application; for example, games and entertainment applications aim to manipulate user emotions, while e-commerce applications have design goals to influence decisions of individual stakeholders and user groups.

Design goals may arise from the need to motivate users to change their behaviour or persuade them towards certain decisions in applications such as healthcare (lifestyle behaviour), marketing e-commerce (purchasing decisions) or social e-communities (persuading people to participate).

4.1   Analysing User Goals and Motivation

Analysis of personal goals will follow conventional interviews and scenario-based techniques augmented with motivation analysis using the taxonomy. At this stage user motivations are identified as an extension of personal goals. For example, personal goals to

Table 2. Motivations, obstacles and responses

Motivation	Obstacles	Potential emotion (possible response)
Safety	Dangerous events, malevolent agents	Fear, hate (remove cause or relocate user, add defences and counter measures to events
Power	Change to authority, responsibility	Anger, shame, resentment (compensation, change people, relationships)
Possession	Reduced resource control, monetary incentives	Anger, jealousy, resentment (reallocate resources, responsibilities, change people)
Achievement	Constraints on goals, actions	Anxiety, frustration resentment (change goals, remove constraints)
Self-esteem	Adverse events, goals not achieved	Shame, anger (re-focus goals, emphasise other achievements)
Peer-esteem	Adverse interactions, events	Rejection, loneliness (focus on +ve social relationships)
Self-efficacy	Limitations on actions and responsibilities	Disappointment, distress (improve opportunities, challenges)
Curiosity, learning	Excessive workload, time, resources	Disappointment, reproach (provide time, change workload)
Sociability	Group conflict, personality and authority clashes	Rejection, resentment, loneliness (negotiate problems, change group membership, responsibilities)
Altruism	Limitations on actions	Distress, disappointment (provide opportunities, rewards)

improve one's diet and take exercise will be related not only to achievement but also to self esteem (feeling good about oneself) and peer esteem (improving standing among friends for having lost weight). Barriers to personal goals will often have motivational implications such as frustrated achievement, power and possession, which in turn may have knock-on effects on self-esteem and peer-esteem. Knowledge of user motivations is also applied to planning system responses to affective situations. Since emotional responses are frequently related to motivations as well as to our short-term goals and aspirations, analysis of motivations, goals and emotions is inevitably intertwined. A summary of motivations and possible obstacles to their realisation, and emotional responses to frustrated motivation, is given in Table 2.

This is used in obstacle analysis to consider the interaction between motivation, emotions and personal goals. The motivations and emotions in Table 2 can be used to prompt questions in both directions. Emotional reactions to a scenario may indicate motivational problems, while obstacles to personal goals and related motivations indicate emotional consequences which will need to be addressed either in the social system or design of information content and artificial agents.

4.2 Identifying Affective Situations

The first step is to identify the range of potential affective situations, then to trace the source responsible for emotional reactions in the system content or environment. Situation analysis is directed towards identifying the possible emotional response and its source, then establishing requirements for system agents and responses using the template illustrated in Table 3.

Table 3. Affective situation requirements template, with notes

Application	Situation ID
Agents and actions	People in the scenario, possible actions and communication
Objects	Objects and design artefacts
Events (previous)	Expected events in the environment, with their source, when known. User memory of previous events
Expected emotions	As identified from the above and obstacle analysis
System response	Remove cause, mitigate effect
Agent requirements	Agents' actions for mitigation
Other requirements	Non-agent responses, avoid cause, etc.

Identifying agents and stakeholder groups is standard practice in RE analysis and modelling [31–33]. Scenarios, use cases and storyboards, all commonly practised RE techniques, can be adapted for "affective situation" analysis with stakeholder groups and individual users. Scenarios describing potential emotion invoking incidents may be elicited from stakeholders or created by requirements analysts to explore user reactions to personal goals and design features. Storyboards and sketches are used to illustrate scenarios and presented to users to capture their responses. Since agent-based technology is now cheap and easy to use, lightweight prototypes can be developed to explore design options with a range of emotional expressions by agents [6]. Some examples of facial expression of emotions using agent prototyping tools are illustrated in Fig. 3.

"You seem to have problems;
can I help you ?.....   All is ok please continue"

Fig. 3. Expression of emotion by agent's face with dialogue excerpts

Facial expression alone is somewhat ambiguous, as might be discerned from Fig. 3, so it needs to be combined with dialogue, for example, "You seem to be having difficulty in placing this order; please select the product again" and "Thank you for your order; please proceed to payment" in a typical e-commerce sequence. Emotional expression is even more effective when prosody (voice tone) is used, and text to speech output with limited tonal expression is provided by agent development tools.

4.3   Analysing Situations and Emotions

Tracing the source of emotions follows the template and OCC decision tree to elicit the reasons for the response, then identifying the source in the system environment, content or the design itself. The OCC decision tree helps to identify potential emotions and their causes by asking questions about the source of the problem (agents' actions, objects' attributes, events), who it affects (self, other stakeholders), and the consequences and impact of the problem, as well as any previous related experiences (expectations). Affective reactions may be caused either by the system design, the content of the design, agents, especially people and other stakeholders, actions, or events in the system environment the user has to deal with. Poor implementation of requirements or missing requirements may evoke frustration and anger in more extreme cases. User reaction to the content of applications and websites may be more complex as the response may be caused by information and messages conveyed by text or speech, images of people or natural phenomena, or even sounds and music. Situations involving the system environment range from other people in computer-mediated communication and social software, to events in the world or user goals that the system has to respond to by advising, persuading or directing the user to take action.

Anger tends to be associated more closely with agents and people, so the presentation of characters, opinion and values that clash with the stakeholder's viewpoint should be investigated. Fear is related to events as well as to specific agents, so events in the system environment or described in the system content (e.g. website information) should be questioned. Disgust is a strong, visceral emotion usually associated with content, for example images of putrefying food. Socially oriented emotions have roots in reactions to people and events, so in this case the stakeholder's relationship with others may need to be investigated, through the history of events involving the user and others in the system environment. Social emotions are also important considerations in social computing applications, with privacy and security implications. For example disclosure of secrets may cause shame (in own behaviour), jealousy (in others), remorse (in injudicious actions which have offended others) and so on. Scenarios of information disclosure and privacy controls can explore the types and strengths of emotional responses.

4.4 Obstacle Analysis

Planning system responses to user emotions can be helped by analysing obstacles to motivations and personal goals. If responses can invoke appropriate user motivations then potential negative emotions might be deflected or converted into positive responses (e.g. convert dislike into like by changing an object or design).

Obstacles to personal goals follow the established practice of inquiry into what assumptions, resources, and events may prevent a goal being achieved [22]. This is extended to investigate users' motivations. Since motivations are long-term goals, obstacles are more general and possibly more persistent than may be expected for short-term personal goals. Table 4 gives some guidance in analysing possible reasons for affective reactions for a sub-set of OCC negative emotions. This contributes to obstacle analysis since the causes (agents, people, events, etc.) may hinder the achievement of personal goals with limited guidance on countermeasures for the obstacles. Barriers to power, possession and achievement may be found in social technical systems as modelling in i* strategic dependency diagrams, where changes are made to responsibility relationships, power and authority, or access to resources by agents. Motivation obstacles indicate possible adverse consequences for human stakeholders. Motivational

Table 4. Emotions, possible causes and responses

Emotion	Obstacles, causes	Possible responses
Hate	Actions of people or things, value clashes	Remove object, agent; change focus to self-achievement
Anger	Offensive events, people, things, values	Remove cause, mitigate reasons
Fear	Threats to self, dangerous objects, situations	Remove threat or user from situation, add protection
Disgust	Offensive objects, people	Remove cause, change location
Jealousy	People's actions, objects	Mitigate reasons, change focus to self
Shame	Own actions self-image	Analyse reasons, change focus to achievement

consequences may be mitigated by design in the social system, for example, poor self-esteem arising from a lack of achievement may be alleviated by improving training, changing the organisation of work, or re-setting targets to make them more achievable.

Emotional responses indicated from motivation obstacle analysis suggest further scenarios for situation analysis where the implications can be explored by role-playing situations in which the generic obstacles are made more realistic and concrete, e.g. being turned down for promotion is an obstacle to achievement and has a negative impact on self-esteem.

4.5 Planning Responses

The source of the emotional response is traced back to the agent action or event, and response scenarios are planned to mitigate the anticipated negative emotion. Once the source is known, requirements to deal with the situation can be specified. There are three main routes: first to remove the source; secondly to reassure the users and diffuse the emotion by reducing the significance or impact of the reaction; and finally planning a system response to change negative affect into its related positive emotion, e.g. fear is converted into relief by explaining that the event's consequences are not what the user expected. Removing the source in content can be achieved by editing to remove the offending image, text or event; however, changing sources in the system environment may not be an option, so a mitigation strategy may be necessary. For example, if resent-ment is felt in response to the success of others, then a better outcome might be to convert this into satisfaction or deflect the negative emotion by urging the user to reflect on their own achievements. Resentment might be reduced by counselling the user to ignore the event as unimportant or reflecting on one's own success rather than envying others.

Hate and its milder manifestation, dislike, may be encountered as a response to missing requirements, poor user interface design, or when users are frustrated by poor design. With content, the causes may arise from a clash between the user's beliefs and values and information or opinions expressed in the content. Adverse reaction to person-alities is another likely cause. Emotional responses to products and designed artefacts are usually easier to deal with since these can be traced back to the feature causing dislike. Disliked features indicate poor design or missing/inappropriate requirements.

Positive emotions are less of a concern in situation analysis since there are fewer implications for system requirements, although when goals for influencing user behaviour are present, then scenarios need to be developed that describe the desired positive emotion, e.g. pleasurable experience for persuading users. To illustrate, in an e-commerce application selling high-quality design goods such as jewellery, the high-level goal is to influence the user to buy the product. The user is a member of the public, objects are the jewellery products, and the intended emotions are curi-osity, pleasure and desire. Requirements for a sales agent virtual character are to empathise with the user, using a smiling facial expression to communicate interest and pleasure in explaining the product, followed by actions to demonstrate product qualities, and use of gesture and gaze to draw attention to these features. In games applications there will a sequence of affective situations, in which the user-player is led through situations with agents and events to evoke fear, anxiety, surprise and relief as the game sequence unfolds. Action scripts and sketches of the game's virtual world amplify the requirements described in the template.

5 Illustrative Case Studies

In this section, implementation of the User-Oriented RE process in two persuasive technology applications in e-health is described. Both applications are at the feasibility exploration stage, so only initial pilot studies have been conducted; however, they do illustrate application of the UORE method and provide preliminary experience.

5.1 Detecting Early Onset of Cognitive Impairment

The system is intended to help early diagnosis of cognitive dementia and Alzheimer's disease among the elderly. Unfortunately, Alzheimer's disease is diagnosed too late in too many people, by which time there is little that medical science can do to help; however, if the disease is detected early, then treatment can delay its onset and ameliorate its symptoms. Early onset can be detected by memory tests, patterns of word use and motor reaction times, so the high-level system goal is to remotely and unobtrusively monitor people's use of home computers and text-based messaging via e-mail and social networking sites. There are many complex requirements involving data and text mining to produce early onset diagnostic indicators, which do not concern this paper; instead, analysis of the users' possible reactions to the system is described, with requirements to persuade elderly users to self-refer for follow-up tests and appropriate medical treatment.

The users' motivation is safety, to avoid Alzheimer's disease if possible, with personal goals to participate as volunteers in the trial for altruistic reasons. Affective situations in this case are an obvious consequence of the design goal to warn the user. The affective requirements problem is to analyse people's potential reaction to system diagnoses. The diagnostic part of the system will not be perfect, hence there is uncertainty about the results and the danger of false positive diagnoses, which could provoke fear about the consequences. Scenarios based on these assumptions were explored. If the system detected signs of dementia then this information could be distressing to the user. This raises questions about how the information should be communicated to the user, and the appropriate system response to different diagnostic signs. Using the OCC model, the source of anticipated emotions of fear and distress are the event (message), which has consequences for self (the user) with a specific impact when the feared expectation (diagnosis of dementia) is confirmed. Relief or fear confirmed are also possible depending on the results of follow-up tests. This may also have a general impact leading to distress and fear of the future. This is summarised in the template shown in Table 5.

The next step is to specify the system response. In this case the mirror emotion (relief) can be explored since the diagnosis is uncertain, so suggestions for follow-up tests can be specified to confirm or negate the initial diagnosis with reassuring messages that many initial signs turn out to be false alarms.

Table 5. Situation template: cognitive impairment diagnosis

Situation: diagnosis of problems, low confidence	
Agents and actions	User, possibly their kin
Objects	Text, graphs feedback presentation
Events (previous)	Message warning about possible cognitive impairment (patient history)
Expected emotions	Anxiety, fear, distress, relief
System response	Mitigate consequences, reassure user, empathise
Agent requirements	Agent sympathises with user, communicates
Other requirements	Supplementary information, communication with doctors, kin and friends.

Consulting medical experts with explanations of tests in memory clinics is another system response. The social emotion of empathy is a further means of dealing with distress, hence requirements for social support might be explored, for instance the acceptability of letting close friends know via a social network. A range of scenarios (see Fig. 4) were developed to explore different means of communicating the potentially distressing message, with system responses ranging from no emotion (just the facts), to expression of empathy by agent characters.

Agent: " Sorry to disturb you, but I have found a few signs of problems with your memory. These might not be significant but I think it would be helpful to try a few follow-up tests: see the following link."

Fig. 4. Scenario and agent storyboard for the weak diagnostic signs situation

Other design requirements involve choice of media to deliver the message (text, voice, agent character plus voice/text), as well as the content and format of the message (polite, sympathetic tone).

Scenario: *You are presented with evidence of memory problems from the computer monitor. How would you feel about the messages presented, and the follow-up advice to complete more self-assessment tests?*

These scenarios, personal goals and motivations were investigated with obstacle analysis to identify possible barriers to system goals (to encourage self-referral for follow-up tests), for example self-denial that the user has a medical problem.

Requirements indicated from preliminary analysis of the storyboard scenarios showed individual differences in affective responses. Some users preferred simple factual communications, whereas others liked the empathetic agent. Older characters were suggested to match the user audience, also using a doctor to evoke more trust. Content requirements included simple explanations of the reasons for diagnosis, with limited disclosure of the information to close friends or kin in the user's social network. All users felt that, apart from letting their very best friend know if the follow-up tests did confirm the problem, any disclosure would cause them distress and unnecessary fear among friends.

5.2 Persuasion for Exercise Conformance

The second application focuses on system initiative to persuade the user to take exercise as part of a recovery programme after hospital treatment for a fall. Analysis follows the planning pathway to persuade the user to carry out a set of exercises. The personal goals are to recover from the fall and achieve mobility. Obstacles may be insufficient motivation or physical difficulty in carrying out the exercises. Requirements are for an agent character-based interface to persuade the user (an elderly patient) to take exercise on a regular basis. The situation template for motivating exercise is shown in Table 6.

Table 6. Situation template: exercise motivation

Situation: exercise conformance feedback	
Agents and actions	User, exercise movements, procedures
Objects	Exercise videos, graphs feedback presentation
Events (previous)	Feedback messages on performance
Expected emotions	Satisfaction, anxiety, fear, distress, relief
System response	Encourage user to complete routine
Agent requirements	Congratulate good conformance, mild displeasure for poor conformance
Other requirements	Progress displays, advice possible group motivation- group progress and communication

The personal goals and motivations are:

- Improve health (top level)
- Perform exercises as best as I can
- Make progress each day
- Achievement, self-esteem, peer-esteem.

The design problem is motivating the user to take exercise, which involves communicating a sense of achievement with the corresponding emotions of satisfaction and pride in their achievement, while also motivating their self-esteem, and in a group context peer-esteem. The agent role is a trainer-tutor to encourage exercise conforming to a set regime. To motivate the patient, the agent needs to empathise with the user's situation, be encouraging, and communicate pleasure when the user achieves their exercise goals. The potential for positive and negative responses by the agent needs to be explored, so if the patient does not take the recommended exercise then disappointment and mild reproach may be necessary, followed by more positive encouragement. The social dimension in this application is setting up a self-help group of users to motivate each other by sharing experience and progress feedback. Privacy concerns may lead to resentment (when others do better). A range of scenarios are created, varying the agent's response from mild to stronger emotions to explore which combinations are more acceptable and effective.

6 Case Study and Lessons Learned

UORE was applied in the SAMS project (Software Architecture for Mental-health Self-management) which is investigating the potential of computer monitoring of user inter-action and e-mail for inferring change in cognitive function to diagnose early signs of dementia and mental health problems. The efficacy and acceptability of the SAMS approach depend critically on discovery of affect-laden user requirements, since diag-nosis of dementia is a potentially stressful situation. The obstacles to understanding the emotion-laden requirements involve new imagined systems where few contemporary analogues exist, and a challenging mix of ethical and emotional factors.

UORE was applied in a requirements discovery process with five workshops that were conducted with a total of 24 participants (14 male, 10 female, age range 60–75, median 66), with a median four participants/session plus two facilitators and one to two moderators from the Alzheimer's Society (AS) or the Dementias and Neurodegenerative Diseases Research Network (DeNDRoN). The method was used to construct scenarios to illustrate design variations to mitigate the fear of diagnosis, as well as addressing

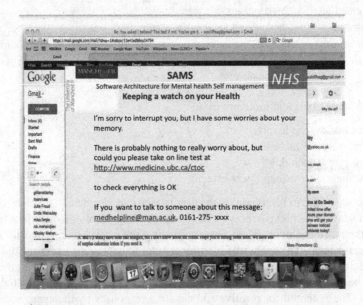

Fig. 5. Storyboard for diagnostic message situation: text version

emotions of despair, anger and frustration which may be felt if there was insufficient explanation for the computer-based diagnosis. The scenarios also explore anxiety that may be caused by invasion of privacy in computer-based monitoring and data security concerns.

The design mock-up illustrated in Fig. 5 shows the simple text message version of the interface, using reassurance to try and ameliorate possible fear, as well as a polite tone to reassure the user.

The ECA version of the feedback interface with additional information to explain the diagnosis is illustrated in Fig. 6. Eight mock-ups were created to explore different design treatments: modality of information delivery (simple text/avatar/video), +/− additional explanation, and tone of the message more/less empathetic. The users were presented with a scenario similar to the one illustrated in Fig. 4, with the variation of imaging the news from a self and other (friend/relative) viewpoint. The scenario mock-ups were presented in sequence either in group workshops or in individual interviews.

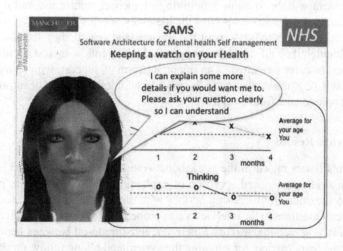

Fig. 6. Storyboard for diagnostic message with added explanation: avatar version

All workshops were structured in two sessions lasting approximately 1 h. In the first session the SAMS system's aims, major components and operation were explained, followed by presentation of eight PowerPoint storyboards illustrating design options for the alert-feedback user interface, such as choice of media (video, text, computer avatars), content (level of detail, social network) and monitoring (periodic feedback, alert only, explicit tests). The second session focused on discussion of privacy issues in monitoring computer use, data sharing and security, ethical considerations, emotional impact of alert messages, users' motivations and likelihood of taking follow-up tests.

6.1 Workshop Results

All participants reported they would feel anxiety and distress over a possible warning message, although the strength of emotional reaction varied, with some people feeling the motivations outweighed the potential distress. Opinion was never unanimous on any design option. There was no consensus on choice of media (text/video/avatar), although a majority in all workshops favoured provision of more detail and availability of regular reports (content). Use of video was favoured in four workshops where participants suggested that self-help (how to cope) and explanatory videos (dementia mitigation treatments) were important motivators for persuading them to take follow-up action. Active monitoring (e.g. quizzes) was favoured by all, but (e.g. card) games were rejected in three of the five workshops. Participants in all workshops suggested that configuration controls for different design options would be welcome.

All participants expressed anxiety over privacy and security arising from monitoring their computer use. Although they were reluctantly willing to share their data with the researchers for analysis, most participants insisted they should have control over their own data. Sharing data with their close kin/friends had to be under their control and the majority would not share information or the alert with their doctor. The majority in all workshops were willing to allow monitoring of their computer use and e-mail text content, suitably anonymised to protect the identities of other parties to conversations. Most participants expected to experience anxiety and fear if they received an alert message, although they all stated that they would take a follow-up test. Contact with a human expert or carer was cited as an important form of support, with connections to support groups (e.g. the Alzheimer's Society) as additional sources of information to motivate people to take follow-up tests.

6.2 Interview Results

Requirements issues raised in the workshops were explored further in 13 interviews following a similar structured approach of explaining the SAMS system, presenting scenarios to illustrate similar design options with discussion on privacy, security and ethical issues. Questions in the interviews also probed users' reactions to different levels of monitoring (e.g. actions, text) and their perceived trade-off between benefits/motivations versus fears/barriers for adopting the system and taking follow-up action after an alert message. Respondents (4 male, 9 female), ranging from 67 to 89 years old (median 72), were all interviewed in their own homes, apart from three sessions carried out in a community centre.

Anxiety, distress and fear (in a few individuals) were the main emotional reactions. The interviews produced less consensus than the workshops for the user interface design requirements. Most respondents (11/13) favoured the plain text alert message over other media options. Active monitoring by a 'cognitive quiz' and a weekly diary was favoured by the majority (11/13) although card games were less popular (8).

The respondents were even more concerned about privacy and security, possibly because three participants had recently experienced phishing attacks on the Internet. However, only two individuals were unwilling to have their e-mail content monitored. Opinions on minimal data sharing and the need to maintain control over their own data were similar to the workshop participants'. The majority of the respondents (11/13) expressed anxiety about being monitored, and they expected to experience discomfort, fear and worry when they received an alert message, although all these 11 participants stated they would take the follow-up test: "better to know the bad news" was a common statement. However, ten respondents reported that they could not realistically imagine how they would react in a real-life situation. Five individuals noted that further explanation after the alert message would be vital and all reported that their main motivation for using the system was efficacy: a feeling of being in control by self-management of their health.

6.3   Summary and Lessons Learned

Several issues which were categorised as values (see [12]) and emotional requirements [24] were discovered to have an important bearing on the requirements and design options:

Trust: in the SAMS system, the universities (system authors), healthcare professionals, follow-up test websites and authors thereof.

Motivations: efficacy, desire for self-control, altruism (participation might help research on dementia).

Emotion: anxiety, distress and fear of negative alert messages, uncertainty over personal reaction.

The UORE method identified the major user goals and non-functional requirements from analysis of emotional reaction to the scenarios and mock-up prototypes. However, the range of values, motivations and emotions which were discovered was modest, even though the analyst was expert in such analysis and actively sought these insights. Fear and anxiety were the main emotions and a sub-group of users emerged who showed stronger emotional reactions, suggesting that these users may be less willing adopters of SAMS. The analysis also discovered another sub-group of users who showed less emotional reaction, which is unusual given the very real prospect of dementia affecting the lives of our senior citizen interviewees. We have two interpretations of this result. Either people find it difficult to imagine how they would respond in reality given a fictitious scenario, or these people may be unwilling to express their emotional response while feeling their motivations (wellbeing, being in control) outweigh the downsides of potentially distressing news.

The UORE method is still being refined, as early experience with storyboard and preliminary requirements analysis leads to improvements in the method. The research has followed an action research approach in which the first version of the method was applied in practice, leading to insight into problems and improvements to the method. The nature and quantity of the advice incorporated in the method is an open question, as analysis proceeds by a team of medical and requirements-human factors researchers. One problem with affect-oriented research is that people are rarely completely candid about expressing emotion [34]. Some users expressed the concern that they only felt emotion in real life and that imagining how they would feel in response to scenarios was not easy. Another problem was negative reaction to the agents; one user preferred to communicate with real people rather than computer images in affective situations. However, motivations and discussion of feelings were productive when assessing responses to different agent designs. The analysis side of the method, eliciting emotional situations which might occur, appears to be more difficult than the synthesis-design side where reaction to specific agent designs is being assessed. Tools for developing proto-type agents have proved successful in demonstrating a range of facial expressions and scripted interactions, so exploration of affective requirements for agent designs does seem to be a promising approach.

7 Discussion

Presentation of situations to explore human motivations, emotions and attitudes is a novel contribution to RE. UORE extends previous concepts of personal requirements [2] as well as addressing requirements for advanced UI technology where agent/char-acter-based interfaces are becoming more common. Motivation and emotion analysis are particularly pertinent to social computing applications where computer-mediated interactions need to be considered. The UORE method is not intended to supplant conventional RE; instead, it is a way of augmenting scenario-based RE with person-oriented and social considerations. Even though the method is in its early stages of development, UORE does show some promise in producing insight into personal problems in applications where individual experience and goals are paramount. It also addresses requirements analysis for the new generation of user interfaces where char-acter/agent-based interaction is becoming widespread, and in applications where system goals aim to influence users [4]. The method fits within RE practices of goal-based and scenario-based RE, amplifying them, especially in personally oriented applications. The method may also be applied to content analysis in websites and requirements for customisable systems where users can choose their own goals and preferences.

While emotions and motivation are psychological constructs which require in-depth knowledge for analysis of human problems, the UORE method delivers a digestible sub-set of psychology, which could be used by non-experts. Experience to date has involved medical personnel who are conversant with the psychology of emotion from their training, so testing the method with non-experts is part of the future research agenda. To deliver the method's advice more effectively we will create a hypertext website so users can explore the links between motivation, emotions, obstacles and possible miti-gations. The scenario and storyboard analysis has demonstrated that affective issues can be explored with users who are not experts.

RE methods for modelling motivation and emotional influences on requirements goals have been proposed [35, 36] following an agent-role, soft-goal modelling approach. However the People Oriented Software Engineering method [35] did not adopt any specific model of emotion beyond Norman's framework of three levels of emotional reaction [15], so their role modelling approach does not provide any specific guidance for analysing the impact of users' emotions on requirements. UORE, in contrast, does provide specific advice based on a sound theory [25]. Emotional require-ments could augment modelling of social influences in i* [30, 31], and UORE could be applied to the goals, skills preferences approach [23] and RE modelling of socio-tech-nical systems. Considering emotions and motivation may help in modelling agents and their relationships, since trust and responsibility are already part of the i* family of models [31, 32]. Knowledge of individual agents may help inspection-based analysis, while emotional analysis can help problem identification in scenario-based investigations. Analysis of emotions may also be applied to requirements monitoring of progress relating to personal goals. Current sensory technology enables body posture and facial expression to be automatically analysed to detect emotional responses such as disappointment when personal goals are not achieved, or dislike of products. The OCC model has been formalised [37] so there is the prospect of creating emotional analysis tools for agent-based specifications. UORE could also extend games-based specification methods [9, 10] and requirements for interactive virtual environments such as SecondLife. In conclusion, UORE has extended a theme in RE which started with a focus on personal goals [2, 3] and the user as a subject of requirements analysis. It also extends earlier work on emotion in RE [38] which analysed the socio-technical implication of affective reactions to inappropriate features, tacit knowledge and managerial changes. Finally, UORE raises questions about how RE deals with new generations of systems where goals are not just functional but relate to human feelings and values.

Acknowledgements. This research was partially funded by EPSRC Grant EP/K015796/1 Software Architecture for Mental-health Self-management (SAMS).

References

1. Thew, S., Sutcliffe, A.G.: Investigating the role of soft issues in the RE process. In: Proceedings, 16th IEEE International Requirements Engineering Conference, pp. 63–66. IEEE Computer Society Press, Los Alamitos (2008)
2. Sutcliffe, A.G., Fickas, S., Sohlberg, M.M.: PC-RE: a method for personal and contextual requirements engineering with some experience. Requir. Eng. **11**, 157–163 (2006)
3. Fickas, S., Robinson, W., Sohlberg, M.M.: The role of deferred requirements in a longitudinal study of emailing. In: Proceedings RE-2005, pp. 145–154. IEEE Computer Society Press, Los Alamitos (2005)
4. Fogg, B.J.: Persuasive Technology: Using Computers to Change What We Think and Do. Morgan Kaufmann, San Francisco (2003)
5. Reeves, B., Nass, C.: The Media Equation: How People Treat Computers, Television and New Media Like Real People and places. CLSI/Cambridge University Press, Stanford/ Cambridge (1996)
6. Artificial Intelligence Foundation. http://alice.pandorabots.com/
7. Preece, J., Maloney-Krichmar, D.: Online communities. In: Jacko, J., Sears, A. (eds.) Handbook of Human-Computer Interaction, pp. 596–620. Lawrence Erlbaum Associates, Mahwah NJ (2003)
8. Kraut, R.E.: Applying social psychological theory to the problem of group work. In: Carroll, J.M. (ed.) HCI Models, Theories, and Frameworks: Toward a Multidisciplinary Science, pp. 325–356. Morgan Kaufmann, San Francisco (2003)
9. Callele, D., Neufeld, E., Schneider, K.: Balancing security requirements and emotional requirements in video games. In: Proceedings, RE 2008, pp. 319–320. IEEE Computer Society Press, Los Alamitos (2008)
10. Callele, D., Neufeld, E., Schneider, K.: Augmenting emotional requirements with emotion markers and emotion prototypes. In: Proceedings, RE 2009, pp. 373–374. IEEE Computer Society Press, Los Alamitos (2009)

11. Thew, S., Sutcliffe, A.G., DeBruijn, O., McNaught, J., Procter, R., Venters, C., Buchan, I.: Experience in e-science requirements engineering. In: Proceedings, 16th IEEE International Requirements Engineering Conference, pp. 277–282. IEEE Computer Society Press, Los Alamitos (2008)

12. Friedman, B.: Value sensitive design. In: Schular, D. (ed.) Liberating Voices: A Pattern Language for Communication Revolution, pp. 366–368. MIT Press, Cambridge (2008)

13. Cockton, G., Kujala, S., Nurkka, P., Hölttä, T.: Supporting worth mapping with sentence completion. In: Gross, T., Gulliksen, J., Kotzé, P., Oestreicher, L., Palanque, P., Prates, R.O., Winckler, M. (eds.) INTERACT 2009. LNCS, vol. 5727, pp. 566–581. Springer, Heidelberg (2009)

14. Hassenzahl, M., Schöbel, M., Trautmann, T.: How motivational orientation influences the evaluation and choice of hedonic and pragmatic interactive products: the role of regulatory focus. Interact. Comput. **20**, 473–479 (2008)

15. Norman, D.A.: Emotional Design: Why We Love (or Hate) Everyday Things. Basic Books, New York (2004)

16. Cooper, A., Reimann, R., Cronin, D.: About Face 3: The Essentials of Interaction Design. Wiley, Indianapolis (2007)

17. Djajadiningrat, J.P., Gaver, W.W., Fres, J.W.: Interaction relabelling and extreme characters: methods for exploring aesthetic interactions. In: Conference Proceedings, Designing Interactive Systems: Processes, Practices Methods and Techniques, pp. 66–71. ACM Press, New York (2000)

18. Picard, R.W.: Affective Computing. MIT Press, Cambridge MA (1997)

19. Bickmore, T., Cassell, J.: Social dialogue with embodied conversational agents. In: Van Kuppevelt, J., Dybkjaer, L., Bernsen, N. (eds.) Natural, Intelligent and Effective Interaction with Multimodal Dialogue: Proceedings of the International Joint Conference on Artificial Intelligence. Kluwer Academic, New York (2004)

20. Cassell, J.: Embodied conversational interface agents. Commun. ACM **43**, 70–80 (2000)

21. Pelachaud, C., Carofiglio, V., De Carolis, B., De Rosis, F.: Embodied virtual agent in information delivering application. In: Proceedings, First International Joint Conference on Autonomous Agents and Multi-Agent Systems, Bologna (2002)

22. Van Lamsweerde, A., Letier, E.: Handling obstacles in goal-oriented requirements engineering. IEEE Trans. Softw. Eng. **26**, 978–1005 (2000)

23. Hui, B., Laiskos, S., Mylopoulos, J.: Requirements analysis for customisable software: a goals skills preferences framework. In: Proceedings IEEE Joint International Conference on Requirements Engineering, pp. 117–126. IEEE Computer Society Press, Los Alamitos (2003)

24. Ekman, P.: Basic emotions. In: Dalgleish, T., Power, M. (eds.) Handbook of Cognition and Emotion. Wiley, Chichester (1999)

25. Ortony, A., Clore, G.L., Collins, A.: The Cognitive Structure of Emotions. Cambridge University Press, Cambridge (1988)

26. Bandura, A.: Social Cognitive Theory of Mass Communication. Lawrence Erlbaum Associates, Mahwah (2001)

27. Maslow, A.H., Frager, R., McReynolds, C., Cox, R., Fadiman, J.: Motivation and Personality. Addison Wesley-Longman, New York (1987)

28. Sandelands, L.E., Boudens, C.J.: Feeling at work. In: Fineman, S. (ed.) Emotion in Organizations. Sage Publications, London (2000)

29. Potts, C.: ScenIC: a strategy for inquiry-driven requirements determination. In: Proceedings, 4th IEEE International Symposium on Requirements Engineering, pp. 58–65. IEEE Computer Society Press, Los Alamitos (1999)

30. Sutcliffe, A.G.: Analysing the effectiveness of human activity systems with i*. In: Yu, E., Georgini, P., Maiden, N., Mylopoulos, J. (eds.) Social Modelling for Requirements Engineering, pp. 1139–1195. MIT Press, Cambridge (2010)
31. Yu, E.S.: Social modeling and *i**. In: Borgida, A.T., Chaudhri, V.K., Giorgini, P., Yu, E.S. (eds.) Conceptual Modeling: Foundations and Applications. LNCS, vol. 5600, pp. 99–121. Springer, Heidelberg (2009)
32. Yu, E.: Introduction to social modelling in RE. In: Yu, E., Georgini, P., Maiden, N., Mylopoulos, J. (eds.) Social Modelling for Requirements Engineering, ch. 1. MIT Press, Cambridge (2010)
33. Sommerville, I., Kotonya, G.: Requirements Engineering: Processes and Techniques. Wiley, Chichester (1998)
34. Fineman, S.: Understanding Emotion at Work. Sage Publications, Thousand Oaks (2004)
35. Miller, T., Pedell, S., Lopez-Lorca, A.A., Mendoza, A., Sterling, L., Keirnan, A.: Emotion-led modelling for people-oriented requirements engineering: the case study of emergency systems. J. Syst. Softw. **105**, 54–71 (2015)
36. Miller, T., Pedell, S., Sterling, L., Vetere, F., Howard, S.: Understanding socially oriented roles and goals through motivational modelling. J. Syst. Softw. **85**, 2160–2170 (2012)
37. Adam, C., Herzig, A., Longin, D.: A logical formalization of the OCC theory of emotions. Synthese **168**, 201–248 (2009)
38. Ramos, I., Berry, D.M.: Is emotion relevant to requirements engineering? Requir. Eng. **10**, 238–242 (2005)

Personas for Requirements Engineering

Opportunities and Challenges

Cindy Mayas, Stephan Hörold[✉], and Heidi Krömker

Media Production Group, Technische Universität Ilmenau, Ilmenau, Germany
{cindy.mayas,stephan.hoerold,heidi.kroemker}@tu-ilmenau.de

Abstract. Knowledge about users is often used as a prerequisite for the identification of requirements, but it is not systematically integrated into the requirements engineering process. Personas provide a tool for the adequate documentation of users' attributes and support the development team throughout the entire development process. Based on five research and development projects using personas, this approach describes the opportunities and challenges of the integration of personas and the persona creation process within the different activities of requirements engineering.

Keywords: Personas · Requirements engineering · Software engineering

1 Introduction

The development process of software, products and services can be structured differently, e.g. in a linear way, following a waterfall model [1], or in an iterative way, following a spiral model [2]. Nowadays, an increasing use of agile, iterative or incremental software development processes can be observed [3], which result from different workflows and changing attitudes towards development. Within these kinds of development processes, some decisions don't have to be made at the beginning and can be adjusted along the development. These adjustments often result from technical issues and challenges, or from incorporate phases of coordination with clients. While technical or organizational adjustments are realized, it is essential to validate them with user requirements. Therefore, knowledge about users is a prerequisite to keep up with these changes. However, this valuable knowledge about users is often neglected after the requirements specification [6].

Providing access to this original knowledge about users along the development process can support an agile, incremental, or iterative development. In this regard, personas [4], which are commonly used in user-centered design and human-computer interaction activities, are not only a suitable method for the adequate documentation of users' attributes, but also a tool for empathizing with users' aims and needs [5]. Personas can be used by the development team for requirements engineering activities throughout the entire development process and in addition to user-centered design activities.

A. Ebert et al. (Eds.): UsARE 2012/2014, LNCS 9312, pp. 34–46, 2016.
DOI: 10.1007/978-3-319-45916-5_3

The integration of personas, as a kind of user description, in the requirements engineering activities, improves two aspects of the development: (1) considering multifaceted user needs in the early phases of development, when functional key decisions are taken, (2) continuous integration, verification and revision of user requirements to evaluate developed prototypes and intermediate products.

In the following, the opportunities and challenges of the integration of personas in the different activities of the requirements engineering process are described, based on the practice of five research and development projects using personas. The described approach is based on the work of Schneidewind et al. [6] and extends this work in regard to the entire development process, using the persona method as a tool for keeping requirements vivid along the development process.

2   Requirements Engineering Activities

Requirements engineering provides "a structured set of activities, which are followed to derive, validate and maintain a system requirements document" [7]. These requirements engineering activities are often described as a linear process, which results in a

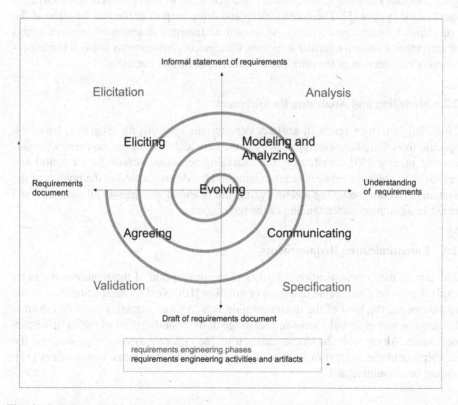

Fig. 1. Spiral model of the requirements engineering activities (based on the approaches of Kotonya and Sommerville [7] and Nuseibah and Easterbrook [10])

validated final requirements document, used as a basis for system planning and implementation [8]. Within the further development process, additional managing activities have to be undertaken, in order to react on changing needs of stakeholders or changing environmental or organizational conditions [7].

These requirements management activities are closely related to the requirements engineering activities. In addition, agile development processes also demand a more dynamic dealing with requirements. Especially in the context of software development, prototyping, testing, and evaluation of the system might implicate changes of the requirements documents, which have to be replicable and revisable [9]. The approach of Nuseibah and Easterbrook [10] not only considers the developing activities of requirement documentation but also these evolving activities to adapt changes. In order to emphasize the incremental character of these activities, this approach is transferred to the spiral model of Kotonya and Sommerville [7], as shown in Fig. 1. As a consequence, the following activities [10] have to be undertaken iteratively.

2.1 Eliciting Requirements

The elicitation activities provide methods and techniques to capture information about goals, domain knowledge, stakeholders and actors, as well as the operational environment of the system [8]. The core eliciting activities are part of the first iteration of the requirements engineering process. As a result, an informal statement of requirements is developed as a basis for further activities. Changes of requirements imply a reinterpretation or recollection of the information material in further iterations.

2.2 Modelling and Analyzing Requirements

Modelling activities result in abstract descriptions respectively diagrams, based on specific modelling languages, and present the core activities of the requirements engineering process [10]. In addition, the analyzing activities include the detection and resolving of conflicts between requirements and the determination of the bounds of the system [8]. Both, modelling and analyzing, are essential activities in all iterations and result in a common understanding of the requirements.

2.3 Communicating Requirements

The aim of the communication activities is the description of the requirements in an explicit and comprehensible language or notation [10]. Next to the specification of the requirements, the kind of the documentation in a logic or natural, formal or informal language is also essential for the further usage of the resulting draft of the requirements document. Along with the documentation of the concrete system requirements, the description of the context of use, including users, tasks, and usage environment [11], should be communicated.

2.4 Agreeing Requirements

The agreeing activities are often called validation, with the aim to check the requirements document for consistency and completeness [7], for instance via requirements reviews. Moreover, the agreement with all stakeholders and the consideration of their goals and conflicts [10] is an essential basis for the beginning of the following iterations.

2.5 Evolving Requirements

The evolving activities include methods and tools for the management of changes. A very important precondition for this requirements management is the traceability to check the impact of changes to further requirements [12]. These activities have to accompany all the other activities of eliciting, analyzing, communicating, and agreeing continuously, in order to recognize potential risks of changes during the whole process.

3 Challenges of User Requirements

According to IEEE, requirements are "a documented representation of a condition or capability" that either "must be met or possessed by a system or system component" or is "needed by a user to solve a problem or achieve an objective" [13]. In contrast to system requirements, which are derived from organizational, domain and platform restrictions [14], user requirements are based on the user needs [15]. In development processes, user requirements are often neglected or reduced to design aspects of the user interface [16, 17]. However, user requirements include information about users, tasks, and the environment [11], which concern not only usability aspects but also key decisions of system design and functionality.

As a consequence, user requirements can provide a basis for the system development and the evaluation process. This approach requires a holistic integration of user needs into the requirements engineering process. But the characteristics of user needs involve some challenges for the requirements engineering process. The challenges have been identified within five research and development projects. The projects differ in their duration, team size, goals, and their area of application, as shown in Table 1.

Table 1. Overview of research and development projects

Project	Duration	Team size	Goal	Area of application
Project A	3.5 years	20 members	Communication standard	Public transport
Project C	2.5 years	7 members	Mobile planning application	Logistics
Project B	2 years	5 members	Predictive diagnosis system	Automotive industry
Project D	2 years	3 members	B2B system	E-commerce
Project E	0.5 years	2 members	Public display user interface	Public transport

Elicitation Challenge: User Needs Are Independent from the Planned Solution.
The expectations of users often depend on their previous experiences with systems [18].
As a consequence, users are not able to imagine innovative system solutions or interactions, which differ from their current workflows. In order to provide flexible, open,
and unbiased user requirements, it is important to identify the core goals and tasks of
the users in detail, independently from current or future solutions. Otherwise, there is
the risk of anticipating planned solutions, without considering the real user needs.

**Analyzing Challenge: User Needs Are Rather Imprecise and Vague and Partly
Even Contradictory and Illogical.** User needs often concern a complex task or goal
of a user [18], which might be reached by different means and ways. Especially, systems,
which are developed for several user groups, have to meet different user needs. But these
needs respectively wishes might be inconsistent or illogical, not only in regard to
different user groups, but also in regard to a single user. It is the responsibility of the
usability and requirements engineers to solve these conflicts according to the best solution for the user, in order to reach the core goals and solve the tasks.

**Communication Challenge: User Needs Leave Scope for Interpretation Along the
Development Process.** The development and design process of a product integrates
different stakeholders and developers with different opinions. Cooper et al. point out,
that the user can be used to justify different personal opinions within a discussion,
without having the user needs in mind, but the own idea of the product [5]. Therefore,
a common understanding of the user based on real user data is needed, which can be
understood by all involved stakeholders.

These mentioned challenges lead to the result, that there is a high potential to improve
the user descriptions for requirements engineering activities. Current user descriptions
are modeled in a very structured way, which is not sufficiently vivid and flexible. For
instance, user roles focus on the tasks, but neglect the users' motivation and actions as
well as the context of use [11]. These approaches give a short overview, but do not enable
the developer to feel empathy with the user, in order to also consider user needs into
new upcoming development decisions. When key decisions are only taken from the
developers' point of view or even the developers interpret their own needs as user needs,
the project risks failing to meet the real user needs.

4   Describing Users with Personas

Software, requirements and usability engineering have a set of different methods to
describe users in regard to the needed detail level and purpose of the description.
Personas provide a method to communicate typical behavior, motivation and goals of
users in order to personify a group of users [4]. Personas are archetypes, which are
derived from the dispositions and behavior of real people, but describe fictitious and
clearly distinguishable characters. Compared to other methods for user descriptions, the
strengths of personas [5] are:

- User-oriented determination of product characteristics based on goals and tasks,
- Universal communication tool for different stakeholders within the development process, especially to discuss challenges and solutions, based on a common understanding of the users,
- Ad hoc evaluation tool, to reflect decisions and changes from a users' point of view.

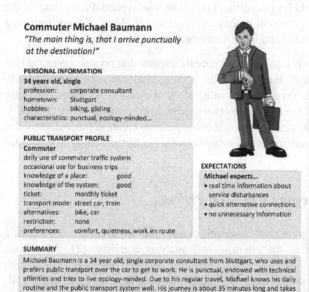

Commuter Michael Baumann
"The main thing is, that I arrive punctually at the destination!"

PERSONAL INFORMATION
34 years old, single
profession: corporate consultant
hometown: Stuttgart
hobbies: biking, gliding
characteristics: punctual, ecology-minded...

PUBLIC TRANSPORT PROFILE
Commuter
daily use of commuter traffic system
occasional use for business trips
knowledge of a place: good
knowledge of the system: good
ticket: monthly ticket
transport mode: street car, train
alternatives: bike, car
restriction: none
preferences: comfort, quietness, work en route

EXPECTATIONS
Michael expects...
- real time information about service disturbances
- quick alternative connections
- no unnecessary information

DAILY ROUTINE
Every day Michael takes the street car to his place of work in downtown Stuttgart. He knows his daily travel routine by heart. He must transfer once every 20 minutes. Michael has attempted the same journey by car, but the constant traffic jams and the cumbersome search for a parking space became too stressful in the long run. In addition, he wants to travel ecology-minded and sees his best travel opportunities in public transport, in order to fulfill this desire. Public transport enables Michael a worry free daily routine. His monthly ticket enables him to travel stress free: the journey in general actually affords him relaxation in comparison to travel by car. He has gotten used to short delays and has scheduled 5 minutes of spare time, so as to get to his office at the latest by 8 o'clock. Major delays always get him in trouble with his boss and Michael's day schedule gets completely mixed up. This often continues to aggravate him on his way back home.

SUMMARY
Michael Baumann is a 34 year old, single corporate consultant from Stuttgart, who uses and prefers public transport over the car to get to work. He is punctual, endowed with technical affinities and tries to live ecology-minded. Due to his regular travel, Michael knows his daily routine and the public transport system well. His journey is about 35 minutes long and takes him to the center of Stuttgart. During his journey he has to transfer once and therefore he predominantly uses the street car, which gets him to work and back quickly.
Michael does not want any unnecessary information during his daily way to work, which already is familiar to him. He only uses passenger information in the event that something would not work out as planned. In that case, Michael expects that he would be informed about disturbances as soon as possible, ideally before setting off on a journey, so that he is able to avoid the disturbance by using an alternative connection.

Fig. 2. Example of a persona

In general, the activities of the process for creating personas vary slightly between different authors [5, 19]. But all creating processes focus on the described strengths of personas and are based on qualitative and quantitative data, derived from analysis and statistics. Therefore, the approaches follow the same basic steps [20] starting with an identification of variables and values, followed by an identification of patterns, and the description of the persona, e.g. as shown in Fig. 2, and its validation. The following overview presents the core activities of each step of the persona creation:

1. **Identifying variables and values** includes the operationalization of the activities, attitudes, aptitudes, motivations and skills [5] of the potential users, in respect to the product. The values represent specific manifestations of a variable, which differ from user to user and are revealed by qualitative and quantitative user research methods, for instance in interviews and observations, statistical reviews.
2. **Identifying patterns** maps the processed user data to a value of each variable. As a next step, the most frequent combinations of values are analyzed and classified

into typical behavioral disposition. These patterns build the basis for the creation of the "skeleton" of the persona.

3. **Describing personas** enriches the patterns with demographic variables. Next to a name, age, and hobbies, some attributes of the character, a personal story, and a picture are added to the persona, in order to encourage more empathy with the user.
4. **Validating personas** includes the verification of the final typical dispositions of the personas as well as the agreement process with the stakeholders of the system and their political, organizational and legal restrictions.

The integration of personas into the requirements engineering process concerns two fields of work. Firstly, the creation process of the persona itself has to be integrated into the requirements engineering process. This integration of working activities is mainly related to the first iteration of the requirements engineering process, as shown in Sect. 5. Secondly, the usage of the personas, as a result of the persona creation process, provides advantages for several requirements engineering activities in further iteration, which are described in Sect. 6.

5   Integrating the Persona Creation Process

Current approaches to integrate user descriptions into the requirements engineering process are largely limited to the eliciting and analysis activities [21, 22]. Some approaches also suggest the integration of several user-centered design activities, such as user studies and usability testing, into the requirements engineering process [23, 24]. The usage of personas as user descriptions were suggested by Castro et al. [25], who developed an advanced persona technique and integrated the identified detailed creation activities within the whole requirements process. In this way, the developed persona is an additional result at the end of the requirements engineering process.

In contrast, we recommend to create the persona in the first iteration of the requirements engineering process, in order to provide the results of the persona creation as an added value to the majority of the requirements engineering activities in further iterations.

The development of personas is a creation process, which consists of different activities, as described in Sect. 3. These activities of persona creation are comparable to the requirements engineering activities, and transferable to the requirements engineering process, as shown in Fig. 3. Within the first elicitation phase, information about the context of use is collected, which build an important basis for both, the development of personas and further requirements. By these means, the variables and values defining the characteristics of the personas are identified, next to the first informal statement of requirements. As a next step, the elicited information is structured and analyzed for the identification of behavioral patterns of personas. The typical language to communicate personas is the textual form in combination with a picture (cf. Fig. 2), which should be added to the draft of the requirements document. Finally, these descriptions are validated and can be agreed with the stakeholders in combination with other requirements documents.

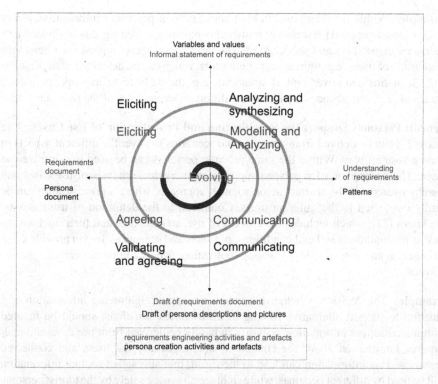

Variables and values
Informal statement of requirements

Eliciting

Analyzing and synthesizing

Eliciting

Modeling and Analyzing

Requirements document

Understanding of requirements

Persona document

Patterns

Evolving

Agreeing

Communicating

Validating and agreeing

Communicating

Draft of requirements document
Draft of persona descriptions and pictures

requirements engineering activities and artefacts
persona creation activities and artefacts

Fig. 3. Integration of personas into the requirements engineering process

6 Opportunities of the Integration of Personas into the Requirements Engineering Activities

The integration of the created personas provides benefits for the different requirements engineering activities. Each benefit is supported by an example from a research and standardization project on passenger information in public transport, which provides a context of use with different actors, tasks and systems in a mobile environment. Therefore, the examples focus on a complex field of applications, which is similar to other fields of applications where the mentioned challenges typically arise.

6.1 Eliciting Requirements

Benefit: Personas Support the Identification of Actors and Scenarios. Often, the development process focuses not only on one type of user in a specified scenario, but also on several actors within the context of use. Personas support the identification of these actors, based on their characteristics, and describe them from a holistic point of view. Therefore, scenarios can be derived more easily and different aspects of the usage and accompanying contexts can be addressed.

Example. Within the mentioned field of application of passenger information, actors include passengers and personnel of transport companies, which e.g. can be divided into operators, dispatchers and service staff. The term "passengers" represents a heterogonous group of users, e.g. tourists and commuters, which can be described with personas [20]. Scenarios can cover typical situations, e.g. the daily route to work, or special situations, e.g. disturbances, including the different perspectives of the personas [26].

Benefit: Personas Support the Specification and Prioritization of Use Cases. Use cases [27] can be derived from personas and scenarios to cover the different aspects in a more abstract way. Within the same process, personas can be used to prioritize use cases. The description of a persona supports an individual analysis of use cases and thereby overcomes the abstract actor oriented approach, where a prioritization can be hardly connected to the different users. Compared to the definition of use cases by Cockburn [27], which includes the context of use, stakeholders and their interests, as well as preconditions and end conditions, personas and scenarios already provide these information and extend them by adding motivations, goals and other personal characteristics.

Example. The decision, whether a function to support sightseeing information or a function to support alternative routing in disturbances situations, should be favored within a passenger information system, can hardly be derived from use cases alone. It requires information about the context of use, especially the users and connected scenarios. This information can lead to the result, that alternative routing information will be used by different personas, while sightseeing is used solely by the tourist persona. Therefore, the alternative function will most likely receive a higher priority.

6.2   Modelling and Analyzing Requirements

Benefit: Personas Support the Prioritization of Requirements. Requirements are usually not all equal in their priority. Priorities can be given in regard to clients' wishes, technical feasibility or user needs. The comprehensive knowledge, combined within the persona descriptions, facilitates the comparison of the requirements of different users for the development team. In addition, personas serve as a neutral and agreed basis for discussion.

Example. Within passenger information systems, different time related information can be found. Therefore, the list of requirements will include a number of requirements focusing on this time related information. A decision, as to whether the remaining minutes to departure or the time of departure should be used, or if real-time information is needed, can be made based on the needs of the personas.

Benefit: Personas Support the Deeper Understanding of Requirements. In order to manage development challenges and requirements changes, the development team should have a deeper understanding of the requirements. In contrast to separated requirements lists, personas can provide additional information to get a holistic view of the requirements. Therefore, an adequate traceability of requirements and personas is an important prerequisite.

Example. The development of the passenger information system included a set of requirements, which focuses on information and different presentation functions. Personas support developers implementing these functions by providing a context for the requirement. In a passenger information system not only the mere information, but also the combination with other information provides useful support for the passenger.

6.3   Communicating Requirements

Benefit: Personas Support the Comprehensible Communication of Requirements to Stakeholders. As described in the previous benefits, the memorable and comprehensible descriptions of personas in natural language and pictures can play an important role for the eliciting and analyzing activities. The same advantages support the identification with users, their needs and goals for the different stakeholders. An integration of the personas into the requirements document therefore improves the understanding of the whole requirements document.

Example. The developed personas for users of a passenger information were presented in a booklet [26]. The persona booklet was easy to handle and permanently available to all developers and stakeholders. In addition, further types of information, such as presentations, positioned figurative representations, or integrations into the daily routines also support the communication and the memorization of personas for the developers.

6.4   Agreeing Requirements

Benefit: Personas Support the Validation of Requirements. The usage of personas during validation activities ensures the consideration of the user perspective during requirements reviews or testing. Thereby, personas can not only indicate an incompleteness of requirements, but also help to solve conflicts between the stakeholders.

Example. In order to validate the requirements for a passenger information system, typical user requests to the system were derived from each persona. Subsequently, the requirements were checked to ensure a response to these requests, according to the specific user needs and expectations. In later iterations, these user requests could also be used for system and component tests, in order to ensure the correct responses to the requests.

6.5   Evolving Requirements

Benefit: Personas Support the Tracing of Requirements. Along the development process, requirements are changed due to different reasons, e.g. technical issues or results of usability evaluations. Personas can not only support the decision and evaluation process of these changes by integrating the users' perspective, but also keep track of related requirements and influences resulting from these changes. In addition, persons can be used to measure the compliance to requirements from another perspective. In regard to the final product, the persona perspective provides more reliable results, as the perspective is already based on the final users.

Example. Even when a function is rated with high priority, situations along the development process can arise, where the requirements related to this function are questioned, due to different reasons. For instance, the departure timer within a mobile passenger application was questioned within the development process. The assessment of neglecting this function using the personas revealed that this function can be considered as an added value for several personas, but the departure timer does not represent a key function to solve a task. As a result, the requirements of the departure timer were removed.

7   Conclusion

Today, requirements engineering lacks a well-established process to combine personas as a type of user descriptions and requirements engineering activities. However, personas are already used to overcome different challenges along the development and requirements engineering process [28–31]. Therefore, personas can be considered as a powerful method to provide vivid descriptions and requirements along the development and requirements engineering process. In addition, the persona method bridges the gap between requirements engineering, user-centered software development and human-computer-interaction.

Based on the experiences of development and research projects of different scale and content, the described approach shows solutions to integrate the persona creation process and the persona artefacts in the requirements engineering activities. The benefits of the usage of personas and their exemplary application are described for well-established methods of requirements engineering. However, the validation of these findings still requires a systematical analysis of the requirements engineering activities in further development projects.

Personas provide a user-oriented overall context, which includes tasks, values, and motivations, for single requirements. The integration of personas into development projects ensures the consideration of the user needs in all requirements engineering activities and supports the solution of conflicts between requirements, as described by Miller and Williams [28]. By these means, personas support the requirements engineering process, serve as a stable reference for agile and iterative development processes and increase the usability of the final products.

Acknowledgements. The application example is part of the IP-KOM-ÖV project, which was funded by the German Federal Ministry of Economy and Technology (BMWi) grant number 19P10003L.

References

1. Royce, W.W.: Managing the development of large storage systems. In: Technical Papers of Western Electronic Show and Convention (WesCon), Los Angeles, USA (1970)
2. Boehm, B.W.: A spiral model of software development and enhancement. ACM SIGSOFT Softw. Eng. Notes 11(4), 14–24 (1986)
3. Sommerville, I.: Software Engineering, 9th edn. Addison Wesley, Harlow (2011)
4. Cooper, A.: The Inmates are Running the Asylum. Macmillan, New York (1999)
5. Cooper, A., Reimann, R., Cronin, D.: About Face 3: The Essentials of Interaction Design. Wiley Publishing, Inc., Indianapolis (2007)
6. Schneidewind, L., Hörold, S., Mayas, C., Krömker, H., Falke, S., Pucklitsch, T.: How personas support requirements engineering. In: Proceedings of the First International Workshop on Usability and Accessibility Focused Requirements Engineering (UsARE 2012), pp. 1–5. IEEE Press, Piscataway (2012)
7. Kotonya, G., Sommerville, I.: Requirements Engineering – Processes and Techniques. Wiley, Chichester (1997)
8. Abran, A., Moore, J.W., Bourque, P., Dupuis, R.: Guide to the Software Engineering Body of Knowledge (SWEBOK). IEEE Computer Society, Los Alamitos (2004)
9. Sawyer, P., Sommerville, I., Viller, S.: Capturing the benefits of requirements engineering. IEEE Softw. 16(2), 78–85 (1999). doi:10.1109/52.754057
10. Nuseibah, B., Easterbrook, S.: Requirements engineering: a roadmap. In: Proceedings of the Conference on The Future of Software Engineering (ICSE 2000), pp. 35–46. ACM, New York (2000). doi:10.1145/336512.336523
11. ISO-International Organization for Standardization: ISO 9241-210:2010: Ergonomics of human-system interaction - part 210: human-centred design for interactive systems (2010)
12. Hofmann, H.F., Lehner, F.: Requirements engineering as a success factor in software projects. Softw. IEEE 18(4), 58–66 (2001). doi:10.1109/MS.2001.936219
13. IEEE Standards Board: IEEE Standard Glossary of Software Engineering Terminology. IEEE Press, New York (1990). IEEE Standard 610.12-1990
14. Bruegge, B., Dutoit, A.H.: Object-Oriented Software Engineering: Using UML, Patterns, and Java, 3rd edn. Pearson, Boston (2010)
15. ISO-International Organization for Standardization: ISO/IEC TR 25060: Systems and software engineering – Systems and software product Quality, Requirements and Evaluation (SQuaRE) - Common Industry Format (CIF) for usability: General framework for usability-related information (2010)
16. Jackson, M.: Software Requirements & Specifications. Addison-Wesley, Harlow (1995)
17. Heiskari, J., Kauppinen, M., Runonen, M., Mannisto, T.: Bridging the gap between usability and requirements engineering. In: 17th IEEE International Requirements Engineering Conference, 2009, RE 2009, pp. 303–308 (2009)
18. Hackos, J.T., Redish, J.: User and Task Analysis for Interface Design. Wiley Computer Publishung, New York (1998)
19. Pruitt, J., Adlin, T.: The Persona Lifecycle: Keeping People in Mind throughout Product Design. Elsevier, Amsterdam (2006)
20. Mayas, C., Hörold, S., Krömker, H.: Meeting the challenges of individual passenger information with personas. In: Advances in Human Aspect of Road and Rail Transportation, pp. 822–831. CRC Press, Boca Raton (2013)
21. Whitehead, J.: Collaboration in software engineering: a roadmap. In: Proceedings of International Conference on Software Engineering (FOSE 2007), May 2007, pp. 214–225 (2007). doi:acm.org/10.1145/1253532.1254720

22. Ferré, X.: Integration of usability techniques into the software development process. In: Proceedings of ICSE 2003 Workshop on Bridging the Gaps Between Software Engineering and Human-Computer Interaction (ICSE Workshop on SE-HCI), pp. 28–35 (2003)

23. Paech, B., Kohler, K.: Usability engineering integrated with requirements engineering. In: Proceedings of ICSE 2003 Workshop on Bridging the Gaps Between Software Engineering and Human-Computer Interaction (ICSE Workshop on SE-HCI), pp. 36–40 (2003)

24. Sousa, K.S., Furtado, E.: RUPi - a unified process that integrates human-computer interaction and software engineering. In: Proceedings of ICSE 2003 Workshop on Bridging the Gaps Between Software Engineering and Human-Computer Interaction (ICSE Workshop on SE-HCI), pp. 41–48 (2003)

25. Castro, J.W., Acuña, S. T., Juristo, N.: Enriching requirements analysis with the personas technique. In: Proceedings of the International Workshop on Interplay between Usability Evaluation and Software Development (I-USED 2008) (2008)

26. Mayas, C., Hörold, S., Krömker, H.: Internet Protokoll basierte Kommunikationsdienste im öffentlichen Verkehr: Das Begleitheft für den Entwicklungsprozess - Personas, Szenarios und Anwendungsfälle aus AK2 und AK3 des Projektes IP-KOM-ÖV, urn:nbn:de:gbv:ilm1-2012200028 (2012)

27. Cockburn, A.: Writing Effective Use Cases. Addison-Wesley, Boston (2000)

28. Miller, G., Williams, L.: Personas: Moving Beyond Role-Based Requirements-Engineering. Microsoft and North Carolina State University (2006)

29. Sim, W.W., Brouse, P.S.: Empowering requirements engineering activities with personas. Procedia Comput. Sci. **28**, 237–246 (2014)

30. Aoyama, M.: Persona-and-scenario based requirements engineering for software embedded in digital consumer products, In: Proceedings of the 13th IEEE International Conference on Requirements Engineering, pp. 85–94. IEEE Computer Society (2005)

31. Lopez-Lorca, A.A., Miller, T., Pedell, S., Mendoza, A., Keirnan, A., Sterling, L.: One size doesn't fit all: diversifying "the user" using personas and emotional scenarios, In: Proceedings of the 6th International Workshop on Social Software Engineering (SSE 2014), pp. 25–32. ACM, New York (2014)

Experiences with User-Centered Design and Agile Requirements Engineering in Fixed-Price Projects

Edna Kropp[1,2(✉)] and Kolja Koischwitz[1,2]

[1] akquinet, Berlin, Germany
{edna.kropp,kolja.koischwitz}@akquinet.de
[2] Institut für Informatik, Freie Universität Berlin, Berlin, Germany
edna.kropp@fu-berlin.de

Abstract. Efficiently incorporating usability and user experience (UX) in agile requirements engineering (RE) remains a challenge. We introduce a team role called 'On-site User Experience Consultant' (osUX consultant) which supports integrating user-centered design (UCD) firmly in agile RE under the constraints of fixed-price software development projects. Our experience shows that such changes in processes cause tensions. These tensions can arise around issues such as the power dynamics within the team, budgets as well as effectively using insights gained from usability tests. We name methods and practices of osUX consulting and how they fit into different phases of an agile RE process. Additionally, we discuss who within a team is ideally suited to occupy this role. Finally, we describe how old habits in the development process have to be adapted to establish this approach within the project team and with the client.

Keywords: User-centered design · UCD · User experience · UX · On-site UX consultant · Requirements engineering · RE · Agile software development process · Dual-track process

1 Introduction

The efficient combination of agile software development projects [8] and usability measures [17] is still an unresolved issue for researchers [15,19] and industry [1,6,16,18]. At akquinet we are doing mostly fixed-price software development with explicit focus on UX. These projects, despite of being delivered for a fixed price, are subject to change in the sense that the stories or features implemented in the final solution are not necessarily those agreed upon in the initial contract. Requirements, their details, and their priorities often change throughout the projects. Typically, projects are for business-to-business (B2B) solutions of niche products such as web applications for manufacturers of machines and the domain is complex and not well known. Unlike with business-to-consumer (B2C) solutions we do not interact with our users directly. In our case users are

© IFIP International Federation for Information Processing 2016
Published by Springer International Publishing Switzerland 2016. All Rights Reserved
A. Ebert et al. (Eds.): UsARE 2012/2014, LNCS 9312, pp. 47–61, 2016.
DOI: 10.1007/978-3-319-45916-5_4

employees or customers of our clients. Therefore, we need alternative ways, such as user-centered design (UCD), to ensure the users' acceptance and benefits from our solutions.

We introduce a role in the development team called 'On-site User Experience Consultant' (osUX consultant). Typical roles in our project teams are project manager (PM), who is also doing most of requirements engineering (RE), several developers with one dedicated architect role, and a designer (only working part time on the project). The role of an osUX consultant helps us to successfully combine agile RE and a user-centered design (UCD) approach in our development projects. The UCD approach, also known as Human-Centered Design (HCD) [5], allows RE to focus on users' experience (UX), as well as their needs, and expectations [17]. The information gathered and used by the osUX consultant constantly adds to the understanding of requirements and the overall goals. Additionally, the osUX consultant ensures that the target user groups and their usage requirements are at the center of attention at all times, especially for RE and during implementation.

In this paper we describe the strategies and UCD activities we use to firmly integrate the osUX consultant in agile RE. Our experience shows that such changes in the development process cause tensions. These tensions can arise around issues such as the power dynamics within the team, cuts to the UCD budget as well as how to report usability issues while being mindful about budgetary constraints. Moreover, we discuss who within the team, e.g. the PM or one of the developers, is ideally suited to occupy this role. Additionally, we share our experience on how habits of clients and the project team need to be adapted to establish a UCD approach in agile RE.

2   The Role of UCD in Our Agile RE

The basis for integrating UCD in agile RE is to establish a process so that information about the users and evaluation of solutions from a user's point of view become part of the development. In this section we describe how UCD and agile RE are permanently integrated in our fixed-price projects, what our UCD approach contains, e.g. planned methods and best practices, and who should take on the role of osUX consultant.

2.1   Project Management in Fixed-Price Projects with UCD and Agile RE

As described in more detail in one of our latest blog posts [10][1], in our agile projects the initial contract consists of a set of rough descriptions of features with their basic, initially known requirements and a clause permitting the client to ask for changes during the project. Such changes will be accommodated, provided that the total estimate required to implement changed requirements either does

---

[1] Written in German.

not exceed the estimates before the change or an additional agreement is set up to cover the additional efforts. Together with the agile principle of releasing early and often, this gives the clients optimal conditions to meet their goals without being obliged to exactly define every detail in advance. This approach allows the project to stay within the predetermined or adjusted budget.

The central topic of communication and interaction between the PM, the development team, and the clients throughout the entire development process revolves around RE [7]. Requirements are typically gathered and documented once and refined iteratively in one or more cycles during planned interviews and workshops with the client. Then, the requirements are further enhanced within the project team (consulting with the client when necessary) in ramp-up meetings. This happens in a sprint before the corresponding features are implemented - comparable to a dual-track process [3,12] - as well as during development, when necessary.

During the course of the project our project managers (PM) communicate intensively with the client. The procedures and rules to do so are set individually for every project and client. The initial goal of the PM is to establish the most suitable communications and documentation for a given project. Communication also depends on how tech-savvy, demanding, and confident the clients are. The integration of UCD in the development process depends on whether the clients have prior knowledge or experience with it.

Feasibility in agile projects is based on solid quotes [4]. These will dictate the day-to-day work of the project team and determine the overall success. Quotes are usually done by the PM, an experienced developer, and the osUX consultant. A good estimate covers all labor needed to develop a feature. From our experience estimates (including an explicit budget for usability measures) comprise of the following:

- The cost of calculating the quote itself
- RE and UCD (up to 15 %)
- Implementation
- Testing and bug-fixing (up to 20 %)
- PM and communication (10–20%)
- A budget for contingencies

The initial estimate of a feature set is typically part of the contract and is based on an initial rough RE and conceptual work before and during estimation. Its main purpose is to give the project team and the clients a foundation for all upcoming communication.

2.2   UCD Approach - Methods and Practices of an OsUX Consultant

The osUX consultant brings a UCD approach to the agile RE process. This includes input on usability and UX throughout the whole RE process and hence throughout the whole development process [14]. UCD activities can be grouped for each feature in four phases: initiation, conceptualization, implementation, and follow-up. Below we have listed crucial UCD activities in each phase. There may be other, exceptional phases in our development process such as bug-fixing or release phases which are not included in this list of phases due to their irregular appearance. The further the projects progress the less the influence and the greater the expenses of UCD activities [2].

UCD in Initiation

- Project planning - within project team
  - Setting goals for UCD
  - Estimation on initial requirements from a UCD point of view
- Contextual inquiry - with potential users and other stakeholders
  - Research on users, domain, and context
- Visualization and modeling of users in their context and domain
  - Personas - concrete user representatives
  - Work-flow analysis
  - Scenarios - nontechnical description of use
- UCD moderated requirements workshop - with client, potential users, and other stakeholders

UCD in Conceptualization

- Allocate and analyze all existing information about a planned feature or requirement
- Concept of design and interaction
  - Transform requirements and scenarios into use cases
  - Transform use cases into concepts - scribbles, wire frames, paper prototypes
  - Match concepts with existing style guide and patterns
  - Allocate feedback from client, potential users, and other stakeholders
- Ramp-up meeting - break down complex tasks within team

UCD in Implementation

- Formative evaluation
  - Expert reviews on preliminary results
  - Paper prototype tests
- Feedback about UX to team and client on preliminary results

UCD in Follow-up

- Summative evaluation
  - Expert reviews on existing features
  - Usability tests (UT) - with potential users
- Reporting about UX to team and to clients
  - Summary of the overall usability of the solution
  - Suggestions for future improvements

The **initiation phase** comprises all UCD activities which need to be conducted before conceptualization and development can begin. Visualizations and models of contextual information help to communicate about overall goals and concrete requirements. Some activities in the initiation phase such as initial estimations and contextual inquiry are performed once and most of their results apply throughout the entire development process. Most other UCD activities are applied repeatedly depending on the feature or functionality to be developed in the agile project setting. Meetings in the initiation phase, e.g. requirements workshops, and just before implementation, e.g. ramp-up meetings, help to transfer knowledge between stakeholders supported by the osUX consultant and UCD activities. For vital, large, and complex requirements a requirements workshop is conducted. The workshop is moderated by the osUX consultant who provides a well structured approach and keeps focus by avoiding unnecessary discussions. The structured approach includes identifying user roles through personas, writing scenarios, specifying requirements, their details, their limits and priorities with clients, potential users, and other stakeholders.

Sometimes there are several months between RE workshops and the **conceptualization phase**, hence good documentation during initiation is needed. In preparing of the concept for a planned feature all relevant information, such as information gathered during contextual inquiry about users, given requirements, created scenarios, need to be collected.

The **implementation phase** starts with a ramp-up meeting. An informal meeting with the PM, the osUX consultant, and the developers who plan to start a task that is part of the current sprint. These meetings are not planned ahead. They are initiated by a developer, if the task is complicated or information is missing. Activities in this meeting are information gathering, knowledge exchange, writing down missing scenarios, discussing issues, and finding a consensus about possible solutions. In this phase the osUX consultant is an advocate for the users, when conducting e.g. reviews or giving feedback to the developers on preliminary results. All these efforts are still included in the quotes for implementation. The developers' willingness to make changes is greater during this phase as opposed to when the task is declared completed. Once the developers declare the feature to be finished and ready for a final review or a usability test, there is usually neither the budget nor the willingness for changes due to usability issues or UX recommendations.

In the **follow-up phase** UCD activities can help to check whether requirements are fulfilled and the quality of the solution provides good UX e.g. through usability testing and summative evaluation, e.g. expert reviews. In this phase only usability issues of the highest priority i.e. show stoppers are fixed by developers, because the release is close. The removal of minor usability issues or UCD recommendations then depends on the priorities of the client and the management of the PM. Usually, they are gathered by the osUX consultant and communicated as future improvements to the client.

There are conditions under which it is especially demanding to properly integrate UCD activities in the project phases described above. During initiation the clients present a rough set of requirements. These are usually feature-driven and do not have a specific focus on users' needs or expectations. This leads to situations in which important UX requirements and risks can easily be overlooked. For standard tasks, e.g. sign-in processes or user administration, overall quotation and initial conceptualization is easy. But for complex tasks and individual solutions, e.g. complex UI elements such as calendars, time bars, or charts, the project team has to invest additional time to analyze the clients' input from a UCD perspective and check for hidden complexity before proceeding with quotation and conceptualization.

During the implementation phase the team follows UCD methods presented above, e.g. initial concepts and ramp-up meetings, as long as they are within the estimated budget. Conflicts arise when there are additional demands from clients, which often emerge with a tangible solution, but not enough time or resources to adequately handle them. This leads to short-cuts in the process which are prone to weaken the already achieved usability of the current solution. Similar effects are observable in the release and the bug fixing phases. With limited resources and deadline pressures, quick fixes are made without usability considerations. Most times these have unforeseen implications on the usability of the current solution.

2.3   Who Should Take on the Role of On-Site UX Consultant?

When considering who is suited to take on the role of osUX consultant, it is necessary to look at the skills this person should have. Among many others, these are:

Trained in UCD methods and practices - The osUX consultant is well trained in UCD methods and practices and knows most state of the art UCD procedures. Hence, she or he can make decisions such as what UX evaluation method, e.g. formative or summative, usability test or expert review, etc., should be used in what stage of the process. And she or he can perform them without additional supervision.

Availability - The osUX consultant should be available throughout the entire development process. Hence, she or he knows about every initial request or change in requirements, knows about existing styles and patterns and the reasons they were chosen, always looks out for potential optimization (for better UX and solutions that fit into budget), can choose from best fitting UCD methods and practices/ state of the art UCD procedures, and can support the team with fast solutions. Alternatives to having an osUX consultant role or person available throughout the entire development process are to outsource to an agency or an inhouse service for conceptualization and evaluation, and other variations to those approaches. The advantage of having an osUX consultant is that open issues and questions are dealt with immediately or at least within the specified deadlines.

Responsibilities to users and self-assigned tasks - The osUX consultant focuses on the quality of the software solution concerning UX. This includes the initiation of the right UCD activities despite any skepticism of other project members and to be an advocate of users' needs and expectations even when the project suffers from pressure in time or budget. Her or his objective is to satisfy the user's needs (not the client's) in the best interest of the client. The responsibilities and assigned tasks of the osUX consultant are limited. She or he can only introduce recommendations and offer her support to the project. Thus, the PM and the client make final decisions on how to use the budget. Also, the developers decide when and if to ask for help and advice. Additionally, all initial plans and quotes, such as conducting a usability test or using 10 % of the planned budget for UCD methods, are always at risk of omition through pressures of time and budget.

Introduction of improvements - The osUX consultant has typically the unpleasant role to point out weaknesses of existing requirements or solutions. Also, she or he has to formulate recommendations that have to prove their worthiness to the user. This requires some distance to the development process as well as a lot of diplomatic skills. Sometimes, the client's wishes have to be questioned or at other times solutions have to be challenged by e.g. usability tests.

Besides the personal skills of the osUX consultant, it is important to consider what position, i.e. responsibilities and authority, the person has within the project.

The advantages to assigning the role of an osUX consultant to a team member such as the PM or a designer are substantial. The PM is already a fixed role in any project for the entire duration. Additionally, the PM typically has deep insight into requirements, because she or he is in charge of RE. UCD activities are then more likely to be conducted, because next to the client the PM has the authority to plan the budget and to make final decisions in the project. Assigning the role of osUX consultant to the designer could be favorable as well. It is likely that she or he is at least part-time in the project already and is interested in and acquainted with most of the visual aspects of good usability, e.g. supportive positioning of content or buttons - maybe even some of the interactional aspects, e.g. a supportive navigational structure.

Despite these apparent advantages, our experience shows, however, that in reality, it is preferable not to have a current team member, including developers, in the role of osUX consultant. They each have their own focus and responsibility which generally collides with the responsibilities and assignments of an osUX consultant. It was observable that, even with an osUX consultant on the team, the PM would omit UCD activities, among others, in the face of time or budgetary pressures. Also, in a B2B project it is the PM's first priority to please the client, not to satisfy the users' needs who are e.g. employees of the client. This might be different when looked at in contexts other than fixed-price projects for B2B solutions, e.g. when revenue is generated directly by a B2C platform. Additionally, none of the above mentioned team members are trained in UCD methods or practices, because usually training in other areas, e.g. project management, technology, graphics tools, etc., have higher prioritiy. Also, it was observable and reported by the team members such as architects, designers, and developers that they get a sort of 'tunnel vision' and therefore lack the necessary distance to adopt a usability perspective. When they focus and spend a lot of time with a task, even the most complex concepts seem intuitive. They tend not to take the users' context into account any more.

3 Breaking Old Habits for UCD in Agile RE

One might assumed that little would stand in the way of a solution with good usability and UX, when clients support a UCD approach by committing up to 15 % of explicit budget for UCD activities, which are fully support by all project team members and management. However, we observed that independent of best intentions old habits of the client, the PM and other team members such as developers have to be addressed first.

3.1 Breaking Old Habits with the Client

Conservative attitude – The typical client (in our case traditional industries such as mechanical manufacturing) is not prepared to participate in an agile project with a UCD approach. Often clients have taken part in more formal and sequential development processes in which the focus is mainly on budget, time and scope, rather than on users' needs and expectations, and hence they are shaped by their experience. Personal habits, expectations, and approaches as well as existing organizational procedures and requirements at the client's side stand in the way of agile development.

Introducing an agile approach which includes UCD and an osUX consultant requires to build a trusting relationship with the client and create success stories. Usually, there is no budget allocated to start over, hence there is are only small margins for errors. It is the PM's task and challenge to convey why the agile way is the better approach, how it is more effective and transparent and why the change from existing approaches to a new one is worth the effort.

In order to maintain an agile and user-centered approach, it is important to establish rules of engagement with the clients that will ensure a focus on these aspects. The following questions should to be answered:

- Are there regular meetings, what is their structure, what is documented by whom, when, and where?
- Given the project plan, how do we approach the features to implement next?
- How do we handle and how do we refine basic assumptions stated by our contract?
- How do we dissolve different interests and opinions?
- What happens when requirements change?

As a result of a development process with a UCD approach RE workshops can be restructured to be more user centered (described in Sect. 2.2). Additionally, other tools, e.g. personas and scenarios, can dissolve some conflicts in communication. Making features tangible through visualization helps with some communication issues.

Solution oriented – Clients tend to think first and foremost of the end-product, e.g. they present a screen shot instead of stating users' needs and usage requirements. This means that they may skip important steps of the UCD approach. Usually, clients do not share the same interests in the solution as the target user groups and hence miss important factors for a solution with good UX. This increases efforts, because the conceptual model and the implementation do not match real requirements. To prevent false assumptions from entering the RE process, presented solutions have to be tested from a user's point of view. The best questions to ask are:

- What problems of the user are solved by the solution presented by the client?
- What part of the solution presented by the client might be irrelevant to users and could be left out?
- What tasks would the user perform to achieve her or his goals?
- How would the user most likely perform her or his tasks, in what order, can content be semantically grouped?

The first thing to learn is to start with getting to know the users and their context. The UCD approach is at first not easy to accept for most clients. Especially, doing interviews, creating personas and describing scenarios seems very theoretical and far from the problems to be solved. The clients start to value those as important first steps of an elaborated problem solving strategy when they experience their importance in requirements workshops. Workshops are expensive and time is usually short. The goal is to make requirements more concrete and find a consensus about their boundaries. Without sticking to personas and scenarios a lot of discipline by all participants is necessary to stay focused and not be lost in discussions about some detail or solution. Habits do not change over night. Defined procedures in e.g. requirement workshops are helpful to avoid e.g. quick solutions that may not have a matching use case or scenario.

In a project we conducted for a machine manufacturer, the client had no possibility to give us access to users due to high competition in the market. Nevertheless, the osUX consultant and the PM insisted to stick with the UCD process by creating and refining personas and scenarios. The approach was new and not plausible for the client. However, the UCD approach proved to be an immediate benefit in the following RE workshop. The task was to define filter options for machine entities. The client began the RE workshop by presenting his solution, a self-made screen shot, consisting of more than 30 different filter attributes each having multiple possible values. This solution was set aside in favor of the UCD approach. We started by collecting all possible use cases for filtering. Then, we only allowed filter options which matched the allocated use cases. Afterwards, only 6 of the formerly presented search attributes remained in the final version. This saved 80 % of development efforts and enhanced the UI's usability by omitting over 24 additional unnecessary filter options.

Unused potential – Clients need to get accustomed to the fact that some UCD activities such as usability tests (UT) or recommendations from expert reviews uncover potential weaknesses or improvements which cannot all be fixed or implemented within the estimated budget. When it comes to costs, the change to agile RE and UCD is likewise demanding. With fixed-price projects, our company takes most financial risks. Of course, we trust our clients not to exploit the offer. In the contract efforts are pinned to roughly described features and when refining them through RE cycles, the client cannot expect to get everything an initial description could have possibly meant. Instead, the estimated budget for a single feature should be seen as a limit. This limit states the capacity to implement as much functionality as possible starting with high priority, must have requirements. Suggestions on how to cope with unused potential are:

- Build up a trustful relationship with your client
- What makes a solution complete? Find mutual agreeable basis for the scope of planned features and emerging improvements.
- Establish definitions to distinguish between issues which are bugs, weaknesses in usability and suggested improvements

With every client we have to build up trust through transparency, constant communication, and close interaction. Transparency is needed on estimated and real efforts, of saved efforts, and overspent time. We notify the client when we want to reserve or push up some budget to e.g. conduct a UT or realize some measures resulting from a UT. Often, newly emerging requirements or improvements to existing features can be postponed to later projects or project phases, keeping the current sprint and milestone stable and allowing to finish in time.

We were surprised by the client's reaction in one of our projects. We planned three milestones each ending with a UT. After the first UT, the client declared all usability issues found as bugs and therefore asked for immediate repair of all findings.

Performing all measures would have gone well beyond all estimates in the contract. Declaring all UT results as bugs and hence assuming to fix them is part of the contract seemed right to the client. Yet, it is wrong in more than one way. In general, it is not advisable to repair every little weakness that is found in a UT. The time spent to make that many changes might prove to be wasted, when in agile projects such as this, requirements may change in the future. Moreover, even the smallest changes in layout or interaction can cause new, unknown, and unwanted effects on UX.

The osUX consultant has the knowledge about the overall goals of the project and is trained to find measures with maximum effect which are minimally invasive. Measures that also best fit in the remaining time and budget. This has to be made visible and understandable to clients to change their thinking about UT results as bugs.

3.2   Breaking Old Habits with the PM

When a UCD approach is added to a project, especially when there is not much prior knowledge about UCD in the team, the PM has a lot to steer during the whole project. A lot of the responsibilities for different parts of the 'traditional' agile development process change with UCD. Before UCD was introduced, RE was mainly performed by the PM in close collaboration with the client, i.e. in regular phone calls without a lot of documentation. The osUX consultant therefore has a tough time participating in RE and acquiring all knowledge necessary for a UCD approach. Often, the limited time available to conceptualize and implement features is not used as effectively and efficiently as could be. The PM is held back by old habits making decisions about usability although this is the task of the osUX consultant. These concepts and the time spent in them reduce the estimated time available for the osUX consultant. Issues to be addressed by the PM, when an osUX consultant becomes a new team member:

- Which parts of the process need to be adjusted to UCD and the osUX consultant?
- What responsibilities and tasks are now assigned to the osUX consultant which were originally performed by other team members?
- Who decides on what UCD activities are planned and performed? Who has the knowledge and the authorization to make those decisions?
- Who should participate in UCD activities? Only the osUX consultant, the client, the project team, or all stakeholders?

The process comprising UCD needs to be adjusted to a dual-track process in which there is an explicit conceptual phase before implementation of important and complex tasks can be started. Also, the osUX consultant has to be integrated into existing communication channels concerning RE. Additionally, the PM needs to refer discussions about usability and UX to the osUX consultant.

There are situations, in which the osUX consultant's role is ignored and work is taken over by the PM. This is the case, when the osUX consultant is not available, the PM is pressured in time, and/ or tasks have to be rescheduled spontaneously. There are also situations, in which the PM has to decide to do without or with limited UCD. As stated in Sect. 2.1, one possible reason to omit UCD activities could be that a feature's implementation is getting out of proportion to its estimation. Other times, UCD activities may not provide immediate benefit or are not as easyly integrated in the development process.

Not all UCD activities can prove immediate benefit and are as easy to be integrated in the development process as e.g. use cases. At one occasion in a project with an alpha-state solution, the osUX consultant recommended to rethink the navigational structure and labels, although no budget was planned for it. The osUX consultant prepared and proposed a card sorting. Although the PM understood the need for restructuring the navigation, he did not feel comfortable to ask the client for authorization. There were no real users available to participate and the PM did not believe that anyone from the client's side could represent real users. In the end, a compromise was to discuss the navigational structure in the next RE workshop. In comparison to personas and scenarios, card sorting remains a UCD activity not established in this project.

At another occasion the PM decided - due to time pressure and the absence of the osUX consultant - to give a developer a new task, drew wireframes for it, and introduced them to the development team not conferring with nor mentioning it to the osUX consultant. This resulted in UI elements which did not comply with existing conceptual patterns. Reorganizing the UI to be consistent to existing patterns was not possible due to limited time and budget.

The osUX consultant is the only team member who has expert knowledge about usability and UCD as well as a complete overview over interaction strategies and conceptual patterns. Hence, the PM should never skip to involve the osUX consultant about issues with requirements concerning the usability. The osUX consultant being a bottleneck could be avoided, though it requires the PM to change his habit of doing all RE by himself and giving the osUX consultant heads up about upcoming tasks and the RE process. As described above, the success of integrating UCD greatly depends on the support the role of the osUX consultant gets from the PM.

The PM learned about particular aspects of usability considerations as far as they concerned issues that arose during the project. However, the issues to solve were specific to the project and different every time. Therefore, it cannot be expected of him to come up with usability considerations apart from the ones he witnessed. More importantly, during the course of the project, the PM understood the UCD approach and its purpose better, got to know some of its benefits and experienced the consequences of omitting it.

3.3   Adapting Old Habits in the Development Team

Introducing and establishing the new role of an osUX consultant is not the same. First it is necessary to introduce the role by advertising UCD activities to all team members including the PM. This can be achieved by offering consulting services whenever possible, e.g. in meetings. The osUX consultant has to find a way to make UCD activities and their results as transparent and accessible to the other team members as possible. The long term establishment of the osUX consultant role is another challenge. Ideally, the osUX consultant should be available to all team members at all times. Due to different office hours this is not always the case. UCD activities can become a bottle neck when the osUX consultant works part-time or other team members work overtime. When the osUX consultant is not available, the team sometimes falls back to old habits and procedures that existed before the osUX consultant was introduced in the team. The following methods can be used to establish the role of an osUX consultant in the development team. The osUX consultant should:

- show positive outcomes of UCD activities, e.g. solutions that are based on existing patterns or general usability considerations that will save developers time

- make usability considerations as transparent as possible, so developers can learn and apply them without feeling patronized
- consider to integrate the whole team in conceptual decisions. So it is less likely that whom ever had a similar role (intrinsic or officially assigned) before will have reason to work against the new approach.

It is advisable for the osUX consultant to sit in close proximity to the developers. Then, the osUX consultant has a better chance to realize when old habits are picked up again or steps in UCD are skipped. Also, the developers and the osUX consultant have a better overview of what the other is doing.

The need for a ramp-up shows that although requirements have been formulated and scenarios for features have been written, there are still enough gaps for the osUX consultant to fill before a developer knows exactly what is asked for. Especially in the implementation phase, the osUX consultant keeps the focus on UX and can give valuable advice to the developers. When developers try to solve technical problems their focus is solely on technical issues. In doing so, they sometimes get a tunnel vision and forget about the users and their context [11]. Then the osUX consultant has to adapt the developers' habits to spend all their time with elaborate technical refinement and consider basic UCD recommendations instead. In these cases, personas and scenarios help the osUX consultant to bring the users back into the developers focus. Placing UCD activities in this manner is less effort than proving obvious weaknesses of UX in a UT and waiting for improvements to be authorized by the client afterwards.

Here, the same examples as mentioned in Sect. 3.2 apply as good examples. The developers asked the PM for advice because the osUX consultant was out of office, when they were not sure about conceptual decisions and the PM made decisions that did not match existing conceptual patterns. Also, the developers accepted wireframes drawn by the PM not complying with existing patterns due to time pressure. Additionally, more than once developers build small add-ons to existing views that were demanded by the client, once the client saw existing solutions. These solutions did not comply with existing patterns such as e.g. static information that was placed at positions reserved for controls, and styled in colors, e.g. in bright yellow, that were not defined in the style guide.

4   Conclusion

In this paper we shed some light on our experiences with agile RE in fixed-price projects in the B2B industry. We point out how a new role called 'On-site User Experience Consultant' (osUX consultant) is introduced and established in the development team. We suggest the role of an osUX consultant to be taken by a separate team member who is trained in UCD methods and practices and who focuses on users' needs and expectations (with respect to clients' wishes) and is available for usability consulting and feedback throughout the entire development process.

Also, we name UCD activities we use to integrate a UCD approach into agile RE, e.g. the usage of personas and scenarios in requirements workshops and the establishment of ramp-up meetings before implementation to break down complex tasks together with developers, the PM, and the osUX consultant. Recommendations made after implementation usually end up as improvements for later milestones. It can be especially demanding to properly integrate UCD activities in some phases of the development process. For example, during the initiation phase estimation and initial conceptualization for complex or individualized solutions are prone to underestimation and hidden complexity. Also, if the clients have additional demands, which often emerge with a tangible solution and which are not included in the estimated budget, this can lead to a lack of usability due to short cuts during the implementation, release, and bug-fixing phases.

Finally, we have demonstrated in what manner old habits of clients, the PM, and the development team remain a challenge and how we have coped with those so far. Although clients accept an agile development process, they are still conservative in project communication and decision making. Also, clients tend to be solution-oriented, i.e. presenting solutions in form of e.g. self-made screen shots instead of describing what problems to be solved. Additionally, clients need to learn to live with unused potential, e.g. results of a usability test should not be treated as bugs in general. Results should be seen as the potential to further improve usability. Before UCD was introduced the PM used to do all the RE by himself. Hence, communication was directly between PM and clients and documentation reduced to a minimum. The PM decided when to forward what information to team members. With UCD the PM needs to change communication habits and enlarge documentation to ensure earliest possible knowledge exchange with the osUX consultant. We learned that introducing and establishing the role of an osUX consultant in the development team are two separate steps. After introduction the osUX needs to advertise UCD services, e.g. usability consulting on specific tasks, to each team member and establish new communication channels for evaluation and feedback on usability, e.g. in team meetings.

In the future, we hope to further explore the existence of generalizable phenomena, i.e. habits to change. It is also planned to incorporate how these phenomena manifest themselves in the process and what their consequences are. Where possible, we will additionally support our findings with a quantitative approach, e.g. how much effort it took or saved to overcome old habits.

References

1. Anitha, P., Prabhu, B.: Integrating requirements engineering and user experience design in product life cycle management. In: First International Workshop on Usability and Accessibility Focused Requirements Engineering - UsARE, Zurich (2012)
2. Bias, R., Mayhew, D.: Cost-Justifying Usability: An Update for an Internet Age. Morgan Kaufmann, Burlington (2005)
3. Cagan, M.: Dual-Track Scrum (2012). http://www.svpg.com/dual-track-scrum/. Accessed 12 Mar 2015

4. Cohn, M.: Agile Estimating and Planning. Prentice Hall PTR, Upper Saddle River (2005)
5. DIN EN ISO 9241-210: Ergonomics of human-system interaction - Part 210: Human-centred design for interactive systems (2010). http://www.iso.org/iso/home/. Accessed 12 Mar 2015
6. Ekelund, J., Levingston, C.: Usability in Agile Development. UX Research, Melbourne (2008)
7. Ekelund, J., Lowe, D.: Using Partial Designs to Elicit Requirements in Web Development a Survey of Commercial Practice. University of Technology, Sydney (2002)
8. Fowler, M.: The New Methodology (2003). http://martinfowler.com/articles/newMethodology.html. Accessed 12 Mar 2015
9. Krug, S.: Rocket Surgery Made Easy: The Do-It-Yourself Guide to Finding and Fixing Usability Problems. New Riders, San Francisco (2009)
10. Kubitz, T.: Agile Festpreisprojekte Risiko oder Chance?, akquinet AG, blog post (2014). http://blog-de.akquinet.de/2014/04/29/agile-festpreisprojekte-risiko-oder-chance-2
11. Lai-Chong Law, E., Hvannberg, E., Cockton, G., Jeffries, R.: Introduction to Agile usability: user experience (UX) activities on Agile development projects. In: Maturing Usability Quality in Software, Interaction, and Value. Springer, Berlin (2007)
12. Lent, J.: Dual-track Agile keeps requirements in check (2014). http://searchsoftwarequality.techtarget.com/opinion/Dual-track-Agile-keeps-requirements-in-check. Accessed 12 Mar 2015
13. Mayhew, D.J.: The Usability Engineering Lifecycle: A Practitioner's Handbook for User Interface Design. Morgan Kaufmann, Burlington (1999)
14. Nielson, J.: Usability engineering lifecycle. IEEE Comput. 25(3), 12–22 (1992)
15. Parsons, D., Lal, R., Ryu, H., Lange, M.: Software development methodologies, Agile development and usability engineering. In: 18th Australasian Conference on Information Systems, Toowoomba (2007)
16. Raison, C., Schmidt, S.: Keeping user centred design (UCD) alive and well in your organisation: taking an agile approach. In: Second International Conference on Design, User Experience, and Usability, Design Philosophy, Methods, and Tools, Las Vegas, pp. 573–582 (2013)
17. Rogers, Y., Sharp, H., Preece, J.: Interaction Design: Beyond Human - Computer Interaction. Wiley, Chichester (2011)
18. Singer, N.: Intel's Sharp-Eyed Social Scientist (or The Watchful Lab of Dr. Bell), p. BU1. New York Times, 16 February 2014
19. Sohaib, O., Khan, K.: Integrating usability engineering and agile software development: a literature review. In: International Conference on Computer Design and Applications (ICCDA), Qinhuangdao, pp. V2-32–V2-38 (2010)

Experience Focused Requirements Gathering with Children and Young People - Balancing Player, Learner and User (PLU) Requirement Needs

Diana Yifan Xu and Janet C. Read[✉]

School of CEPS, University of Central Lancashire, Preston PR1 2HE, UK
{yfxu,jcread}@uclan.ac.uk

Abstract. This chapter is bridging the gap of Human Computer Interaction (HCI) and Requirement Engineering (RE) where the intended users or appropriators of the technology or service are children and young people. The research draws theory and practices from several disciplines: Human Computer Interaction (HCI) and Interaction Design (IXD) but also from psychology, educational technology and games.

Research into children and young people's requirement needs as Player, Learner and User (PLU) is a main theme in Interaction Design for Children (IDC). This chapter focuses on the challenges and issues that arise when conducting requirement gathering with children and young people; it looks at common methods, approaches and methodological innovation in the current research while treating children as research partners in the requirements gathering process

Keywords: HCI · Requirement engineering · Child-Computer Interaction (CCI) · Children · User experience · User-Centred Design (UCD) · Participatory design

1 Introduction: Child-Computer Interaction (CCI), Children's Experience

CCI or Child-Computer Interaction is a reasonably newly established discipline that focuses on Human-Computer Interaction (HCI) where the intended users or appropriators of the technology or service are children and young people. It grew from pockets of work, mainly driven by interests in technology use within education and schools, in its own early years, before developing into an identifiable community within the HCI space which is beginning a process of maturing into its own discipline with its own associated methods and solutions [1] as an IFIP SIG group[1].

Similar to the multidisciplinary HCI, CCI draws theory and practice from several disciplines, and lessons are learned from the current practices of working with children

---

[1] http://www.idc-sig.org/.

A. Ebert et al. (Eds.): UsARE 2012/2014, LNCS 9312, pp. 62–76, 2016.
DOI: 10.1007/978-3-319-45916-5_5

in various fields. It is often inspired by child-centred participatory approaches that originated from child psychology and social science.

The book Researching Children's Experience [2] has provided methods and approaches in developmental psychology: from naturalistic observations to participatory research with children and the humanistic participatory way of working with children is common in childhood studies and social sciences. Some examples of influential works in the field are the 'Mosaic Approach' [3] and 'The Hundred Languages of Children' [4]; they work with the nature of children's expressions: diverse, divergent and intertwining. The recent review on methodology of working with children [5], and investigations on various children's social experiences [6] have raised the common point, that there has been a methodological shift, involving the emergence of new 'participatory' research methodologies, the adaptation of more traditional methods, such as observation, and the development of multi-method approaches.

2   Children and Young People's Requirement Needs

User Experience (UX) is the new usability. Technology for children and young people is increasingly becoming experience focused, and in doing so considers their experiences as Players, Learners and Users (PLU). The PLU model [1, 7] defines how children interact with technology and maps how their three distinct requirement needs as Players, Learners or Users; can be met by technologies that are described as Entertainment, Education, and Enabling. The intended relationship of child to the technology assists in considering how the interactive product may be designed and developed (Fig. 1):

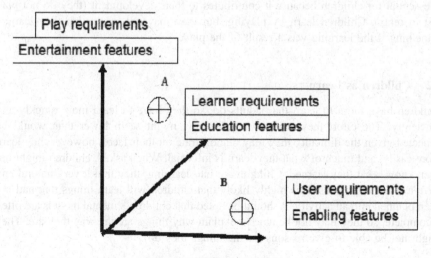

Fig. 1. The PLU model [1]

- **Player Requirements** - The child sees the interactive product as a toy and gameplay thing; the product must amuse or entertain, be fun and challenging. Example technologies are games and interactive toys.
- **Learner Requirements** - The interactive product is a learning tool similar to school or a teacher; the product is expected to instruct, challenge and reward. Typical examples are educational software and Virtual Learning Environments (VLEs).
- **User Requirements** - For the product to be useful it must enable the child and make things easier to do. The examples can be handwriting recognition software, a word processor, an energy use tracker or an interactive TV.

The PLU model demonstrates children's different roles and activities from both children's and adults' perspectives; in picking up a product, the children's concern may be all about play, while adults might place the importance on learning. Most children's products share two or three of the (PLU) requirement features, an example is educational games: these have to be playful, appealing to children and at the same time delivering the expected learning benefit; that is to balance the different requirement needs and to meet the interests of all stakeholders.

To carry out requirements gathering with children and young people, an understanding of some of the differences between adults and children and their use of technology can be established [7]:

2.1 Children as Players

Children find play natural, they have high levels of imagination, so much of their play can be hard to visualize for adults. In requirement gathering, if asked, the children might say that they have been playing, but it can sometimes be difficult to observe. Play is essential for children because it contributes to their development (they do not play just to relax). Children learn by playing, but they may not report that they learned something if the learning was a result of the play.

2.2 Children as Learners

Children have more to learn than adults do, so they have to learn more quickly and efficiently. The effort they report when learning might seem lower than would be expected given the difficulty they may demonstrate on their faces, however they learn more easily, and much of what they learn is informal. When asked, children might not even know what they learned. Children are into learning; they find it very natural and have a lot of curiosities. It is highly likely that children will learn things that had not been planned into an activity. It should be noted that children's mental models are often incomplete, so they may not be able to explain why things are the way they are. They might not be able to give reasons for the things they do.

2.3   Children as Users

Children age more quickly, so their needs for technology keep changing; it is essential to ensure that technology is age appropriate. They have different motivations than adults. They only use technology if they want to; they also have much more discretion than adults. If they don't like what is put in front of them, they may walk away. Children expect more from ordinary products. They may believe that technology is magic, this can lead to high expectations that may not be realized and may discourage the child.

As all the differences suggest, children and young people are NOT simply small adults, their unique requirement needs for interactive products and services should be considered.

3   Establishing Requirements

The activity of understanding what a product should do is variously described as requirements gathering, requirements capture, requirements elicitation, requirements analysis and requirements engineering [8]. The term 'establishing requirements' is often used to describe the process of finding out what users may want or need in a system [9].

Establishing requirements is about understanding the potential users. It provides insight into the many possible solutions in order to select and investigate the best solution from the users' perspective. The requirements gathering phase is the period when the product team must do its initial research in order to determine the direction of the product, which is critical in creating a basis for the design. Poor requirements collection will impact the remaining stages of the product life-cycle, which will end up with misguided products that won't sell, or products that may be unusable and useless to the user and/or the company that purchases them [10].

A requirement is a statement on what a product should do, or how it should behave. Rogers et al. [8] have identified five different types of requirement for systems that are being developed for adults:

- Functional requirement - a statement of what the product should be able to do.
- Data requirement - a statement about the data within the product.
- Environmental requirement - specify the circumstances within which the product will operate; this will include the physical environment, the social environment, the organizational environment and the technical environment.
- User requirement - used to capture the characteristics of the user group; their skills, whether they are novices or experts, whether they will be casual or frequent users.
- Usability requirements - will be concerned with effectiveness and efficiency, accessibility and learnability.

Among the five types of requirement, the first three tend to be more system focused, while the User and Usability Requirements are more about the user and the usage of the product in situ. In many cases, determining requirements is best done with the assistance of real or potential users, especially when the potential users are children [9].

4 Requirements Gathering with Children and Young People

End users' expertise in the development of new applications is acknowledged in user-centred participatory design. Similarly, children's experience of what they find enjoyable and how they learn is a valuable source of inspiration for the design of products intended for them [11]. A child-centred interaction design requires methods suitable to gather information from and about children. Though different opinions about what role children should play range from very active design partner [12, 13] to a less active role as informants [14], most people agree that children can provide useful insights into the design and development of their technology and service [15].

There are a number of common methods and approaches for gathering requirements to inform Interaction Design for Children (IDC): from traditional methods like observations, interviews and questionnaires, to recent methodological innovations that have been specifically tailored to children, such as Drawing Intervention (DI) [16] and Obstructed Theatre [17, 18].

In general, with a user-centred participatory approach, there are three means by which requirements can be gathered:

- Observation: watching children on what they do.
- Interview, focus group and survey: asking children about their opinions.
- Participatory Design: doing design with children.

Most of the time, the three approaches of "watch, ask and do" are combined to achieve a triangulation of the data, e.g. combining observed and reported requirement needs. The following subsections explore some of the common methods and approaches and how they could be applied in practice.

4.1 Observations, Watching What Children Do

One simple approach to working with children is by observing what they do in a realistic setting. Generally speaking, the term observation refers to an examination of a phenomenon that results in a description suitable for the purpose of a research study [7]. For example, field observation combined with low-tech probes has been used for requirement gathering for a multimedia museum environment with 5 to 10-year-olds [19]; and classroom observation followed by surveys was used for understand what is needed for a handwriting recognition interface for children aged 6 to 7 (Read, MacFarlane et al. 2004).

Naturalistic observation is often a preferred approach when working with children, as, compared to working in a lab, children in their familiar environment are more relaxed and at ease, with any observer effect minimised. Also by working in children's natural environments, product use is naturally embedded in their everyday activities and the interactions take place within their social setting and context, which can be hard to replicate or capture in a lab.

In a number of observational studies, a probe or a mock-up of the system is used to prompt technology and non-technology related requirements during the observation. These can be non-functional prototypes made of low-tech materials like paper and cupboards [19] or they could be storyboards that show the basic idea of the technology to be developed [20]. Sometimes the Wizard of Oz technique is used to gather hardware requirements [21] and other times Video prototypes are used to demonstrate how the system, if made, might have worked [22].

Observation can be direct or indirect. Direct observation is done by the observer, who might watch or listen to what children do. Indirect observation can use photos, audio and video recordings. In some research studies, both direct and indirect observations are employed for rich data. A direct observation can be structured or unstructured. In an unstructured observation, open questions may be asked and the record will be rich descriptions of context without a priori limiting of the range of events or behaviours. The advantage of unstructured observation is its open-endedness that welcomes surprises and new discoveries. In practice, though, lack of focus can cause some problems and can lead to a low reliability of results between observers due to subjectivity. The observational data may also be many but irrelevant or contrived and may not serve the goals and difficult to analyse.

As an alternative, a structured observation can be carried out. Compared to an unstructured observation this will be more focused and will directly serve the goal of the requirement study. In [7], the following steps of a structured observation are explained in details:

1. Determine the focus of your observation
2. Develop observation guides and forms
3. Recruit and train observers
4. Carry out the observation
5. Analyse the interpret findings

The focus of the observation is what is being looked for and having a focus means being selective and observing specific events, activities and behaviours. Observers can make more numerous, more detailed, and more reliable observations when they have a specific focus. When developing observation guides and forms, it may be helpful to involve someone with expertise at the particular age of the children, e.g. a teacher, parents and other members of the design team [7].

Encourage Children's Verbalization during the Observation. While observation takes place, it is common to encourage children's verbalization, as this can reveal more of their experience. The verbalization could be children with their peers in a group brainstorming ideas, with discussion, drawings and investigating existing technologies [23]; or an agent could be introduced for eliciting their self-report.

An example of the innovative use of an agent is the 'Mission from Mars' method used alongside a participatory design session [24] Martians are introduced for a shared narrative space with children, providing a first-hand insight into children's practice in a fun and intriguing way. The method is proposed as a supplement to existing descriptive design methods for interaction design and children. Similarly, 'Designing for Mr Hippo' [25] explored metaphoric design for marginalised children, to provide a fun and easy way for children to begin to understand how to design for users who are not the same as themselves. In both cases, the agents are introduced to encourage children's verbalisation, and for improved self-report.

4.2   Interview, Focus Group and Survey, Asking Children Their Requirement Needs

Asking children about their requirement needs can be a challenging task, as children's logic, linguistic, cognitive, and communication skills are still developing. Especially for shy young children, they have great difficulties to articulate to a stranger (researcher) in an alien environment. In the field of CCI, some child appropriate alternatives of the interview and questionnaire techniques have been specifically developed.

An interview is a guided conversation in which the researcher seeks information from a child. Given that interviews are flexible and can be used as a solo activity or in conjunction with other user requirements activities, it is one of the most frequently used user requirements gathering techniques. The end result of a set of interviews is an integration of perspectives from multiple users for a holistic view of the system being designing for [10]. An interview with a child has to be non-threatening, the child to be interviewed may be selected according to his/her verbal communication skills and personal characteristics; for example, the child may be chosen because he/she is articulate and outgoing, it is less common to interview very young children however interviews can be done among children themselves as in KidReporter [15], as this minimises unfamiliarity and increases the relevance, and the chance of there being asked child-understandable questions.

One alternative to interviews is the focus group, where the researcher works with a group of children in a setting children are familiar with. In a study of designing energy saving devices with teenagers (Bell, Toth et al. 2013), a small number of children were brought together for an hour or so to provide information in response to a series of questions, and to provide their subjective response to product demonstrations/concepts. Note that for children, the time used is shorter than the normal 1 to 2 h focus group session with adults, as 45 min to an hour resembles the length of a typical school class. Often children are given tasks to complete with the prototype of the product so that they may have a better frame of reference from which to speak. Presenting the questions or product to a group usually sparks group discussion and can provide more information than interviewing individual alone [10]. Focus groups are best suited to the generation of ideas with children at the initial stage of design.

Questionnaires allow a developer/researcher to ask every child the same questions in a structured manner. These can be administrated on paper or in digital forms; to be given to a class of children, or to be distributed to a large group of children digitally at one time. The advantage of this technique is that it can reach a large demographic however with little room for adaptation. In some design projects, children use questionnaires to contribute ideas and suggestions for future or partially completed designs: e.g. for eliciting their mental models [26] and for gathering requirements for interfaces [9]. There are established guidelines for survey design for children [7]: 1. Keep it short; 2. Pilot the language; 3. Provide assistance for non-readers and poor readers; 4. Limit the writing; 5. User appropriate tools and methods; 6. Make it fun; 7. Expect the unexpected; 8. Don't take it too seriously; and 9. Be nice! The Fun Toolkit is a popular selection of tools that were designed with these guidelines in mind; it use pictures instead of words, and simple children's language instead of technical jargon. The Fun Toolkit consists of a "Smileyometer", a "Fun Sorter" and an "Again-Again table".

The toolkit can be used for sampling children's experience, comparing and ranking activities. It is fun and attractive, and reduces some of the effects of satisfying and optimizing [27].

When it comes to surveying emotions and experiences over time, one approach can be to combine Cultural Probes and Experience Sampling [28], in a design research method for inquiries involving young children in the design of artefacts supporting daily life activities and outside a classroom context [29]. In this study, to sample experiences of a very young child who could not read and write, a probes package including diary/booklet, stickers, a disposable camera, pencils, coloured paper, drawing paper, crayons etc. was used. The difficulties of obtaining self-report by children over time can be overcome by involving parents and by using appropriately defined playful assignments in the form of cultural probes as with Iversen and Nielsen who worked with children 11–13, using mobile phones (digital cultural probes) as a data capture device and found that they provided access to children's everyday lives that was not accessible through other means [30].

4.3   Participatory Design, Design Sessions with Children

Participatory design emphasises user participation in the decisions related to computing systems that have an impact on their lives. An important aspect of this approach is that users act as fully empowered participants in the design process. One technique for doing this is to ensure that users have early exposure to the target implementation technology - even if this must be done through coarse-granularity, relatively static mock-ups [31]. Participatory design has been an established method for designing technology for and with users [31, 32] and has become increasing popular for designing with children [33].

As opposed to simply being observed, in participatory design children are directly asked to work with researchers to collaboratively create "low-tech prototypes" out of paper, glue, crayons, and so on. These tools act as an icebreaker for a more comfortable brainstorming session, new technology possibilities that might not have previously been considered can therefore be identified [33, 34].

An early variation on participatory design is Informant Design [14], in which stakeholders like children or teachers are seen as experts or 'native informants' informing designers of key issues related to their experience, helping to develop early design ideas and testing prototypes in development [35]. For example, informant design sessions with children aged 8 to 10 used mixed media in designing the logical, physical and the interaction of tangible technology for a museum environment [36].

There are some participatory design methods and techniques that have been specifically designed for working with children. One example is Cooperative Inquiry [37], which is a framework for research and design with children, which includes three crucial aspects: a multidisciplinary partnership with children; field research that emphasizes understanding context, activities, and artifacts; and iterative low-tech and high-tech prototyping. Another is KidReporter [15], which uses mixed media, combining a number of techniques for eliciting information from children, such as interviews, drawing and making pictures. Participatory Analogy is another technique developed for designing user-centred security for children [38].

Other Innovative Participatory Approaches. Two recent methodological innovations that are especially developed for working with children, are Drawing Intervention (DI) [39] and Obstructed Theatre [17, 18].

Drawing and sketching has long been a common practice in design, creativity and problem-solving [40], where drawing is seen to belong to the set of 'low-tech', lightweight, communicative and creative tools. Children's drawings are widely used for visualizing ideas in the design processes; e.g. for general requirement gathering [15, 41], Informant Design [14, 36] and Participatory Design [42, 43]. Drawing has advantages in being visual and concrete, without using abstract verbal descriptions [44]. In many cases, drawing has been shown to be useful as a form of low-tech prototyping to allow children (and not only children) to envision and visualise their ideas [34, 36, 45].

In CCI, children's drawings are mostly used as an inquiry tool to elicit children's thoughts and ideas for design and requirements gathering. The drawing activity provides insight into the children's concept, understanding and request of the technologies; they give ideas for future work on the redesign of the systems, concerning the functionality, the content, the types of input and output and the interactions.

Drawing is an inclusive activity; it can be used with children of different ages, gender, language, culture, education, developmental level, etc. An example is a large scale study [46] which had asked over 200 children aged 12 and under across the world to draw their answer to the question: "What would you like your computer or the Internet to do that it can't do right now?". In this case, drawing was used as a universal inquiry tool, overcoming language and cultural barriers, positioning younger people as windows into the future of technology, informing technology experiences of all ages.

In general for working with children, drawing can facilitate communication with them; four different experiments done by [47, 48] demonstrate that children, given the opportunity to draw while they build a narrative, give about TWICE as much accurate, detailed information as those who are not asked to draw. The general usage of drawing can enhance communication through direct visual expression and/or through drawing facilitated verbal expression.

The idea of Obstructed Theatre originated from [49]. In the technique, the research team used a slightly humorous video clip in which one actor described some of the functionality of an interactive device in a conversation with another actor whilst referring to, but not showing, the off-screen interactive device in question [18].

The method is intended to trigger design ideas without biasing the imagination by showing a real object. After the video film, the researchers encouraged the children to think about what the mysterious device could do and what it would look like. No functional constraints were given in this activity: the children were free to imagine any magic behaviour fancied and were facilitated to try to convey their ideas with art and craft material [17]. This separation from the physical device allows discussion of functionality without giving 'too much' away during the design briefing stage.

5 Summary, Challenges and Issues

Children and young people are not simply small adults; they have their unique requirement needs for interactive products and services. The methods and approaches introduced in this chapter show the overall trend of requirement gathering with children as being a child-centred mixed-method approach with a focus on their experience. It raises many possibilities for working with children on gathering their unique requirement needs.

To get a richer context and a deeper understanding, very often, a combination of methods and approaches are deployed. For example: a systematic observation followed by a semi-structured interview for the requirement gathering for a museum environment [19]; technology probes for exploratory use, peer discussion and critique followed by focus group sessions for designing technology to reduce teenager energy use [50]; classroom observation followed by surveying (interview and questionnaire) in requirements for the design of a handwriting recognition interface [9]; obstructed theatre, drawing and emoticons survey with observation for gathering requirement for a mobile music device for social inclusion [17]. With some other examples listed in the following Table 1:

However there are challenges and issues that arise when choosing the most suitable requirement gathering methods and carrying out work in practice:

- Balancing different requirement needs, e.g. for fun, learning, and communication (use); that meet the interests of all stakeholders.
- Ensuring that the methods and approaches for children are playful, motivating and stimulating; child-appropriate and suited for their reading and writing levels, and their preferences for expressing themselves in different ways, e.g. verbally or non-verbally.
- Combining diverse data to optimise the data quality. With adults, but possibly more so with children, it is important to check for consistency of answers, by gathering similar information from different sources. For example, using various methods such as interviews, observations and diary methods.
- Ensuring the technique results in useful information for the design of targeted applications, e.g. on educational games, tangible technology, small devices, mobile, distributed app, service development etc.

To summarise: gathering ideas from children early in the design process has yielded useful insights into what children want in technology in general or in a specific type of application. Druin et al. [12], for example, discovered that children want control, variety, social interaction, and creative tools, and that they pay attention to the appearance, learnability, and "coolness" of an application, as well as on how rich it is in terms of the use of multimedia. Children's early involvement in requirements gathering has revealed clues also about, for example, gender differences in preferences related to technology, children's navigation skills, ways of presenting textual information, application-specific content related preferences, the variety of elements to be included in user interfaces and their structures, and children's desire to personalize their applications [11, 15, 20, 23, 24, 39, 51].

Table 1. Requirement gathering methods and approaches, examples in practice

Technology or service	Requirement gathering methods and approaches used	Age of children	Children as
Interactive museum environment [19]	Observation, semi-structured interview	5–10	Learner
Design of a VLE (Virtual Learning Environment) [20]	Storyboard and observation	8–12	Learner
Computer mediated communication for children and families [22]	Video prototyping, Participatory Design and Cooperative Design	3+	User
Technology to reduce teenager energy use ([49]	Technology probes for exploratory use, peer discussion and critique followed by focus group sessions	10+	User
School classroom Software for encouraging collaborative working [23]	Observation, Brainstorming with low-tech prototyping and storyboarding	7–10	Learner and User
Interactive educational game [15]	KidReporter that combines many techniques like interviews, drawing and making pictures	9–10	Player and Learner
Game-Based Learning Environments [11]	User interface (UI) drawings, idea maps, and evaluations of existing learning environments	7–9 11–12	Player and Learner
Electronic school bag (eBag) for a shared narrative space [24]	Mission from Mars	10–11	Player and User
Affective input-device design (SenToy) [21]	Wizard of Oz prototyping	14+	Player and User
Handwriting recognition interface [9]	classroom observation followed by surveying (interview and questionnaire)	6–7	Player, Learner and User
Mobile music device for social inclusion [17]	obstructed theatre, drawing and emoticons survey with observation	5–10	Player, Learner and User

6   Conclusion

Nowadays the design and development of children's and young people's technologies has been focusing on their experience at home, school and public spaces. Research into their requirement needs as Player, Learner and User (PLU) are one of the main themes in Interaction Design for Children (IDC).

This chapter introduces this unique research domain, presents an overview of the current practice in requirement gathering with children and young people. It shows a variety of common methods and approaches, and child-appropriate methodological innovation in the current research. This:

- Presents a broad range of requirement gathering methods and approaches;
- Provides insights on when to apply the various requirement gathering methods for various requirements and shows how methods can be also applied to a more general HCI context;
- Includes new research on requirement gathering methodological innovations applicable for novel technologies, e.g. Tangible Technologies (TanTech) and portable devices;
- Describes new methodological innovations;

This chapter hopes to give an overview for researchers and practitioners in the field for carrying out requirement gathering research with children and young people.

References

1. Read, J.C., Bekker, M.M.: The nature of child computer interaction. In: Proceedings of the 25th BCS Conference on Human-Computer Interaction, pp. 163–170. BCS, Newcastle-upon-Tyne, United Kingdom (2011)
2. Greene, S., Hogan, D.: Researching Children's Experience Approaches and Methods, p. 304. Sage Publications Ltd, Thousand Oaks (2005)
3. Clark, A., Moss, P.: Listening to Young Children: The Mosaic Approach, 2nd Revised edn, p. 83. National Children's Bureau Enterprises Ltd, London (2011)
4. Edwards, C.: The Hundred Languages of Children: The Reggio Emilia Experience in Transformation, 3rd edn. Praeger, Westport (2011)
5. Fargas-Malet, M., et al.: Research with children: methodological issues and innovative techniques. J. Early Child. Res. 8(2), 175–192 (2010)
6. Mauthner, M.: Methodological aspects of collecting data from children: lessons from three research projects. Child. Soc. 11(1), 16–28 (1997)
7. Markopoulos, P., et al.: Evaluating Children's Interactive Products: Principles and Practices for Interaction Designers, p. 400. Morgan Kaufmann, San Francisco (2008)
8. Rogers, Y., Sharp, H., Preece, J.: Interaction Design: Beyond Human-Computer Interaction. Wiley, New York (2011)
9. Read, J.C., MacFarlane, S., Gregory, P.: Requirements for the design of a handwriting recognition based writing interface for children. In: Proceedings of the 2004 Conference on Interaction Design and Children: Building a Community, pp. 81–87. ACM, Maryland (2004)
10. Baxter, K., Courage, C., Caine, K.: Understanding Your Users: A Practical Guide to User Requirements Methods Tools and Techniques. Morgan Kaufmann Publishers, San Francisco (2005)
11. Nousiainen, T., Kankaanranta, M.: Exploring children's requirements for game-based learning environments. Adv. Hum.-Comput. Interact. 2008, 7 (2008)
12. Druin, A., et al.: Children as our technology design partners. In: Druin, A. (ed.) The Design of Children's Technology, pp. 51–72. Morgan Kaufmann, San Francisco (1999)

13. Kafai, Y.B.: Children as designers, testers, and evaluators of educational software. In: Druin, A. (ed.) The design of children's technology, pp. 123–145. Morgan Kaufmann Publishers Inc, San Francisco (1998)
14. Scaife, M., Rogers, Y., Aldrich, F., Davies, M.: Designing for or designing with? Informant design for interactive learning environments. In: CHI 1997. ACM, Atlanta (1997)
15. Bekkera, M., et al.: KidReporter: a user requirements gathering technique for designing with children. Interact. Comput. **15**, 187–202 (2003). Elsevier
16. Xu, D.Y., et al.: Children and 'smart' technologies: can children's experiences be interpreted and coded? In: Proceedings of BHCI 2009 the 23rd British HCI Group Annual Conference on People and Computers: Celebrating People and Technology, Cambridge, United Kingdom, pp. 224–231 (2009)
17. Mazzone, E., et al.: Considering context, content, management, and engagement in design activities with children. In: Proceedings of the 9th International Conference on Interaction Design and Children, pp. 108–117. ACM, Barcelona, Spain (2010)
18. Read, J.C., Fitton, D., Mazzone, E.: Using obstructed theatre with child designers to convey requirements. In: CHI 2010 Extended Abstracts on Human Factors in Computing Systems, pp. 4063–4068. ACM, Atlanta, Georgia, USA (2010)
19. Mazzone, E., Horton, M., Read, J.: Requirements for a multimedia museum environment. In: Proceedings of the Third Nordic Conference on Human-Computer Interaction, pp. 421–424. ACM, Tampere, Finland (2004)
20. Hall, L., et al.: Using storyboards to guide virtual world design. In: Proceedings of the 2004 Conference on Interaction Design and Children: Building a Community, pp. 125–126. ACM, Maryland (2004)
21. Andersson, G., et al.: Using a Wizard of Oz study to inform the design of SenToy. In: Proceedings of the 4th Conference on Designing Interactive Systems: Processes, Practices, Methods, and Techniques, pp. 349–355. ACM, London, England (2002)
22. Hutchinson, H., et al.: Technology probes: inspiring design for and with families. In: Proceedings of the SIGCHI Conference on Human Factors in Computing Systems 2003, pp. 17–24. ACM, Ft. Lauderdale, Florida, USA (2003)
23. Jones, C., et al.: Experiences obtained from designing with children. In: Proceedings of the 2003 Conference on Interaction Design and Children, pp. 69–74. ACM, Preston, England (2003)
24. Dindler, C., et al.: Mission from Mars: a method for exploring user requirements for children in a narrative space. In: IDC 2005, Proceedings of the 2005 Conference on Interaction Design and Children, pp. 40–47. ACM Press, Boulder, Colorado (2005)
25. Read, J., et al.: Designing for Mr Hippo – introducing concepts of marginalisation to children designers. In: The 8th International Conference on Interaction Design & Children, ACM, Como, Italy (2009)
26. Read, J.C., MacFarlane, S., Casey, C.: What's going on?: discovering what children understand about handwriting recognition interfaces. In: Proceedings of the 2003 Conference on Interaction Design and Children, pp. 135–140. ACM, Preston, England (2003)
27. Read, J.C.: Validating the fun toolkit: an instrument for measuring children's opinions of technology. Cogn. Technol. Work **10**, 119–128 (2007)
28. Kubey, R., Larson, R., Csikszentmihalyi, M.: Experience sampling method applications to communication research questions. J. Commun. **46**(2), 99–120 (1996)
29. Riekhoff, J., Markopoulos, P.: Sampling young children's experiences with cultural probes. In: 7th International Conference for Interaction Design and Children, IDC 2008, ACM, Chicago, USA (2008)

30. Iversen, O.S., Nielsen, C.: Using digital cultural probes in design with children. In: Proceedings of the 2003 Conference on Interaction Design and Children, pp. 154–154. ACM, Preston, England (2003)

31. Muller, M.J.: PICTIVE—an exploration in participatory design. In: Proceedings of the SIGCHI Conference on Human Factors in Computing Systems, pp. 225–231. ACM, New Orleans, Louisiana, USA (1991)

32. Muller, M.J., Wildman, D.M., White, E.A.: Participatory design through games and other group exercises. In: Conference Companion on Human Factors in Computing Systems, pp. 411–412. ACM, Boston, Massachusetts, USA (1994)

33. Druin, A., Solomon, C.: Designing Multimedia Environments for Children. Wiley, New York (1996)

34. Druin, A., Hanna, L., Risden, K.: The Design of Children's Technology, 1st edn. Moran Kaufmann Publishers, Inc., San Francisco (1998)

35. Facer, K., Williamson, B.: Designing Educational Technologies with Users, NESTA Futurelab (2004)

36. Xu, D., Mazzone, E., MacFarlane, S.: Informant design with children - designing children's tangible technology. In: International Workshop Re-thinking Technology in Museums, Limerick, Ireland (2005)

37. Druin, A.: Cooperative inquiry: developing new technologies for children with children. In: The SIGCHI Conference on Human Factors in Computing Systems, pp. 592–599. ACM, Pittsburgh, Pennsylvania, USA (1999)

38. Read, J.C., Beale, R.: Under my pillow: designing security for children's special things. In: Proceedings of the 23rd British HCI Group Annual Conference on People and Computers: Celebrating People and Technology, pp. 288–292. BCS, Cambridge, United Kingdom (2009)

39. Xu, D., et al.: Experience it, draw it, rate it: capture children's experiences with their drawings. In: Proceedings of IDC 2009, The 8th International Conference on Interaction Design and Children, pp. 266–270. ACM, Como, Italy (2009)

40. Buxton, B.: Sketching User Experiences: Getting the Design Right and the Right Design, p. 448. Morgan Kaufmann, San Francisco (2007)

41. Yarosh, S., Chew, Y.C.D., Abowd, G.D.: Supporting parent–child communication in divorced families. Int. J. Hum. Comput Stud. 67(2), 192–203 (2009)

42. Lindquist, S., Westerlund, B., Sundblad, Y., Tobiasson, H., Beaudouin-Lafon, M., Mackay, W.E.: Co-designing communication technology with and for families – methods, experience, results and impact. In: Yuan, F., Kameas, A.D., Mavrommati, I. (eds.) The Disappearing Computer. LNCS, vol. 4500, pp. 99–119. Springer, Heidelberg (2007)

43. interLiving: Interactive Thread (2002). http://interliving.kth.se/publications/thread/index. html. cited 25 Oct 2013

44. Hemmert, F., et al.: Co-designing with children: a comparison of embodied and disembodied sketching techniques in the design of child age communication devices. In: Proceedings of the 9th International Conference on Interaction Design and Children, pp. 202–205. ACM, Barcelona, Spain (2010)

45. Stringer, M., Harris, E., Fitzpatrick, G.: Exploring the space of near-future design with children. In: Proceedings of NordiCHI 2006, The 4th Nordic Conference on Human-Computer Interaction: Changing Roles, pp. 351–360. ACM, Oslo, Norway (2006)

46. Reinis, J., et al.: Children's Future Requests For Computers & The Internet, A Study by Latitude (Phases 1 & 2), in Kids Innovation & Discovery Studies (KIDS). Latitude, Sudbury (2011)

47. Butler, S., Gross, J., Hayne, H.: The effect of drawing on memory performance in young children. Dev. Psychol. 31(4), 597–608 (1995)

48. Gross, J., Hayne, H.: Drawing facilitates children's verbal reports of emotionally laden events. J. Exp. Psychol. Appl. **4**(2), 163–179 (1998)
49. Briggs, P., Olivier, P., Kitson, J.: Film as invisible design: the example of the biometric daemon. In: CHI 2009 Extended Abstracts on Human Factors in Computing Systems, pp. 3511–3512. ACM, Boston (2009)
50. Bell, B.T., et al.: Teenagers talking about technologies: designing technology to reduce teen energy use. In: CHI 2013 Extended Abstracts on Human Factors in Computing Systems, pp. 1491–1496. ACM, Paris, France (2013)
51. Bilal, D.: Draw and tell: children as designers of web interfaces. Proc. Am. Soc. Inf. Sci. Technol. **40**(1), 135–141 (2003)

Accessibility

Web Accessibility for Visually Impaired People: Requirements and Design Issues

Mexhid Ferati[1(✉)], Bahtijar Vogel[2], Arianit Kurti[3,4], Bujar Raufi[5],
and David Salvador Astals[6]

[1] Oslo and Akershus University College of Applied Sciences, Oslo, Norway
mexhid.ferati@hioa.no
[2] Malmö University, Malmö, Sweden
bahtijar.vogel@mah.se
[3] Linnaeus University, Växjö, Sweden
arianit.kurti@lnu.se
[4] Interactive Institute Swedish ICT, Norrköping, Sweden
arianit.kurti@tii.se
[5] South East European University, Tetovo, Macedonia
b.raufi@seeu.edu.mk
[6] Universitat Autònoma de Barcelona, Barcelona, Spain
david.salvador@e-campus.uab.cat

Abstract. Access to web content continues to be a challenge for the visually impaired, as the needs of such community are very diverse. The access is further hindered by the fact that designers continue to build websites non-compliant with Web Content Accessibility Guidelines (WCAG). To better understand the needs of the visually impaired community, three workshops were organized with various stakeholders coming from three different countries. The results from the workshops suggest that one-solution-fits-all model is inadequate without considering the levels of visual impairment when providing customized web experience. A set of requirements devised from the workshops guided the process of building a middleware prototype. Using eight adaptation techniques, the prototype provides the required user experience based on users level of visual impairment. Preliminary evaluation of the middleware suggests that several adaptation techniques perform better with non-WCAG compliant websites compared to those being compliant.

1 Introduction

The increased portability and wide adoption of diverse web content and mobile technologies have resulted in the fact that computers are not anymore perceived as distinct technological objects, but more as integrated tools to support our everyday activities [17]. The ubiquity of these environments creates the possibilities for people to communicate across multiple computational devices at the same time. These trends provided the opportunities for the evolvement of the web toward a fully-fledged software platform [18]. The main idea behind this view is the fact that people are actively engaged by contributing with digital content on the web through the use of different web and mobile applications and platforms across diverse devices [1].

© IFIP International Federation for Information Processing 2016
Published by Springer International Publishing Switzerland 2016. All Rights Reserved
A. Ebert et al. (Eds.): UsARE 2012/2014, LNCS 9312, pp. 79–96, 2016.
DOI: 10.1007/978-3-319-45916-5_6

All these developments result in new ways for people to create, share, manage everyday life, as well as communicate with their friends and family. The different levels of accessibility of these solutions directly affect their use by diverse user groups. Primarily this creates challenges for user groups with special needs. One such user group is the community of visually impaired people, which is usually marginalized. Some of their challenges include lack of proper access to the different web content that could facilitate their everyday activities.

Considering that this community is highly diverse, such as, in terms of levels of impairment, poses an additional challenge when addressing their needs. One way to better understand their needs was to consider different societies and levels of impairment when identifying the requirements. Moreover, considering various user interaction modalities and adaptation techniques, we believe helps in mitigating the problems when visually impaired users access web content.

Motivated by these challenges and research trends, in this paper we report our efforts on the web accessibility issues for the visually impaired community. The main effort is to understand the key requirements and provide initial solutions that could be utilized for providing access to web content for this marginalized group. To this end, we provide exploratory insights on the accessibility requirements identified through three workshops held in Macedonia and Sweden [6]. This was followed with the design activities and development of a middleware using contemporary web technologies in order to adapt a given website based on user needs. A preliminary user evaluation of the middleware prototype was conducted in Spain, which is reported in details in Sect. 6.

In the following sections of this paper we present our research approach followed with an overview of the accessibility requirements identified via realized workshops. Afterwards, we give details of initial design issues discovered and addressed in a prototype. At the end, we discuss initial findings from the prototype user evaluation and provide some challenges for future efforts.

2 Background

The idea of web accessibility is to make the web open to disabled people [8]. Contemporary web technologies also play a crucial role in this area [9, 23]. However, web access suffers from interoperability and usability problems that make interaction of disabled users difficult [8, 23]. Moreover, the need to improve the web browsing experience by adapting and personalizing the software to user preferences and device characteristics has become evident [8].

To ensure universal design and equal access to web content by all users, the World Wide Web Consortium (W3C) developed the Web Content Accessibility Guidelines (WCAG). These guidelines in many cases help mitigate problems that visually impaired users face when accessing web content. The current version of WCAG 2.0 was published on December 2008 as a W3C Recommendation and includes 12 guidelines organized in four principles [8]. However, WCAG 2.0 seems to not completely address the accessibility issues, where the low level guidelines (e.g., level A) are not fulfilling the needs of visually impaired users [14]. This research shows that the application of WCAG is often insufficient for visually impaired users, because of the overlooked factors, particularly in terms of efficiency and satisfaction.

An interesting issue is that the implementation of WCAG 2.0 is still poor in most of governmental and news agencies websites [7]. Therefore the most used assistive technologies today are the screen readers which most of them are proprietary software in nature [3]. In this manner, most of the screen readers fail to notify in an efficient way that new content has appeared on the web site. This does not allow visually impaired users to fully experience and benefit from dynamic websites. A change in the overview of website design and a stronger inclusion of accessibility is needed given that visually impaired users still cannot fully benefit from the advantages of contemporary web technologies. Thus, there is a need for a new approach on "assisting" the assistive technologies that are open and that allow customizations in terms of personalized accessibility features.

With respect to these developments and as suggested by [10] there is a need for adaptation in enhancing web accessibility for visually impaired users. The advances of web technologies (such as HTML5 and web frameworks) offer a wide variety of adaptation possibilities that can be utilized to increase web accessibility. New web technologies offer a wide range of approaches and techniques for adaptation that were not possible when the WCAG 2.0 was developed. These developments bring new possibilities for increased accessibility of the web content. In this context, web adaptability encourages the development of web-based services that can be resilient to the diversity of uses of such services as well as target audiences [10, 11]. These recent advances in the web technologies increase the possibilities for the adaptive approaches to better follow user preferences and get the most of the visual and navigation aspects by facilitating the interaction with the web content. Nevertheless, the web content adaptation becomes challenging especially when it needs to be applied to the specificities of the visually impaired users. In this manner we have identified two primary lines of adaptation when it comes to visually impaired users: content and modality adaptation approaches:

- **Content adaptation approach** involves displaying and transforming the web content in a more accessible way suitable to user preferences in a specific context [4, 11, 22].
- **Modality adaptation approach** involves alternative content representation (often non-visual) that facilitate the content accessibility using voice narrators and other non-speech sounds [4, 5, 11].

These adaptation approaches can be instantiated with a number of techniques especially by utilizing advances in the web technologies in order to increase accessibility of web content.

3   Research Approach

The rich technological landscape, in which we live in, enables us to use different devices to deploy, invoke, and represent web content that are related to our everyday context. These developments bring a palette of new opportunities to support an increased accessibility of the web content for the visually impaired users [20]. But in order to utilize and gain full benefit from these advances, a proper domain analysis of the visually impaired users' requirements is essential [13]. This type of analysis is defined as a process that acquires, classifies and analyzes all requirements of domain stakeholders [15].

Having in mind that visually impaired community is rather a diverse group, we have utilized a need-driven approach based on active user participation in order to identify the needs in this domain. Another motivation for choosing a need-driven and user-oriented approach was the need to reduce the risk of over engineering as well as avoiding defective requirements [2]. Motivated from this and trying to get the best grasp of the domain analysis, we organized three workshops with different stakeholders from various ethnic, cultural, professional and socio-demographic backgrounds. Workshops have been organized in Macedonia (one) and Sweden (two).

The aim of the first workshop held in Macedonia was to enable an in depth understanding of the needs and requirements of the visually impaired community. Whereas, the aim of the second and third workshop held in Sweden was to validate the identified requirements in the first workshop and bring the diverse research expertise on the domain. These three workshops have been followed with a discussion activity with Optic and Optometry specialists in Spain. The purpose of this activity was to understand how different optical deficiencies could be compensated by utilizing the advances of the web technologies. The overall flow of the research activities conducted in this study is depicted in Fig. 1.

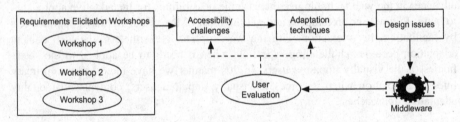

Fig. 1. Depiction of this study flow.

3.1 Workshop Settings and Stakeholders

The first workshop was held at South East European University in Tetovo, Macedonia and gathered various participants starting from research community, visually impaired people, and non-governmental organizations (NGO's) working especially with visually impaired people. The workshop hosted a total of 21 participants (12-researchers and students from the web and mobile technologies and Human-Computer Interaction (HCI) fields; 4-representatives of educational establishments; 2-NGO representatives; and 3-visually impaired students).

The second workshop was held in Kalmar at Linnaeus University, Sweden. The added value of this workshop was the inclusion of additional stakeholders from the fields such as eHealth and Optometry. In total it gathered 11 participants (3-eHealth; 1-optometrist researcher; 1-visually impaired; and 6-researchers from various fields of web and mobile technologies and HCI).

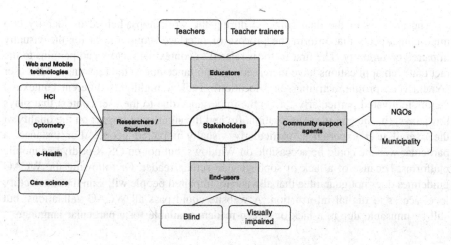

Fig. 2. Ecosystem view of the stakeholders [6].

The third workshop took place at Blekinge Institute of Technology in Karlskrona, Sweden. This workshop included additional stakeholders coming from the fields of Applied Health Technologies, Interaction Design and Caring Sciences. In total it gathered eight participants (3-health technologies; 1-Informatics; and 4-from various fields of Computer Science).

These three workshops helped us identify various accessibility challenges and adaptation techniques, which were later implemented in a middleware prototype that utilized a number of adaptation techniques to increase the web content accessibility. Furthermore, in a direct discussion with a specialist from Terrassa School of Optics and Optometry of the Universitat Politècnica de Catalunya we have further specified the exact adaptation techniques that would be used to determine key functional require-ments of the middleware. A follow up user evaluation of the middleware was then conducted with visually impaired users from the same institution.

In order to gain a better insight of different stakeholders involved in the research activities, an ecosystem scheme of the stakeholders is depicted in Fig. 2. The ecosystem view became a confluence between educators, researchers, community support agents and most importantly, the end users, i.e., the visually impaired. This research approach enabled us to build up knowledge about different accessibility challenges, adaptation approaches and techniques when dealing with visually impaired user needs.

4   Web Accessibility Challenges

The discussion with stakeholders during the three workshops provided a good empirical base to understand the main challenges that keeps the visually impaired as a marginalized community (especially in Macedonia and the surrounding region). List of all challenges identified in the workshops are detailed in [6], while in this paper we mainly emphasize on the web content accessibility challenges for visually impaired people.

The analysis of the data gathered during the workshops, helped us identify two important aspects that inform the process of interface requirements for the visually impaired community. The first factor is related to contextual factors and pertains to the fact that web applications have increased in importance due to the relevance of the user context (i.e., profile, activities, and location). Table 1 highlights different contextual factors motivated particularly for (a) the importance due to the user context that plays nowadays, (b) the end-user satisfaction, (c) and the significant impact on the quality of the overall user experience, particularly visually impaired people. For instance, a particular website could be accessible on Windows, but not on OS X or diverse mobile platforms, because of a lack of sophisticated screen reader. Or following the WCAG guidelines does not guarantee that all visually impaired people will gain the satisfactory level access to digital information. A website could pass all WCAG validations, but still be unusable due to a lack of screen readers available for a particular language.

Table 1. Contextual factors [6].

Factors	Description	Testing activities
Day/time of use	The impact of natural light and time of day in user's activities	Functionality testing
Location	User activity influenced by his location (indoor, outdoor, in a car, train, etc.)	Mobility testing
Device/platform	The impact of device type, size and platform in user's activities	Interoperability and/or compatibility
User profile	The level of user disability	Optometric testing/survey testing
Accessibility	An overarching factor that ensures achievement of all previous factors	Heuristics/usability/field testing

To overcome situations when contextual factors play negative role in achieving satisfactory user experience, in our previous studies we have used non-speech sounds to deliver content to visually impaired users. In the process of auralizing content and deliver it in a non-visual form, we have successfully developed and evaluated *audemes* as a novel non-speech sounds to deliver educational content in experiments conducted with K12 students in a visually impaired school in U.S. [5]. *Audemes* are brief non-speech sounds created of music and sound effect sound snippets referring to natural, artificial or abstract sounds, even popular music.

An interesting insight from one of the workshops revealed the second factor that highlights the necessity to "teach" visually impaired how to make the best use of their remained sight. An optometrist present at the workshop argued that many visually impaired people could pass the legally blind threshold by learning techniques of using peripheral vision [12]. Designing interfaces for visually impaired users familiar with such techniques would require understanding their specific needs, rather than treating them as homogenous group.

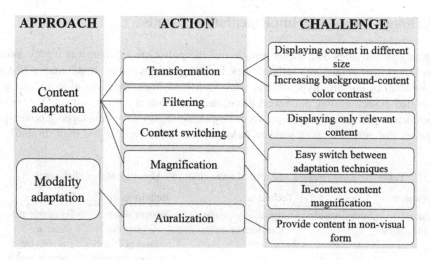

Fig. 3. Accessibility challenges, actions and adaptation approaches for BVI users.

While various web adaptation techniques could be used to deliver usable content to visually impaired users, the one-size-fits-all model, however, does not provide satisfactory solution. Hence, a specific user requirement should be gathered to apply the specific adaptation technique suitable for the user. Based on user's level of impairment, a particular solution should be suggested. To achieve such goal, as a result of the workshops we have identified specific challenges different users face when accessing web content. Figure 3 lists these challenges along with the actions and approaches anticipated to address them.

All these challenges identified from the workshops had as a common denominator, the need to access diverse web content in a more accessible way, and beyond the WCAG guidelines. This inspired the idea of a middleware that would enable applying adaptation techniques of existing web content primarily possible due to the advances in the web technologies.

In order to identify the best adaptation techniques to be implemented into the middleware, we have discussed our ideas with an optician specialist. The result of this discussion indicated that some visually impaired users feel more comfortable with a different contrast rather than the usual black over white. This inspired the idea of color transformation as part of our middleware solution. Furthermore, it is desirable to offer the flexibility of increased text and other content on the web site, but this should not be on the expenses of losing the navigational context of the page. For that reason this inspired us to implement an amplifying text lens that enables the visually impaired user to read the text with an increased size, but without losing the context of the entire web page. All this served as a solid background to initiate our prototyping efforts for the design and implementation of the middleware solution.

5   Design Issues and Implementation Details

The design activities and implementation of the prototype solution was highly motivated by contemporary web technologies. Both, the design and the requirements (listed
in Table 2) of our prototype design, were motivated from: the adaptation approaches
identified in section two, three workshops, and individual meetings with an Optics and
Optometry specialist. Considering these requirements, we have developed a prototype
solution that adapts a given website based on user's preferences and their disability.

Table 2. Requirements and related techniques to address identified challenges.

Approach	Action	Technique	Requirement	Rationale
Content adaptation	Transformation	Image transformation/resizing	System must display the images of the requested page into a more accessible way	To enable the user to recognize an image and it in the given context
		Text transformation	System must have the option of transforming the text in a more accessible way	Enable the user read the content easily
		Color transformation	System must have the option of changing the contrast of chosen website	Enable user differentiate between text and background
	Filtering	Image filtering	System must have the option of filtering the images to be shown by size	Enable the user differentiate between relevant and irrelevant images in the website context
		Content filtering	System must have the option of showing in the adapted page only the main content of the requested page	Enable the user identify the main content of the website
	Context switching	Switching control	System must have a control to allow dynamic	Enable the user to switch between

(Continued)

Table 2. (*Continued*)

Approach	Action	Technique	Requirement	Rationale
			changes of the adaptation features	adaptation modes depending on their need.
	Magnification	Amplifying lens	System must have a lens to amplify the text and images of the website	Enable the user better reading of desired content
Modality adaptation	Auralization	Voice narrator	System must have a voice narrator (text-to-speech) to navigate and read the content in an auditory format	Enable the user consume the content in an auditory form

In order to provide a fully accessible web content, our solution transforms any available web site by making it WCAG 2.0 compliant. Moreover, one of our goals with our solution was to reach the following:

1. To offer different types of visual adaptations for various levels of impairment.
2. To provide the best personalized user experience for the existing web content (such as governmental portals, news agencies and other).

Table 2 lists the requirements identified, which essentially address challenges listed in Fig. 3. In addition, this table lists the technique and rationale for each requirement. Given these requirements and the related technique needed to be implemented into our prototype, the architectural choice was motivated following the software architectural pattern, the Model-View-Controller (MVC) that lately is being highly used in modern web technologies. This architectural pattern is composed of three parts: the Model - corresponds to the data, the View - is the representation of the data, and the Controller - manages the data.

The reason of utilizing this pattern is that it allows decoupling the visual representation of the data and its management. As such, it provides solutions to flexibly address the requirements identified in Table 2, and in the future extend our solution with new features in a more flexible manner. The solution prototype is implemented by utilizing contemporary web technologies in terms of HTML5, CSS, JavaScript and PHP as well as external libraries including: HTML DOM, Modernizr, jQuery, Web Speech API, Lens effect, TextScrolling, and contextJS (source code: https://github.com/davidsalvador/degree-project).

All adaptation techniques identified in Table 2 are carefully implemented into our solution. Figure 4, presents the architectural overview of our prototype solution. The "Controller" and the "View" play a central role in our solution. The "Controller" usually manipulates the "Model" elements and updates the "View". The "Model" of the solution is formed by all HTML elements. The "Content extractor" component in the "Controller" uses a third-party library (HTML DOM), which belongs to the "Model" part. The HTML DOM parser makes it possible to manipulate the HTML elements of a certain web page and its content. The "Data controller" component manages the data extracted from "Content extractor" and afterwards applies different adaptations (see details in Fig. 4). The "View" is responsible for representations. It gets the adaptations and presents them to the user. Usually the "Controller" applies the static changes, whereas the "View" allows the user to change the options and automatically reload the page to display the new content by using the "contextMenuLoader" component. In general, the "View" allows to dynamically change and adapt the web content to different styles and features without reloading the page.

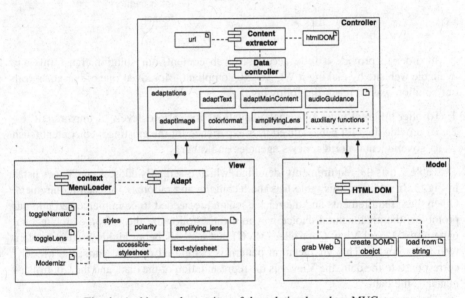

Fig. 4. Architectural overview of the solution based on MVC.

To better understand our solution prototype, a usage scenario is presented in Fig. 5. The typical steps depicted in the use case diagram are:

1. The user enters the URL of the page to browse into the prototype along with the types of adaptations selected (preferences).
2. The solution requests the original website (gets web content and data) and applies the adaptations requested.
3. Finally the adapted page is presented based on the chosen user preferences.

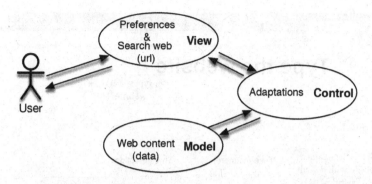

Fig. 5. Use case diagram.

In order to conserve the adaptations chosen by the user, persistent adaptation is applied, enabling that in every subsequent browsing instance, the requested page will be adapted based on the same chosen preferences as the last browsing experience. Before the user searches the web, session cookie is initiated where the features chosen by the user will be stored. The "href" attribute of every anchor HTML element is modified by appending "adapt?web" string to the URL. Using this, all links will refer the "adapt" page where the adapted web content is received as a GET parameter. In this way, every petition that the "adapt" page receives, the session features (variables) are read from the cookie and the adaptations are made available based on the preferences chosen by the user (see Fig. 6). In other words, for each URL submission the adapt.php is called. We must clarify that at this stage, the two-way communication of form handling (e.g., searching) has not been implemented.

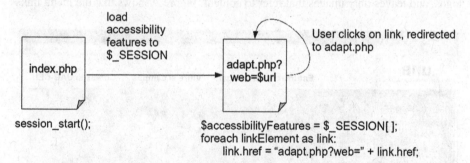

Fig. 6. Persistent adaptations.

In order to rationalize the design and implementation, Fig. 7 presents the screen shot of the prototype solution. The simple and user-friendly interface shows a textbox for typing the requested site and two buttons. The button "Take me there!" takes the user to the desired website with default adaptations. The button "Change options" offers the user the ability to alter the default settings in a wizard-like fashion by guiding them through each adaptation. If users right-click anywhere on the page, a context menu is shown giving them the option to directly apply a desired adaptation, e.g., change the text size.

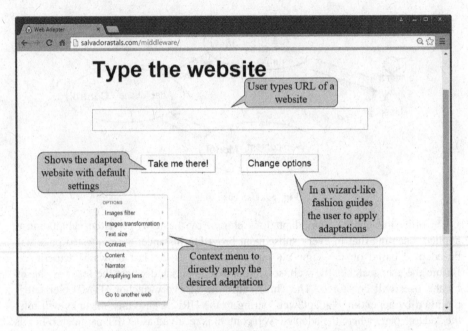

Fig. 7. Prototype homepage and contextual menu.

To better illustrate the effects of adaptation of a given website, in Figs. 8 and 9 we show the original and adapted version of the University of Barcelona website with default adaptation settings. The prototype solution removes irrelevant images, such as logos, and leaves only images that refer to content. Figure 9 shows that the menu links

Fig. 8. The University of Barcelona website without adaptation.

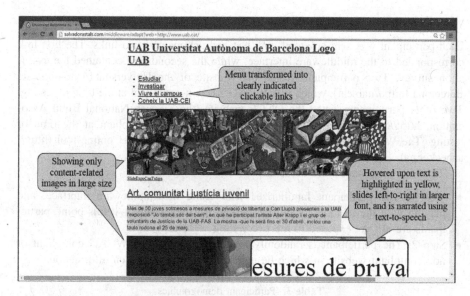

Fig. 9. The University of Barcelona website with default adaptations applied.

are transformed into a form that more clearly indicates them being clickable links. When users hover with a mouse over a given paragraph, such as the one highlighted in yellow in Fig. 9, the content will show and slide left-to-right with a bigger font on a small window below the paragraph. As the content slides, it is also read at loud using a text-to-speech voice narration. The middleware prototype can be accessed at: http://salvadorastals.com/middleware/.

6 Prototype Evaluation

The user evaluation of the middleware was conducted involving four visually impaired users from the Terrassa School of Optics and Optometry of Universitat Politecnica de Catalunya. The evaluation process consisted of three phases. Initially, the participants were given time to familiarize with the middleware and discover its features. Afterwards, participants were asked to find a particular information from a given website. To accomplish this task, each participant chose the middleware settings of their choice. Finally, after participants completed the tasks, they were interviewed to record their feedback about their experience with the middleware.

6.1 Participants

Individual characteristics of each participant is given in Table 3 below. Participants were between 28 and 70 with various types of disability, years of low vision and internet usage per day. One common factor among all participants was that they used the Window Eyes screen reader.

6.2 Procedure

Each participant was sent an email with test instructions and two links. The first link corresponded to the middleware interface, while the second link contained the evaluation survey. Two participants tested the website of the Universitat Autonoma de Barcelona (http://uab.cat), which was WCAG 2.0 non-compliant at the time of testing. Two other participants tested the ONCE website (the Spanish National Blind Association, http://once.es), which was WCAG 2.0 level AA compliant at the time of testing. The WCAG compliance was checked using the achecker online tool (http://achecker.ca).

The following steps were involved:

- Step 1: The participant familiarizes with using the middleware interface, and playing with the features to find the best fit for their needs. (At this point, participants are not yet exposed to the two testing websites.)
- Step 2: The participant is randomly assigned to either the WCAG compliant or non-compliant website in which he is instructed to find a given information.

Table 3. Participant demographics.

PID	Age	Hours of internet per day	Assistive software	Years of low vision	Pathology
A	45	4	Window eyes	12	Magna myopia
B	65	2	Window eyes	2	Glaucoma
C	70	1	Window eyes	5	Age Related Macular Degeneration (ARMD)
D	28	5	window eyes	28	Retinitis pigmentosa

- Step 3: After the participant accomplishes the task, he is instructed to answer the survey, which consisted of three parts: (i) questions gathering information about participant's demographics including their experience with technology and the type and level of visual impairment; (ii) questions highlighting whether the participant was able to find the information required from the given website, indicating Yes, No or Partially Found; and (iii) using a combination of Likert scale and open-ended questions participants were required to evaluate the usability of the middleware interface.

6.3 Results and Discussion

Participants were successful in finding the required information from the randomly assigned website. Only one out of four participants was not able to find the information required, to whom a WCAG 2.0 non-compliant website was assigned.

Two adaptation techniques, *text transformation* and *amplifying lens*, were rated with maximum score (6.0) by all participants whether using a WCAG 2.0 compliant or non-compliant website. This result proves that these two techniques were well accepted by participants regardless of the level of WCAG compliance the website had.

A technique that the WCAG compliance of the website had the most effect was *Image filtering*, which was rated very differently depending on whether participants used a non- or compliant website. Participants using non-compliant website rated this technique with maximum score (6.0), while participants using a compliant website rated it with a minimal score (2.0). We believe this result indicates that the website does not need to be WCAG 2.0 compliant for an adaptation technique to be useful. Developing an accessible website typically requires extra amount of work, which due to financial aspects, forces decision makers to often opt against the implementation of WCAG. Hence, this result suggests that the middleware eliminates the necessity for a website to comply with WCAG.

The *content filter* technique received high rating from three participants, while one participant using a WCAG compliant website gave a poor rating. The *image resizing* and *contrast transformation* techniques received below the average rating. Further studies need to be conducted in order to identify reasons that make these techniques less successful. The only technique addressing a non-visual (auditory) requirement was the *voice narrator*. This technique was rated average by all but one user, who gave it a maximum score using a WCAG compliant website. Summarized quantitative values of the results are given in Table 4.

Table 4. Prototype evaluation results.

Participants	Middleware feature/adaptation technique							WCAG 2.0 compliance
	Image filtering	Image resizing	Text transformation	Contrast	Content filter	Voice narrator	Amplifying lens	
A	2	2	6	3	2	2	6	Yes
B	2	2	6	1	5	6	6	Yes
C	6	3	6	3	6	3	6	No
D	6	3	6	2	6	2	6	No
Mean	4	2.5	6	2.25	4.75	3.25	6	-

Few participants gave negative comments concerning aspects of the middleware homepage. One participant requested that the font size of the contextual menu be higher, while another participant stated that it would be easier to use the middleware as a search engine, rather than requiring to input the entire URL into the box.

7   Conclusion and Future Work

In this paper we presented requirements gathered from three workshops held with different stakeholders to identify the needs of visually impaired users. The novelty of this study was the identification of two important factors relevant when addressing the needs of visually impaired people. The first factor identified was the context of use, which influences the accessibility of digital content for the visually impaired users. The second factor was the need to evaluate user's level of visual impairment before applying any adaptation technique on the existing web content.

The outcome of the realized workshops was the generation of requirements that guided the development of a middleware prototype that made websites usable by adapting them based on user's visual impairment level. The user evaluation of the middleware indicated that several adaptation techniques perform better with non WCAG compliant websites than with those being compliant. Overall, adaptation techniques were useful to our participants.

Although this study used just four participants, it is still important because of two reasons. First, it gives an indication that requirements gathered and the middleware built are an approach in the right direction. The user testing provides some initial insights both regarding the middleware prototype as well as validating the approach in gathering requirements using workshops. Second, it is typical that studies involving people with disabilities are conducted only with several participants. Limitations in terms of mobility and skill qualification of these people are usually the underlying reasons [19]. To an extent, this study is an effort in addressing this issue by giving greater access to information to visually impaired users.

In line with such efforts, we are currently investigating Massive Open Online Course (MOOC) as a means to provide quality education to visually impaired people [16]. Future efforts need to gather requirements for building accessible MOOCs and the skills required for the users to have in order to be able to access web content. Moreover, building and evaluating how different adaptation techniques contribute toward achieving greater web content accessibility will present a step in the direction to increase the number of visually impaired community participating in online education.

In the future, in order to increase content accessibility, new adaptation approaches could be investigated by leveraging open data and standards together with emerging web technologies. In addition, this would enable architectural solutions that are capable to deal with dynamic requirements and heterogonous environments in web and mobile technologies [21]. These two lines of action represent important future research challenges, as we believe that they are key aspects to influence accessibility needs and emerging technologies in general, and in particular of the visually impaired community.

Acknowledgments. We thank all participants from Kosova, Macedonia and Sweden that attended our workshops. We thank the eHealth Institute in Kalmar and Blekinge Institute of Technology in Karlskrona, for hosting our workshops. Furthermore, we thank the professor of UPC – FOOT, Eulalia Sánchez, for her scientific, optical and optometry approach and counseling during the assessment study. Finally, we thank the Swedish Foundation for International Cooperation in Research and Higher Education for supporting this research.

References

1. Berners-Lee, T.: Long live the web: a call for continued open standards and neutrality. Sci. Am. **303**(4), 56–61 (2010)
2. Braude, E.J., Bernstein, M.E.: Software Engineering: Modern Approaches, 2nd edn. Wiley, Hoboken (2011)
3. Brown, A., Jay, C., Chen, A.Q., Harper, S.: The uptake of web 2.0 technologies, and its impact on visually disabled users. Univ. Access Inf. Soc. **11**(2), 185–199 (2012)
4. Brusilovsky, P.: Adaptive hypermedia. User Model. User-Adapt. Interact. **11**, 87–110 (2001)
5. Ferati, M., Pfaff, M., Mannheimer, S., Bolchini, D.: Audemes at work: investigating features of non-speech sounds to maximize content recognition. Int. J. Hum.-Comput. Stud. (IJHCS) **70**(12), 936–966 (2012)
6. Ferati, M., Raufi, B., Kurti, A., Vogel, B.: Accessibility requirements for blind and visually impaired in a regional context: an exploratory study. In: Proceedings of 2nd IEEE International Workshop on Usability and Accessibility focused Requirements Engineering (UsARE 2014), Karlskrona, Sweden, 25–29 August 2014, PP. 13–16 (2014)
7. Hanson, V.L., Richards, J.T.: Progress on website accessibility? ACM Trans. Web **7**(1), 2:1–2:30 (2013)
8. Harper, S., Yesilada, Y. (eds.): Web Accessibility: a Foundation for Research. Human Computer Interaction Series. Springer, London (2008)
9. Johari, K., Kaur, A.: Measuring web accessibility for persons with disabilities. In: 2012 4th International Conference on Computational Intelligence and Communication Networks (CICN), pp. 963–967. IEEE (2012)
10. Kelly, B., Nevile, L., Sloan, D., Fanou, S., Ellison, R., Herrod, L.: From web accessibility to web adaptability. Disabil. Rehabil. Assist. Technol. **4**(4), 212–226 (2009)
11. Knutov, E., De Bra, P.M.E., Pechenizkiy, M.: AH 12 years later: a comprehensive survey of adaptive hypermedia methods and techniques. New Rev. Hypermed. Multimed. **15**(1), 5–38 (2009)
12. Lewis, P., Rosén, R., Unsbo, P., Gustafsson, J.: Resolution of static and dynamic stimuli in the peripheral visual field. J. Vis. Res. **51**, 1829–1834 (2011)
13. Ludi, S., Canter, A., Ellis, L., Shrestha, A.: Requirements gathering for assistive technology that includes low vision and sighted users. In: 2012 1st International Workshop on Usability and Accessibility Focused Requirements Engineering (UsARE), pp. 25–31 (2012)
14. Power, C., Freire, A.P., Petrie, H., Swallow, D.: Guidelines are only half of the story: accessibility problems encountered by blind users on the web. In: CHI 2012, Austin, Texas, USA, 5–10 May 2012, pp. 1–10 (2012)
15. Qiu, F.L., Yin, L.: Research on domain requirement analysis method used ontology. In: 2nd International Symposium on Computational Intelligence and Design, ISCID 2009, vol. 1, pp. 299–301 (2009)
16. Rizzardini, R.H., Chang, V., Gütl, C., Amado-Salvatierra, H.: An open online course with accessibility features. In: Herrington, J., et al. (eds.) Proceedings of World Conference on Educational Multimedia, Hypermedia and Telecommunications, pp. 635–643. AACE, Chesapeake (2013)
17. Sheth, A.: Computing for human experience: semantics-empowered sensors, services, and social computing on the ubiquitous web. IEEE Internet Comput. **14**(1), 88–91 (2010)
18. Smith, K.: How digital outcasts can pilot the future of health care. World Future Rev. **5**(2), 127–134 (2013)
19. Stevens, R.D.: Principles for the design of auditory interfaces to present complex information to blind people. D.Phil. thesis, Department of Computer Science, University of York (1996)

20. Terven, J.R., Salas, J., Raducanu, B.: New opportunities for computer vision-based assistive technology systems for the visually impaired. Computer **47**(4), 52–58 (2014)

21. Vogel, B., Kurti, A., Mikkonen, T., Milrad, M.: Towards an open architecture model for web and mobile software: characteristics and validity properties. In: Proceedings of 38th Annual International Computers, Software and Applications Conference (COMPSAC 2014), 21–25 July 2014. IEEE, Västerås (2014)

22. Watanabe, W.M., Candido, A., Amâncio, M.A., De Oliveira, M., Pardo, T.A.S., Fortes, R.P. M., Aluísio, S.M.: Adapting web content for low-literacy readers by using lexical elaboration and named entities labeling. New Rev. Hypermed. Multimed. **16**(3), 303–327 (2010)

23. Zhou, X.C., Xia, X.: Design and research for mobile web learning platform accessibility. In: 2010 International Conference on Artificial Intelligence and Education (ICAIE). IEEE (2010)

Augmentative Requirements Engineering

Getting Closer to Sensitive User's Needs

Hrvoje Belani[1(✉)], Željka Car[2], and Marin Vuković[2]

[1] Croatian Health Insurance Fund, Margaretska 3, 10000 Zagreb, Croatia
hrvoje.belani@hzzo.hr
[2] Department of Telecommunications, Faculty of Electrical Engineering
and Computing, University of Zagreb, Unska 3, 10000 Zagreb, Croatia
{zeljka.car,marin.vukovic}@fer.hr

Abstract. The widening digital divide in today's interconnected world is more than an access issue in terms of technology availability and affordability. Concerns like media accessibility, information mobilization and consciousness need to be approached comprehensively, especially when dealing with sensitive user groups. Discovering, understanding and efficiently implementing proper requirements for augmentative and alternative communication is essential for supporting the users with complex communication needs in their everyday life, from work engagement to personal settings. By enforcing the usage of information and communication technologies to help solve these issues, users' needs and desires have to be analyzed carefully, by learning from educational, psychological and rehabilitation methods from other fields already deeply involved with life-care for these people. Augmentative requirements engineering is a requirements engineering framework that provides a holistic view on requirements for augmentative and alternative communication services, concerning sensitive users' abilities and needs, service domain and associated intermediary users. The new paradigm is experience-driven from a series of concluded projects and implemented applications for various user groups in Croatia.

Keywords: Augmentative and alternative communication · Requirements engineering · E-accessibility · Appropriate technology · Complex communication needs

1 Introduction

Over the past few years, the interconnected world has witnessed continued growth in the uptake, availability and affordability of information and communication technologies (ICTs). At the end of 2013, around 2.7 billion people have been using the Internet, while the number has gone up to 3 billion by the end of 2014 [1]. Even though the progress is evident on a yearly basis, there are digital divide challenges that still need to be addressed: 4.3 billion people are still not online, and 90 % of them live in the developing world. Moreover, the digital divide is not just an access issue, but also concerns with information accessibility, information utilization and information receptiveness.

A. Ebert et al. (Eds.): UsARE 2012/2014, LNCS 9312, pp. 97–116, 2016.
DOI: 10.1007/978-3-319-45916-5_7

More than just accessibility, individuals need to know how to make use of the ICT tools once they exist within a community [2].

In order to bridge the gap, a multidiscipline approach is needed to provide means in helping sensitive users, like persons with complex communication needs (CCNs), learn and utilize the technologies to which they do have access, but fully accepting the health and well-being status of every individual, along with his/her capabilities. Understanding users' needs becomes even more challengeable when developing ICT solutions for people with disabilities. Even more, it seems that ICT has the potential both for enhancing access to different services for people with disabilities and for creating more division and new forms of exclusion. Therefore, it seems crucial to continuously address the issues of accessibility and usability as technology continues to develop and spread and as new technologies emerge [3]. As ICT inevitably plays an essential role in supporting daily life in today's digital society, European e-inclusion policy [4] aims to achieve that "no one is left behind" in enjoying the benefits of ICT, focusing on participation of all individuals and communities in all aspects of the information society. E-accessibility is considered a key priority in various global programs for supporting ICT innovations, which recommends that additional efforts need to be made to promote the development of assistive technologies that are tailored to help people with special needs access ICTs. Web accessibility is stated as one of the main building blocks for establishing e-accessibility, in order to entail major social and economic gains for people with disabilities, among others, making them more active as workers or consumers. Although public strategies and policy recommendations cover this topic to some extent [5], and some solutions are offered [6], many methodological and practical challenges regarding the ICT development process still exist, especially for its earliest phases, like requirements gathering, specification and verification, and ICT service design.

Bridging the gap from requirements to design and implementation of proper software solutions is often a challenge dealt with methods and tools that tend to trace the status of requirements throughout the software development cycle, but these approaches do not help when requirements are gotten wrong at the first place. Quarter of a century ago, Frederick Phillips Brooks, Jr. made the following statement in his well-known and widely discussed IEEE Computer journal paper [7]: "The hardest single part of building a software system is deciding precisely what to build. No other part of the conceptual work is as difficult as establishing the detailed technical requirements, including all the interfaces to people, to machines, and to other software systems. No other part of the work so cripples the resulting system if done wrong. No other part is more difficult to rectify later."

Surely, research and practice in the requirements engineering area, for a few decades now, fully acknowledge the importance of planning and analysis in early phases of software development. However, gathering the right requirements and providing solutions for them in a traceable and manageable manner has to be achieved through an optimal development pace, resulting with shippable software systems people will gladly use [8]. In order to provide a qualitative and quantitative ground for building more usable and accessible ICT services for people with CCNs, this paper proposes a requirements engineering (RE) framework that provides a holistic view on requirements for augmentative and alternative communication services, concerning sensitive users' abilities and needs, different service domains and associated intermediary users.

The structure of the paper is the following: Sect. 2 provides a context of augmentative and alternative communication, while Sect. 3 gives a background on relevant last year's statistics regarding people with disabilities in Croatia, and corresponding inclusion policies, both national and European. Section 4 discusses the requirements engineering approach to this challenge, while the next section provides a experience-driven overview of concluded projects and applications implemented in Croatia that support augmentative and alternative communication for various user groups in different service domains. Section 6 describes the principles of so-called augmentative requirements engineering. The last section summarizes the findings and comments future work in the area of ICT-assisted augmentative and alternative communication.

2 Augmentative and Alternative Communication

Communication is essential for active participation in everyday life, from work engagement to personal settings. Nevertheless, some people may not have the communication skills to meet all of their needs, due to their developmental (e.g. Down syndrome, cerebral palsy) or acquired disabilities (e.g. multiple sclerosis, stroke). Significant impairments prevent these persons to communicate in a conventional manner. In order to cope with their disabilities and support their complex communication needs, the area of clinical practice called augmentative and alternative communication (AAC) has been established to improve effectiveness of communication by using symbols, aids, techniques and strategies [9]. Augmentative and alternative communication (in some literature referred as "alternative and augmentative communication") represents a set of tools and strategies that individuals, not being able to rely on their natural speech to communicate, use to solve everyday communication challenges. Everyone uses multiple forms of communication, such as speech, a shared glance, text, gestures, facial expressions, touch, sign language, symbols, pictures, and speech generating devices, based upon the context and the other party in communication, in order to make them understand each other [10].

AAC is considered one of three main categories ICTs can play in fulfilling educational needs of children with disabilities, along with the compensation uses (e.g. technical assistance that enables active participation in reading or writing) and didactic uses (e.g. using ICTs as a didactical tool to enable a more inclusive learning environment) [11]. Such special educational requirements of children with disabilities caused by a functional limitation are often called special educational needs (SENs), and are both diverse and varied [12]. Some usability studies [13] show that even though product features are considered "accessible", consumers with disabilities may still have difficulty using it easily and efficiently. It is recommended to consider access issues as the products are being tested and developed, and measure both accessibility and usability in tests that include people with a broad range of disabilities. It is often the case that the cost of specialized, aided AAC devices is too high for the limited functionality they offer. It seems reasonable to build AAC services based on information and communication technologies (ICTs) [14], especially for mobile computer devices.

3 Croatia: Overview on Disability

As defined by the International Classification of Functioning, Disability and Health (ICF), disability is the interaction between individuals with a health condition (e.g. cerebral palsy, Down syndrome and depression) and personal and environmental factors (e.g. negative attitudes, inaccessible transportation and public buildings, and limited social supports). Based on the estimations of the United Nations (UN), more than 1 billion people or 15 % of the world's population are living with disabilities today. In all regions, persons with disabilities are disproportionately represented among the poorest segments of society. Additionally, it is estimated that 80 % of persons with disabilities reside in developing countries [15]. The World Health Organization (WHO) reports the number of persons with disabilities is on the rise, partially due to aging populations, chronic health conditions and improved access to health care [16].

According to the Croatian "Census of Population, Households and Dwellings 2011", the total population of Croatia is 4,290,612. The population density is 75.8 inhabitants per square kilometer, and the overall life expectancy in Croatia at birth is 75.7 years. Since 1991, Croatia's death rate has continuously exceeded its birth rate; the natural growth rate of the population is currently negative [17].

According to the Croatian Disabilities Registry [18], by March 12, 2015, there were 508,350 disabled persons living in Croatia, from which 306,614 were male (60 %), and 201,736 were female (40 %). Therefore, around 12 % of Croatian population are disabled persons (male 7.1 %; female 4.7 %), compared to 16.6 % in EU27. Croatia is also one of 25 EU Member States that have accepted the UN's Convention on the Rights of Persons with Disabilities (CRPD), with the core concepts of self-determination, participation and inclusion for people with disabilities, namely "those who have long-term physical, mental, intellectual or sensory impairments which in interaction with various barriers may hinder their full and effective participation in society on an equal basis with others".

As seen in Table 1, the most common types of impairments that people with disabilities in Croatia have are locomotor system impairments and psychological disorders. Around 28 % of people with disabilities in Croatia have multiple impairments, which presents even a greater challenge to provide means of augmentative and alternative communication to them.

4 Requirements and Design Approach

Discovering, understanding and efficiently implementing proper requirements for augmentative and alternative communication is essential for supporting the users with complex communication needs in their everyday life, from work engagement to personal settings. Many traditional software engineering (SE) approaches are documentation-oriented, usually conforming to some heavyweight processes. On the other hand, agile

Table 1. The number (and percentage) of persons with disabilities in Croatia, by the type of their impairments; data on March 12, 2015, adopted from [18]

Type of impairment	Number of persons	%
Locomotor system impairment	146,359	28.8
Multiple impairments	143,192	28,2
Psychological disorder	124,080	24,4
Other organs and organic system impairment	114,225	22,5
Central nervous system impairment	90,878	17,9
Cognitive impairment	23,618	4,6
Speech and language impairment	20,471	4
Visual impairment	17,039	3,4
Hearing impairment	12,633	2,5
Peripheral nervous system impairment	11,946	2,3
Congenital anomalies and chromosomopathies	9,253	1,8
Pervasive developmental disorder (autism)	1,461	0,3

approaches declare customer satisfaction as their highest priority, through early and continuous delivery of valuable solutions, while embracing requirements change, even late in development [19]. Practically all requirements engineering (RE) paradigms put the customer in central place, trying to deal with other challenges in the same time, like requirements change, too complex specifications, not testable requirements, etc. Considering specificity and the sensitive nature of target user groups, as well as their limited abilities and special needs, and required service features also, it is necessary to make a thorough analysis and define challenges and potentials of adequate requirements elicitation techniques that would properly incorporate multidisciplinary approach during development process.

The following analysis of issues and challenges is given for the requirements engineering phase within the AAC service development for people with complex communication needs, taking into consideration both functional and nonfunctional service requirements:

- Requirements gathering – usual methods, such as interviewing or role playing, cannot be universally applied. The crucial fact for people with complex communication needs is that every person has his/her special needs and specific abilities, not allowing for them to be treated the same way as other AAC service users. Some directions can be driven from experiences of educational, psychological and rehabilitation methods from other fields already deeply involved with life-care for these people.
- Requirements specification – regarding to some extent limited abilities of this target group, it seems reasonable to assume that they need "as simple as possible" set of functional requirements (FR) in order to use some service. However, this does not mean simply reducing already existing set of functions for non-disabled people using the same service, but establishing full understanding which functions are necessary for them, what is the order of function usage, their possible combinations

allowed and/or disallowed, etc. Also, non-functional requirements (NFR), such as those regarding performance, security and trust, have to be carefully considered and analyzed, first separately and then in combination with the set of FRs, in order to provide a robust, but trustworthy and yet usable AAC service.

- Requirements verification – if a presumption that the functional requirements dropping in a number and complexity shows to be valid for ICT services for people with complex communication needs, then some formal methods (e.g. Event-B [20]) and tools (e.g. ProR [21] and Rodin [22]) can be utilized in order to prove the simple formal requirements models for logical correctness. Nevertheless, these statements need to be thoroughly checked through experiments and case studies.

Regarding the design phase within the AAC service development, there are certain issues regarding the production cost and active user participation using "Design for all" principle. User centered design in this case has to be planned carefully, accepting common approaches from other involved fields and experts, including educators, rehabilitators, caregivers, etc. These experts are not mandatory well-skilled with advanced AAC services or ICT services at all, so educating them also seems as a challenge. Design of AAC systems and services should cope with all of person's major disabilities, in order to provide a mean for successful communication, but not emphasizing some other user's inability in the same time. For example, if a non-talking child with severe motor impairments is given a communicator application [23] to e.g. pick his favorite food, the major button on user interface should be adjusted in a way that the child can reach it [24], otherwise the service is not usable for him.

In order to match the type of given impairment with desired AAC functionalities, we have put together a brief mapping of AAC service features and person's impairments that shows which service feature is more suitable to be used as input or output by

Table 2. Input and output AAC service features most suitable for each person's impairment

Type of impairment	Input Features	Output Features
Locomotor system impairment	Adjustable GUI; Execution by a voice command; Stylus pens as pointers (hand-held, mouth sticks, mounted on the head, etc.)	Text-to-speech; Sound effects
Psychological disorder	Picture selection; Object tracking (e.g. eyeball, human position, body parts, etc.)	Visual attention; Sound imitation
Cognitive impairment	Known photos and symbol selection	Photos, symbols; Audio messages
Speech and language impairment	Sign-to-speech; Signs, message composition; Icon sequencing	Texting; Speech; Symbol composition
Visual impairment	Vibration-by-selection; Simple GUI with large elements; Voice commands	Sign-to-speech; High-contrast
Hearing impairment	Text and symbols; Touch and vibrate; Texting, word prediction	Text and symbols; Visual effects

which impairment. Table 2 shows the most common types of impairments, along with typical input/output features of AAC services.

Some other existing impairments, such as central or peripheral nervous system impairments, other organs and organic system impairments, and congenital anomalies and chromosomopathies, may partially find suitable AAC service features among the ones given, but previously have to be thoroughly analyzed on case-by-case basis. Special consideration should be given to pervasive developmental disorders, like autism, in order to fulfil these person's needs and wants. Also, for persons with multiple impairments, it is advisable to prioritize which impairment is the most necessary to be augmented, and to develop the AAC service with such given input and output features. Further evaluation of such AAC services while in usage can guide further user interface development and customization.

Regarding the type of AAC devices, introduction and wide-spreading of new mobile devices, such as tablets and smart phones, can serve as enabler for these AAC services. It is inevitable fact that mobile computers are getting more popular and affordable by the continuous growth and availability of ICT infrastructure worldwide [1]. The goal of AAC is utilizing the most effective communication possible to aid AAC user express his/her needs and wants, and conduct social contacts.

5 ICT-Assisted AAC in Croatia

Half a decade ago, there were practically not any ICT-assisted AAC services and applications being developed for Croatian market and Croatian cultural environment, although the need was eminent [18], especially with around 10 % of all elementary school children being children with special needs, according to Croatian Association for Professional Help to Children with Special Needs statistics. Therefore, multidisciplinary scientists in electrical engineering and computing, graphic technology, education and rehabilitation, speech pathology and psychology have joined forces in developing interoperable and scalable platform for symbol based communication services capable of implementation on various user devices [25].

As one of the results of the project "ICT systems for people with complex communication needs", financed by the University of Zagreb Development Fund, The AAC Body of Knowledge has been developed, containing basic information needed for effective development and implementation of AAC systems based on ICT. It is available in Croatian only, serving as a multi-disciplinary repository of definitions and references to existing sources of information related to AAC, referencing all previously stated research fields [26]. Its sole purpose was to be a reference point for introducing interested stakeholders in the domain of AAC, and to be continuously updated with the new results in research, development and practice for ICT-assisted AAC.

As described in previous section, AAC systems and services can offer various communication methods, depending on the type and severity of user's disability. In order to adjust the graphical user interface (GUI) to users' needs, skills and limitations, AAC services can recognize and quantify user's skills on using the interface, like in the developed Calibrator service [23]. Calibration process here was being done by calculating UI parameters to optimize the symbol size, object position on screen, contrast and background, and choosing the most suitable symbol gallery (Fig. 1).

Given the fact that specialized, aided AAC devices, by that time available on the market, have provided foreign language support only (e.g. "Talking Photo Album" in English) and had to be specially ordered from abroad, it was reasonable to set a common ground for building a national ICT-assisted AAC research and development community in close cooperation with users and user representatives, like parental organizations, associations for people with special needs, etc.

One of the most used AAC applications developed within the project was Mathematical Carousel (shown on Fig. 2), which helps preschool and school-aged children learning and exercising the basic mathematical operations, involving three activities: counting, equality of sets and basic math operations using numbers or symbols.

Based on the results of successful academic cooperation, the "ICT Competence Network for Innovative Services for Persons with Complex Communication Needs" has been established [27, 28] with participation of higher education institutions and knowledge-based small and medium enterprises. They aimed to make a joint effort in development, customization, and maintenance of ICT-assisted AAC services to be used by caretakers or organizations for inclusion of persons with CCN, such as inclusive preschools, primary and secondary educational institutions, social welfare institutions, specialized hospitals, polyclinics and specialized day-care centers. In the following table (Table 3), we have provided an overview of some implemented ICT-AAC applications by their input and output features, and supported platforms and operating systems. Applications developed for Android and iOS can be used on smartphones and tablets running these operating systems. The main interaction with all applications is done by the touch interface on device screen.

Parents and representatives of parental organizations for children with developmental delays, based on their daily experiences living with and taking care of their children, recommended that AAC applications use big images without distracting

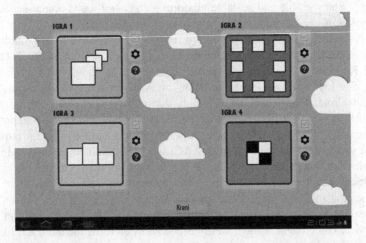

Fig. 1. The Calibrator service, for optimizing: the symbol size (1), object position on screen (2), choosing from the most suitable symbol gallery (3), and contrast and background (4); from [23]

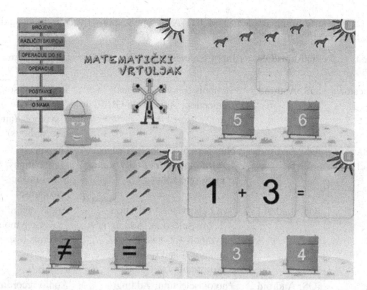

Fig. 2. The Mathematical Carousel, developed for iOS and Android and as a Web application

details, and avoid secondary motives. Also, simple and visually clear font, such as Arial, should be used, while the red color is advisable for emphasizing individual letters or words, being the quickest to reach the child's brain due to its frequency [29]. Among high priority requirements related to the teaching materials for children complex communication needs are incorporated pictures, text and audio records, such as voice recordings or text to speech, prepared and categorized according to the communication disabilities and frequency of use. In order to collect and analyze all these requirements efficiently, and also manage them through the AAC service development cycle, we have looked into RE applicability for ICT-assisted AAC.

6 Requirements Engineering for ICT-Assisted AAC

When supported by ICT services, the field of AAC suitably falls into human-computer interaction (HCI), a mature research discipline that offers numerous approaches for development of efficient user interfaces and means of people interacting with technology. In order to develop such services that support and enhance AAC, principles of requirements engineering have to be applied. We can refer to ICT-based AAC services as services that enable symbol-based human-to-human communication and human-computer interaction in a networking environment [30]. We are tackling needs and perspectives for using such services to supplement, not replace, some of the aids usage by persons with disabilities, which can be especially helpful for the ones with multiple impairments.

This represents a HCI design challenge regarding the technology in domestic life, community settings as well as working surroundings, with significant RE challenges that call for proper design and usage of questionnaires and surveys, as well as some

Table 3. Overview of some implemented ICT-AAC applications by their input and output features and supported platforms/OSs

Application name	Platforms/OSs	Input features	Output features
Communicator	iOS, Android	Symbols (photos, images) selection; Adjustable GUI	Voice and sound representation of symbols (audio recordings)
Mathematical Carousel	iOS, Android, Web	Numbers or symbols (images) selection; Setting only some math operations	Graphical animations; Sound and music response
Letters	iOS, Android	Symbols (visual) selection; Terms selection; Adding new symbols (photos, images, auditory) and terms; Adjustable GUI	Audio recording for every symbol; Terms overview
e-Gallery	iOS, Android	Photos selection; Adding photos and related text and audio recordings; Adjustable GUI	Audio recording for every photo
Mathematical playground	iOS, Android, Web	Numbers or symbols (images) selection; Adjustable GUI	Sound representation of correct or incorrect answers
Vocals	iOS, Android, Web	Symbols (visual) selection; Adjustable GUI	Audio recording for every symbol
Memory	iOS, Android	Symbols (visual) selection; Adding new symbols and words; Adjustable GUI	Sound representation of symbols and words (pronunciation)

other ethnographically-inspired methods such as narrative-based methods and mixed methods, taking also the ethical concerns into account.

In order to tackle this challenge, we propose new paradigm of requirements engineering for AAC, or so-called augmentative requirements engineering (ARE) [31], that will allow holistic view on AAC service requirements concerning users abilities and needs, service domain (such as communication, education, entertainment) and associated user supporters (such as rehabilitators, educators, family). Directions for augmentative requirements engineering for ICT-assisted AAC services for the target groups should strive towards user-centered design principles. Although user-centered design is an established area of HCI research and practice, we are proposing some additional and other-angle insights to the topic.

By building-up the ARE framework (as shown in Fig. 3) from the basis of already outlined usability requirements taxonomy [32], here we provide an overview of what we consider to be influential factors for proper usability and accessibility requirements specification for an AAC service planned to be developed for a person with complex communication needs.

The ARE framework is described in more details in the following subsections, providing insights for each of four framework aspects in dealing with AAC service requirements:

- Contexts of use of an AAC service by a primary user, a person with CCNs,
- Users and their interactions, both with an AAC service and intermediated users,
- Design principles: describing Simplicity (or Low-Tech), Supplementing (or Add-On), Trustworthiness (or Believe) and Prototyping (or Feedback) design principles of the AAC service, and
- Collection and analysis methods: commenting on qualitative, quantitative and mixed methods usage for AAC service requirements collection and analysis.

6.1   Contexts of Use

If we observe a target user of AAC service to be a minor, e.g. Down-Syndrome child, we can recognize at least three contextually different locations (in terms of the context as constantly changing user environment [33]) of his/her daily life:

- Home, as a place of living in a family surroundings with at least one other person,
- School (educational and/or rehabilitation center), as a place of making educational and rehabilitation efforts for the person's benefit,
- Other social places, such as places for neighborhood and community gatherings, shops in the nearby area, etc.

Usability requirements for an AAC service can be very different, depending on the context of the AAC service usage. E.g. classroom can already have several high-tech aids and solutions for communication support, which can be sufficient for communication in this context. Home is the place where user presumably has developed the highest social closeness with others, and communication with no technology support at all or with low-tech methods could successfully apply. In some other social places user behaves by engaging in social etiquette routines, where some suitable and simple AAC services could be of great help.

6.2   Users and Interactions

There are few ways in which user can typically interact with an AAC service [34]:

- Direct interaction between the primary user and a service,
- Intermediated interaction, where intermediary user stands as a helping hand between a primary user and a service, because of some inability of a primary user to bring out a direct interaction.

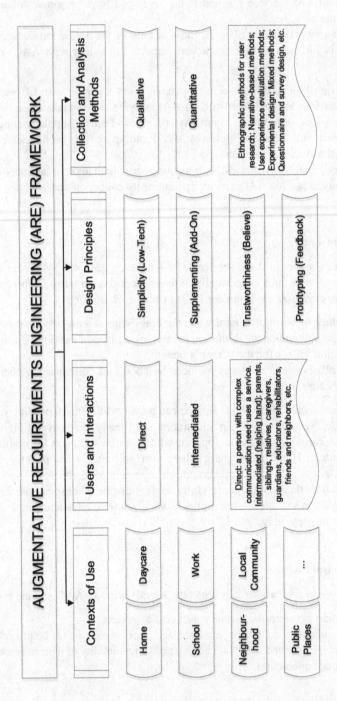

Fig. 3. Augmentative Requirements Engineering (ARE) framework overview

Examples of intermediary users of mobile AAC service are: parents and relatives, caregivers and guardians, educators and rehabilitators, friends and neighbors, etc. Studies have shown [34] that intermediated access creates a multiplier effect for the benefits of technologies through sharing, with intermediary-users acting as gateways between unconnected households and ICTs. The notion of intermediary user introduced into AAC service environment has a direct impact on usability and accessibility requirements, being considerably different than in the direct interaction scenario. Designing AAC services for multiple users that take part in various interactions puts up even more challenges in the whole AAC design and development process.

6.3 Simplicity (or Low-Tech) Principle

In order to gain a valuable insight to the users' needs, it is advisable to take some time observing reactions from their surroundings to the emerging communication needs. E.g. experienced parents and caregivers, knowing their protégés well, can show us practical guidelines and even fully operational solutions to the specific communication challenge in a simple, "pen-and-paper" environment (similar to low-tech prototyping) without any significant aid of technology. This could provide us with additional useful information about usability and accessibility needs and perspectives.

6.4 Supplementing (or Add-On) Principle

It should be reasonably stated to all the stakeholders from the beginning of the AAC service development process that development and deployment of new AAC services will not exclude the need for traditional and non-ICT means of daily communication. Moreover, AAC service should be made as a solution simple enough to be accepted by the user, and powerful enough to supplement some specific user' communication needs. In order to gain valuable insights in such interactions, conducting some Wizard of Oz research experiments could be very useful.

6.5 Trustworthiness (or Believe) Principle

Applying one of the known trust models to AAC services, we may consider the services trustworthy if they: (1) have ability to fulfill requests in a given domain, (2) have integrity to provide proper results as stated, and (3) are benevolent – act in user's best interest [35]. Although gaining user's trust in a particular service is influenced by many factors, some common sense relations, like including intermediary users (parents, teachers) into the trust chain can show benefits for accessibility challenges.

6.6   Prototyping (or Feedback) Principle

Integral parts of every proper user experience (UX) design process are wireframes, mockups and prototypes [36]. As the design process is not linear, going back-and-forth using this approaches may be often the case, and also confusing. While the wireframing approach can fit into our Simplicity (or Low-Tech) principle, mockups should be used to show the basic functionality of AAC application, while adding visual richness, and prototypes should allow users to experience actual content and interact with the UI.

6.7   Qualitative Methods

Some core qualitative user research methods, like observations and interviews, are widely known to research communities around the world, and their applicability to AAC service design is also inevitable. In order to understand users and their behaviors in the everyday contexts, ethnographic methods have been adopted and adapted into software requirements discipline [37]. Ethnographic methods for user research is the common name for ethnographically-informed user research methods used for the purposes of technology design and evaluation.

Another set of qualitative methods are narrative-based methods, used to elicit narratives or small stories from participants. The approach uses various specific techniques, like critical incident technique, diary studies, cultural probes [38] and explorations of user-generated content, such as that shared online. Narrative-based methods seem more appropriate to be used with intermediated users, than the primary users themselves. Their insights are surely valuable to inform AAC service design and/or AAC service in use.

6.8   Quantitative Methods

Quantitative methods have been commonly used in HCI research, such as using statistical methods, or experimental design [39]. Experimental design starts defining the intended contribution of the research agenda, following with experimental design and variables definition, continued by analysis of data, and discussing the issue of reliability and validity of given results.

Some user experience evaluation methods may deal with quantitative data collection, if e.g. the purpose of the AAC service evaluation deals with pragmatic factors such as time and financial constraints [40]. Also, if structured properly, surveys, questionnaires [41], and scales can be very useful methods for getting the quantitative data from the stakeholders, which should include primary and intermediated users.

6.9   Mixed Methods

Mixed methods approach combines quantitative and qualitative techniques at all stages of designing the research or development study. Designing such a study involves setting up the research questions, sampling and data collection and analysis, and reporting of the results.

The holistic framework for understanding the design of any piece of empirical research [42], including qualitative, quantitative and combined, can be consulted in order to find the set of techniques most suitable for planning a particular AAC service design research.

7 Discussion

Natural language requirements may be too demanding for managing throughout the development process, so it is advisable to provide a tool with an appropriate, machine-processable way of specifying and storing them [14]. One of the industry-candidates for requirements specification is Requirements Interchange Format (ReqIF), the emerging standard that provides interoperability with other authoring requirements management tools in industry [21]. ReqIF is basically XML-based file format used to exchange requirements, along with its associated metadata, in an open, non-proprietary and tool-independent manner. One of the main ReqIF features is hierarchically structured specification of uniquely identified requirements that have associated attributes to them and established relations between them. ProR is Eclipse-based tool for requirements engineering that supports ReqIF, aiming to provide reliable traceability between natural language requirements and formal models [22].

On the example of a symbol-based e-mail client [46], we have provided for people with special needs as a communicator service run on a tablet, we present a part of usability requirements (in the form of title: description) for this AAC service, regarding the following usability requirements types:

- Accessibility, e.g. Position of the screen: "User has a possibility to choose which position or positions of elements on the screen are the most accessible to him/her",
- Aesthetics, e.g. Symbol gallery: "User has a possibility to choose which set of symbols to use from a gallery of available symbols",
- UI consistency, e.g. Size of GUI elements: "User has a possibility to choose from different sizes for GUI elements",
- Ergonomics, e.g. First entry field focus: "When a symbol-based dialog box is opened, the focus shall be on the first entry field, in the top position of the dialog box",
- Ease of use, e.g. Help options: "The application has to offer a "Help" menu with proper instructions for users".

In the process of building requirements specification in ReqIF format, every requirement has a certain number of attributes that specify it in more details, e.g. requirements source, creation date, owner and status. The given requirements specification can be exported as the corresponding ReqIF file, which serves as an input for further design and development process [47], e.g. selection process from the AAC component pool, which can ease and speed-up process of finding and evaluating software components matching specified usability requirements [32, 48].

After configuring, customizing and using the ProR tool to gather and specify service requirements into the ReqIF project, the example of these usability requirements specification for a given AAC service is shown on Fig. 4.

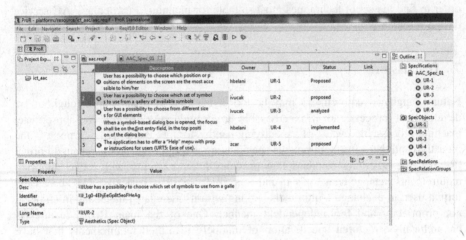

Fig. 4. Requirements specification in ReqIF format in ProR tool

8 Conclusion

In this paper we have discussed the appropriateness of known requirements engineering techniques, inherited from software and systems engineering, for developing information and communication technology (ICT) services for people with complex needs. We have outlined augmentative requirements engineering (ARE) for ICT service development process, which should strive to fulfill the principles of user-centered design (UCD), in a broader sense than accessible design or barrier-free design: equitable use, flexibility in use, simple and intuitive, perceptible information, tolerance for error, low physical effort, size and space for approach and use.

Aiming to answer the challenge regarding the technology in domestic life, community settings as well as working surroundings, for users with complex communication needs, this requirements engineering framework aims to incorporate educational, psychological and rehabilitation methods from other fields already deeply involved with life-care for these people, as well as other ethnographically-inspired methods. Moreover, this book chapter will provide data evidence gathered from a series of concluded AAC projects and implemented applications for various user groups and service domains.

Future work plans involve developing an ARE toolset for platform-based ICT-assisted AAC service development and establishing proper development processes accordingly, in terms of efficiency and effectiveness. For collecting and maintaining the knowledge about requirements for a shared set of AAC service functionality and software assets using a common means of production, the research from the area of software product lines may be applicable [43]. Requirements engineering for platforms is a discipline full of challenges [44], and some platform models for symbol based communication services are already being introduced [25] and user devices evaluated for AAC applications usage [45].

One of the research directions could focus on component development with effective user interface design for persons with complex communication needs, along with developing a software tool supporting the method. The ARE model will take into account the context of service usage, the user profiles and their interaction possibilities with the service as well as service design principles emphasizing usability and accessibility. By systematic usage of accessible interface elements according to the universal design principles, the proposed method will aim to help development process stakeholders in decision making about design possibilities of user interfaces in order to facilitate effective development of software service significantly adjusted to the person with complex communication needs.

Acknowledgments. The part of this work is supported by the Science and Innovation Investment Fund (SIIF)-IPA IIIc, within the "ICT Competence Network for Innovative Services for Persons with Complex Communication Needs" project.

References

1. ITU: Measuring the Information society report 2014. International Telecommunication Union (ITU), Geneva, Switzerland (2014). ISBN 978-92-61-15291-8
2. Kim, M.-C., Kim, J.-K.: Digital divide: conceptual discussions and prospect. In: Kim, W., Ling, T.-W., Lee, Y.-J., Park, S.-S. (eds.) Human.Society.Internet 2001. LNCS, vol. 2105, pp. 78–91. Springer, Heidelberg (2001)
3. Simpson, J.: Inclusive information and communication technologies for people with disabilities. In: Disability Studies Quarterly (Winter 2009), vol. 29, no.1. The Society for Disability Studies, Washington (2009). http://dsq-sds.org/article/view/167/167. Accessed 15 Apr 2015
4. Sears, A., Jacko, J.A.: The Human-Computer Interaction Handbook: Fundamentals Evolving Technologies and Emerging Applications, 2nd edn. Taylor & Francis Group, New York (2008)
5. eAccess+: The eAccessibility network. http://www.eaccessplus.eu/. Accessed 15 Apr 2015
6. Papunet: Accessible communication. http://papunet.net/. Accessed 15 Apr 2015
7. Brooks Jr., F.P.: No Silver Bullet: Essence and Accidents of Software Engineering. IEEE Comput. **20**(4), 10–19 (1987). doi:10.1109/MC.1987.1663532
8. Tate, K.: Sustainable Software Development: An Agile Perspective. Addison-Wesley Professional, Indianapolis (2006)
9. Justice, L.M.: Communication Sciences and Disorders: A Contemporary Perspective. Pearson Education, Upper Saddle River (2010). ISBN-13: 978-0135022801
10. The International Society for Augmentative and Alternative Communication (ISAAC). http://www.isaac-online.org/. Accessed 15 Apr 2015
11. Edwards, A.D.N., Besio, S., Tokareva, N.: ICTs in Education for People with Special Needs. Specialized Training Course. UNESCO Institute for Information Technologies in Education (IITE), Moscow, Russian Federation (2006). iite.unesco.org/pics/publications/en/files/3214644.pdf. Accessed 15 Apr 2015

12. Connect a School, Connect a Community: Assistive technology by disability type: understanding users' needs. Toolkit of Best Practices and Policy Advice, ITU-D (2009). http://www.connectaschool.org/itu-module-list. Accessed 15 Apr 2015

13. Burgstahler, S., Jirikowic, T., Kolko, B., Eliot, M.: Software accessibility, usability testing and individuals with disabilities. In: Information Technology and Disabilities, vol. X, no. 1–2, EASI (2004). http://people.rit.edu/easi/itd/itdv10n2/burghsta.htm. Accessed 15 Apr 2015

14. Vučak, I., Belani, H., Vuković, M.: AAC services development: from usability requirements to the reusable components. In: Jezic, G., Kusek, M., Nguyen, N.-T., Howlett, R.J., Jain, L. C. (eds.) KES-AMSTA 2012. LNCS, vol. 7327, pp. 231–240. Springer, Heidelberg (2012)

15. United Nations Expert Group Report on Disability Data and Statistics, Monitoring and Evaluation: The Way Forward, a Disability Inclusive Development Agenda towards 2015 and Beyond. UNESCO Headquarters, Paris, 8–10 July 2014

16. World Health Organization: Disability and health–Fact sheet N°352, Reviewed December 2014. http://www.who.int/mediacentre/factsheets/fs352/en/. Accessed 15 Apr 2015

17. Belani, H., Ljubi, I., Balković, M.: Information and communication technology services for augmentative and alternative communication: a croatian perspective. In: Proceedings of HCI 2012: The 26th BCS Conference on Human Computer Interaction - People & Computers XXVI. Birmingham, UK, 12–14 September 2012

18. Benjak, T., et al.: (editors-in-chief): Report on persons with disabilities in the Republic of Croatia. Croatian National Institute of Public Health, Zagreb, Croatia (2015). http://www. hzjz.hr/wp-content/uploads/2014/09/bilten_invalidi_2014.pdf. Accessed 15 Apr 2015

19. Leffingwell, D.: Agile Software Requirements: Lean Requirements Practices for Teams, Programs, and the Enterprise. Pearson Education, Boston (2011)

20. Abrial, J.-R.: Modeling in Event-B: System and Software Engineering. Cambridge University Press, England (2011)

21. ProR: Requirements Engineering Platform. http://www.pror.org/. Accessed 15 Apr 2015

22. Event-B and the Rodin Plarform. http://www.event-b.org/. Accessed 15 Apr 2015

23. Blagajic, I., Semanjski, I., Saric, T., Janda-Hegedis, Z., Vuković, M., Car, Ž.: e-accessible service system: calibrator and communicator. In: Jezic, G., Kusek, M., Nguyen, N.-T., Howlett, R.J., Jain, L.C. (eds.) KES-AMSTA 2012. LNCS, vol. 7327, pp. 241–250. Springer, Heidelberg (2012)

24. Pavliša, J.I., Ljubešić, M., Jerečić, I.: The use of AAC with young children in croatia– from the speech and language pathologist's view. In: Jezic, G., Kusek, M., Nguyen, N.-T., Howlett, R.J., Jain, L.C. (eds.) KES-AMSTA 2012. LNCS, vol. 7327, pp. 221–230. Springer, Heidelberg (2012)

25. Car, Ž., Vuković, M., Vučak, I., Pibernik, J., Dolić, J.: A platform model for symbol based communication services. In: Proceedings of the 11th International Conference on Telecommunications – ConTEL 2011, pp. 141–148. IEEE (2011)

26. Stančić, J.Z., Škrinjar, J.F., Ljubešić, M., Car, Ž.: Multidisciplinary collaboration and ICT services for people with complex communication needs. In: Proceedings of the MIPRO 2011. IEEE Press (2011)

27. ICT Competence Network for Innovative Services for Persons with Complex Communication Needs. The project is financed by European Union under the Science and Innovation Investment Fund Grant Scheme. http://www.ict-aac.hr/. Accessed 15 Apr 2015

28. Lovrek, I.: Value network for ICT-assisted augmentative and alternative communication. In: Proceedings of the 12th International Conference on Telecommunications - ConTEL 2013, pp. 229–234. University of Zagreb, Zagreb (2013)

29. Vučak, I., Belani, H., Vuković, M.: AAC services development: from usability requirements to the reusable components. In: Jezic, G., Kusek, M., Nguyen, N.-T., Howlett, R.J., Jain, L.C. (eds.) Agent and Multi-Agent Systems/Technologies and Applications. LNCS, vol. 7327, pp. 231–240. Springer, Heidelberg (2012). doi:10.1007/978-3-642-30947-2_27

30. Car, Ž., Vuković, D., Bjelčić, N., Karas, G., Karas, V.: Introducing session on ICT-based alternative and augmentative communication. In: Jezic, G., Kusek, M., Nguyen, N.-T., Howlett, R.J., Jain, L.C. (eds.) KES-AMSTA 2012. LNCS, vol. 7327, pp. 219–220. Springer, Heidelberg (2012)

31. Belani, H.: Augmentative requirements engineering for trustworthy and usable ict-based services. In: Holzinger, A., Ziefle, M., Hitz, M., Debevc, M. (eds.) SouthCHI 2013. LNCS, vol. 7946, pp. 815–818. Springer, Heidelberg (2013)

32. Belani, H.: Towards a usability requirements taxonomy for mobile AAC services. In: 2012 First International Workshop on Usability and Accessibility Focused Requirements Engineering (UsARE), ICSE 2012 Workshops, Zurich, Switzerland, June 4, pp. 36–39 (2012)

33. Abowd, G.D., Dey, A.K.: Towards a better understanding of context and context-awareness. In: Gellersen, H.-W. (ed.) HUC 1999. LNCS, vol. 1707, pp. 304–307. Springer, Heidelberg (1999)

34. Sambasivan, N, Cutrell, E., Toyama, K., Nardi, B.: Intermediated technology use in developing communities. In: Proceedings of The 28th International Conference on Human Factors in Computing Systems (CHI 2010), pp. 2583–2592. ACM Press, New York (2010). doi:10.1145/1753326.1753718

35. Cranor, L.F., Garfinkel, S.: Security and Usability – Designing Secure Systems that People Can Use. O'Reilly Media, Sebastopol (2005). ISBN 978-0-596-00827-7

36. WEb UI Design Process: The Visual Power of Mockups. UNPin Inc. (2015). http://www.uxpin.com/mockups-ux-design-process.html. Accessed 15 Apr 2015

37. Randall, D., Rouncefield, M.: Ethnography. In: Soegaard, M., Dam, R.F. (eds.) The Encyclopedia of Human-Computer Interaction. The Interaction Design Foundation, Aarhus (2013). http://www.interaction-design.org/encyclopedia/ethnography.html. Accessed 15 Apr 2015

38. Connor, G., Rouncefield, M., Gibbs, M., Vetere, F., Cheverst, K.: How probes work. In: Proceedings of the 19th Australasian conference on Computer-Human Interaction: Entertaining User Interfaces (OZCHI 2007), pp. 29–37. ACM, New York (2007). doi:10.1145/1324892.1324899

39. Cairns, P., Cox, A.L.: Research Methods for Human-Computer Interaction. Cambridge University Press, New York (2008)

40. Roto, V., Law, E., Vermeeren, A., Hoonhout, J. (eds.): User Experience White Paper: Bringing clarity to the concept of user experience. Result from Dagstuhl Seminar on Demarcating User Experience, 15–18 September 2010, 11 February (2011). http://www.allaboutux.org/files/UX-WhitePaper.pdf. Accessed 15 Apr 2015

41. Belani, H., Pripužić, K., Kobaš, K.: Implementing web-surveys for software requirements elicitation. In: Proceedings of ConTEL 2005, Faculty of Electrical Engineering and Computing. University of Zagreb, Croatia, pp. 465–469 (2005)

42. Niglas, K.: How the novice researcher can make sense of mixed methods designs. Int. J. Multiple Res. Approaches 1, 13–33 (2008)

43. Gomaa, H.: Designing Software Product Lines with UML: From Use Cases to Pattern-Based Software Architectures. Addison-Wesley, New York (2004)

44. Berenbach, B., Paulish, D., Kazmeier, J., Rudorfer, A.: Software & Systems Requirements Engineering: In Practice. McGraw-Hill Osborne Media, New York (2009)

45. Dolic, J., Pibernik, J., Bota, J.: Evaluation of mainstream tablet devices for symbol based aac communication. In: Jezic, G., Kusek, M., Nguyen, N.-T., Howlett, R.J., Jain, L.C. (eds.) KES-AMSTA 2012. LNCS, vol. 7327, pp. 251–260. Springer, Heidelberg (2012)
46. Dolić, J., Pibernik, J., Car, Ž.: Design and development of symbol based services for persons with complex communication needs. Acta graphica **24**(1/2), 19–28 (2013)
47. Babić, J., Slivar, I., Car, Ž., Podobnik, V.: Prototype-driven software development process for augmentative and alternative communication applications. In: Proceedings of the 13th International Conference on Telecommunications ConTEL 2015. Graz University of Technology, Graz (2015)
48. Vučak, I., Vuković, M., Car, Ž.: Cache and prefetch mechanisms for improving symbol usage in symbol based applications. In: Proceedings of 12th International Conference on Telecommunications (ConTEL). IEEE, Zagreb, Croatia, pp. 223–228 (2013)

Requirements Gathering and Domain Understanding for Assistive Technology to Support Low Vision and Sighted Students

Stephanie Ludi[✉]

Department of Software Engineering, Department of Computer Science,
Rochester Institute of Technology, Rochester, USA
salvse@rit.edu

Abstract. Accessibility often concerns compatibility with third-party software in order to meet the needs of users who are disabled. The AccessLecture/Math project seeks to transform the Apple iPad into a tool to make Math and Science class more accessible to visually impaired students. Accessing lecture material during lecture is a challenge to low vision students, in terms of the limited options that can be costly or can allow access only upon the completion of the lecture. This paper presents the strategies and techniques used to help the team gather the needs and tasks of math/science instructors and visually impaired students. These groups are distributed geographically and represent diverse constituencies. The analysis of the environment, user groups and the tasks related to the course lecture were modeled in order to ascertain domain knowledge and to specify the system's requirements.

Keywords: Component · Accessibility · Elicitation · Visually impaired

1   Introduction

Imagine you have low vision and are enrolled in a math or science course. The instructor writes the course material on the whiteboard. You try to capture notes based on what is said by the instructor but you can't grasp the material until you get a copy notes after class. But after class it is too late to connect what the instructor is saying to the material he/she has written. This is the common state of Math and Science class for visually impaired students in the United States.

Access to science and math education is critical to facilitating science, math, engineering and technology careers. The goal of AccessLecture/Math is to develop a system that provides visually impaired students enrolled in secondary school and at the university level with greater access to science and math presentations in the classroom. The project leverages portable hardware, part of which attaches to a whiteboard that communicates with a computer that archives the lecture and broadcasts it to the tablet. This enables students with low vision to participate in math and science lectures, thus improving achievement. Students will use a portable tablet to enlarge and adjust the material as needed, navigate through material and refer to prior

© IFIP International Federation for Information Processing 2016
Published by Springer International Publishing Switzerland 2016. All Rights Reserved
A. Ebert et al. (Eds.): UsARE 2012/2014, LNCS 9312, pp. 117–132, 2016.
DOI: 10.1007/978-3-319-45916-5_8

material and notes. The real-time presentation of material enables students to ask questions at the time the material and activities are presented.

The AccessLecture/Math (AL/M) project has a hardware side and a software side. For the initial prototype, existing hardware will be used to capture lecture material. The focus of AL/M is the software side, where the whiteboard marker strokes are sent to the iPad for display, annotation, and archiving via a server (the instructor's station for the prototype).

The hardware used for the prototype is commercially available (Mimio Interactive) and uses wireless communication (between the pens and a bar placed on the whiteboard) and USB (between the bar and a computer). The proposed software will be developed for the iPad and will enable the student to use touch to zoom in/out of the captured whiteboard information and to navigate through the lecture material. Student notes are entered via a stylus or through an attached keyboard using USB or the iPad's keyboard.

This paper will present the diverse approaches used to elicit requirements and model both the user classes and tasks for AccessLecture/Math, including working with stake-holders with special needs (geographically distributed, visually impaired). Other research in the area focuses on developing software for use with other assistive technology (e.g. a screen reader), rather than the development of assistive technology itself [15, 16]. The methods used in this paper take elicitation and modeling techniques and applies them to an assistive tool that has two primary user groups.

AL/M users consist of Math and Science instructors and of the low vision students enrolled in their classes. In order to meet the needs of students and instructors, detailed surveys and interviews were conducted at both the secondary school level and university level. The information and process used to attain the user needs, task and environmental information is used to devise detailed user and task profiles. The analysis results have implications for the design and testing of the AccessLecture/Math system itself.

2   Background

STEM (Science, Technology, Engineering, and Math) professionals remain in demand and careers in computing have been identified as professions that will continue to be in high demand for years to come [3]. However, a gap exists in the participation by students with disabilities, particularly with the approximately 93,400 students with visual impairments currently in US schools. The proposed project seeks to better prepare visually impaired students by increasing their access to science and math lecture material. The current lack of access is seen as contributing to the lack of career options for students who are visually impaired [12].

Unlike the statistical data in STEM that is gathered for female and ethnic minority students, very little information is available on the achievement and participation of students with disabilities [7]. The gap is intensified in terms of information on students in specific disability groups, such as students with visual impairments as at best students with disabilities are all grouped together statistically. The 2000 Report of the Congressional Commission on the Advancement of Women and Minorities in Science,

Engineering and Technology Development identifies the lack of precollege preparation for students with disabilities [7]. This lack of preparation shows in high school science and math classrooms, subjects in which students with disabilities take fewer courses, and, when enrolled, typically receive lower grades than students without disabilities [7]. To compound the problems that arise from the visual nature of instruction, often traditional lecture or the addition of active learning components, the visual display of problems and issues with gaining immediate access to the material while instruction is occurring makes math and science content difficult for students with visual impairments to interpret. Students often receive notes after class. The 2000 Report of the Congressional Commission on the Advancement of Women and Minorities in Science, Engineering and Technology Development explored issues throughout the pipeline for women, minorities and people with disabilities. The report states that the Commission favors precollege reform efforts focusing on better preparation, support, and the professional development of teachers [7]. The AccessLecture/Math project focuses on the need for better support, in terms of assistive technology to facilitate the real-time presentation of lecture material to support the learning process and facilitate participation in lecture.

Among all working-age legally blind Americans, the unemployment rate is approximately 70 % [2]. Regardless of visual acuity, a factor contributing to the lack of preparation for the workplace is education. According to American Foundation for the Blind statistics, approximately 93,600 school age children are visually impaired or blind [2]. The high school completion rates vary by race disproportionately to the rate of visual impairment where visually impaired students who are white, African-American and Hispanic graduate with at least a high school education at 62 %, 41 % and 44 %, respectively [2]. Of those who graduated from high school, students who are legally blind are as likely to have completed some college courses as their sighted counterparts; however, students who are visually impaired are less likely to graduate from college [2].

The exact numbers of students with visual impairments who pursue STEM education is not known, but anecdotal evidence suggests the numbers are very low, as statistics either are only filtered for gender and ethnicity or all disability groups are combined. Academic preparation in science and math courses that channel students into STEM careers is low in part due to the difficulty in accessing information, especially the highly abstract and visually oriented information [11]. Many concepts in math and science are highly visual, with diagrams, graphs and equations that are difficult to explain in static text and the dynamic changes are difficult to capture and interpret in isolation. As such, science and math achievement by young students who are visually impaired is less than that of their sighted peers. While groups such as the National Federation of the Blind [9] offer outreach efforts to encourage young people to pursue STEM, such pioneering efforts are sorely in need of the follow-up and classroom support to provide young people the tools to ultimately pursuit STEM careers. Much research focuses on the blind rather than the visually impaired, which includes those with low vision. For example, the audio depiction of information such as math through lecture or calculators has been investigated [6].

The AccessLecture/Math project focuses on the presentation of material conveyed in lecture. Others have explored lecture in terms of distance education such as embedding text-to-speech features in slides used in web-based lecture [4, 10, 13]. In terms of science instruction, research has shown the importance of involving visually impaired students in the classroom experience beyond contrived, trivial experiences/activities that do not challenge the student or include them in the experiences that the rest of the class experiences [5]. AccessLecture/Math seeks to address this gap, in terms of access to material presented on the whiteboard during lecture, enabling the student to ask questions at the time of presentation and participate in class activities that rely on presented material. As such the focus on real-time presentation to low vision students is innovative.

The AccessLecture/Math project focuses on the needs of students who are visually impaired, specifically those with functional, low vision. The phrase, visually impaired, encompasses the spectrum of impaired vision. The term "legally blind" is defined through US federal law, referring "central visual acuity of 20/200 or less in the better eye with the best possible correction, as measured on a Snellen vision chart, or a visual field of 20 degrees or less" [2]. As of 1995, approximately 1.3 million Americans are considered legally blind [8]. "Of these individuals, 80 % (1,040,000) had some "useful vision" (a rate of 40 per 1,000). The other 20 % (260,000) had only light perception or less vision (a rate of 1 per 1,000). Half of these individuals were totally blind (130,000), that is, had no light perception (a rate of 0.5 per 10,000)." [9] The range that this project will focus on is that of students with vision of 20/100 to 20/800, corrected.

Reaching representative users, in this case secondary-school students (grades 6–12) as well as university students is critical in order to provide a usable and useful, accessible system. By targeting students who are low vision, we propose to prototype a solution that supports both increased math and science achievement, and thus increased choices for students in their future endeavors.

AccessLecture/Math may also help Math, Science, and itinerant (VI Support) teachers with strategies to support low vision students. Presentation of math and science material is significant in terms of accessible textbooks, lecture material, or class activities. The AL/M system seeks to enable educators to move from the challenges of material presentation to deeper concept understanding and linking understanding to the material (ultimately with student annotation features that are out of scope in this proposal). Students can have more ownership over their learning and the ability to ask questions based on the immediate material in class, while educators can provide more immediate feedback to visually impaired students in class. Currently this is a difficult dialog to attain either via extensive enlargement of printed material (which may not be exactly what the teacher is presenting on the whiteboard) or through notes that the student must view after class. Current approaches to supporting students who are visually impaired in the classroom consist of note taking by another student or an in-class aide, possibly alongside recording the lecture. The use of tactile tablets and other assistive technologies are very expensive and require extensive teacher training. A study publicized in the Journal of Visual Impairment and Blindness studied the use of various assistive technologies used by teachers in the classroom [1]. The study showed that a majority of teachers are not prepared to use such technologies and thus students are impacted. The AccessLecture/Math system will leverage the skill of writing on the whiteboard, which is common in most math and science classrooms. The intended result will be for little to no training on the teacher's part in terms of presenting material on the whiteboard. Such low overhead will be important for teacher buy-in to use the system.

3   Survey and Interview Design

The population of visually impaired students is a diverse group that is distributed in low numbers across the US. In addition to the socioeconomic diversity of students in general, the varied characteristics include:

- Year in school (for secondary and university students)
- Major (university students only)
- Gender
- Geographical location
- Math education experience
- Degree of visual impairment and implications on the classroom experience
- Experience with classroom accommodations and instructional settings

Two factors, geographical location and the degree of visual impairment's bearing on accommodations to read print, lead to the search for and design of an accessible online survey. A survey was designed over an interview due to the number of participants and the difficulty in scheduling interviews between student participants in different time zones and the student researchers who would have interviewed the participants. If the scheduling issue did not exist, then interviews would have been a preferred method to explore the participant experiences. Many researchers conduct surveys, but we required an online survey that can accommodate participants who use assistive technology (e.g. screen readers, magnification software). At the time, the best solution that allowed for complex, branching surveys and produced useful reports was the Surveymonkey.com service.

A survey was developed to capture students' pre-college (middle school and high school) and university experience in Math and Science courses. The university students' majors were not important given that each student would have had several pre-college Math and Science courses in order to be admitted to their university and non-STEM majors require some college level Math and Science courses. This approach provides a wide view of the varied pre-college and university campuses that the students have attended. The diversity includes rural, urban, and sub-urban campuses in different socio-economic levels across the United States.

3.1   Student Survey Design and Sampling

The design of the survey entailed the questions as well as the answer mechanisms. The survey system selected is accessible to students with low vision who may need to use magnification software or screen readers. Survey services such as SurveyMonkey or RIT's survey service (Clipboard) has a wide array of question types. Although the on-campus survey service was selected due to its commitment to accessibility, careful question type selected was needed in order to balance the type of feedback needed with ease of answering for the participants. The only question type that is considered difficulty to answer is where the respondent needs to drag and drop items in order to present their ranked list. Due to the fact that persons who are blind do not use a mouse, the ranked list type of question is not accessible. However open-ended questions, multiple or single selection questions, or those with a drop-down list are accessible to all users since the questions can be navigated with a keyboard solely if need be.

The questions themselves were divided into general demographic questions, reflection on pre-college math and science classes, and their experience in university math and science classes. For both pre-college and university courses, questions asked about:

- General Information: major in college, year in university, experience with touch screen, multitouch, and smartphone devices
- Pre-college Specific Information: served by an IEP (Individualized Education Program)
- Pre-college and University Specific Information: classes taken in math and science, accommodations used and those that were helpful in accessing material, difficulties encountered in class due to vision-related issues, issues with getting accommodations and working with instructors, assistive technology used and interest level in trying AccessLecture/Math in their Math and Science classes

Gathering information about the diverse backgrounds of students with visual impairments from the students themselves is critical due to the diverse experiences and access to resources that impact their educational experience (in this case in Math and Science). In addition, students' individual experiences and access to resources and support often varies as they progress from one school to another, as well as between K12 schools and the university setting. Part of the variance is due to the more rigorous legal mandates set for pre-college schools.

The survey was primarily of closed-ended questions (single/multiple selection and Likert scale), with some open-ended questions where students could elaborate on answers or provide information on accommodations or issues with them. The focus on the survey is to assess current class accommodations and issues rather than taking an inventory of visual impairments. The team wanted the survey participants to feel comfortable reflecting on their classroom experiences and related technology experience.

The survey was conducted online, through the use of an on-campus survey resource that is accessible. Students in the sample were contacted through the Disabled Student Services office (or related services) at their respective institutions. The survey was shared with three American universities varying in size and location but whose minimum size is 15,000 students in order to provide a likelihood of a critical mass of students with visual impairments. The team also found that larger universities were more likely to have a larger number of students with visual impairments due to the support infrastructure that is in place to support students with various disabilities.

Eleven students responded to the survey. The students represented a variety of majors including English, Mechanical Engineering, Psychology, and Computer Science. All but one student was an undergraduate student. The analysis of the results will follow.

3.2   Instructor Interview Design and Sampling

The resources and infrastructure in both the pre-college and university settings vary across the US. As such, the team needed to gather environmental and instructional information from the educator's perspective. Due to the need to gather the idea of the broad landscape for instruction and interaction, the educators did not necessarily need to have worked with students who are visually impaired (though some coverage was sought). Also, the instructor participants were not the instructors who taught any of the student participants.

The interview approach was taken after the team found that instructors did not want to take surveys. Instead instructors wanted to be interviewed either on the phone or in-person by the student researchers (depending on the instructor's location and availability). Interviews also had the advantage of allowing for the exploration of topics in-depth in a semi-structured manner.

The questions focused the following areas of the educator's day-to-day experiences:

- Description of the classroom environment
- Use of instructional technology in the classroom
- Teaching and lecture style in content presentation and how technology is used
- Writing style when conveying material on the board (directionality)
- Experience in working with visually impaired students in terms of strategies and logistics rather than student performance
- Division of lecture to recitation/lab
- Degree of access that students are given to teacher notes
- Willingness to allow visually impaired students to use an iPad in class

The interview was highly structured though primarily open-ended questions to enable the instructors to elaborate on their style, preference, and experience. The researchers followed a consistent process for conducting the interviews in terms of question coverage.

Interviews were conducted with eight Math, Science, and Computer Science instructors across the middle school, high school and university level. The student researchers contacted past instructors, in addition to other instructors that they located on departmental Website at those schools. The middle and high school instructors are from the Northeast region, representing both urban/suburban and rural schools. Most of the instructors had no experience with working with students with low vision. A couple of the instructors had experience working with one or two students with low vision over the course of several years.

The pre-college instructors were as open with their answers as the university instructors. As the instructors were self-selected there was little surprise that even when no experience existed with working with visually impaired students, the instructors were generally amenable to accommodating these students. The one exception was one university-level computer science instructor who was less amendable and was against the use of the system. While further analysis would provide more data from computer science instructors, the participant's views were noted as being representative of his personality than of computer science instructors as a population.

Given that personal experience of some of the authors in seeking accommodations, most university computer science instructors are have a more positive attitude. The analysis of the results will follow.

4   Domain Analysis

Complimentary to gathering information about the students and instructors, information also needs to be gathered regarding the domain of math and science education, specifically the classroom environment and related education concepts. The constraints are middle school, high school, and university level math and science education. Middle school is considered to be in grades 6 to 8, where students are typically 11–14 years old. High school is considered to be grades 9 to 12, where students are between the ages of 14 to 18.

Student researchers gathered information about environmental and presentations factors that are relevant to understanding the users and their tasks, in addition to the deployment of AccessLecture/Math.

4.1   Classroom Environment

Educational settings are varied in terms of several organizational, logistical and environmental factors. The factors were determined initially by taking an inventory of the environmental components in a typical classroom at Rochester Institute of Technology. The student members of the research team added additional factors. As a partial bottom-up approach, some factors (e.g. chalkboards, use of interactive whiteboards such as Smartboard and document projects such as the ELMO) were added during analysis of the instructor interview data. Environmental components include:

- Student capacity
- Type and number of chalkboards/whiteboards, and whether the boards are movable (generally vertically)
- Use and placement of a projector, Smartboard, or related technology
- Types of desks (full desk, half desk, tables)
- Location of the instructor's desk/table
- Location of electrical outlets
- Whether there is wireless communication available to the students
- Duration of the class meeting and how often the class meets per week

Due to the diverse nature of the classroom, for pre-college or college use, instructors and students alike were asked about their learning environment in math and science classes. Both perspectives are needed as part of user and task analysis. Each group was questioned separately since the students were not expected to be enrolled in the classes of the instructors who were interviewed.

The results of the interviews are presented in Table 1, where pre-college and college results are categorized.

Table 1. Classroom environment interview results.

Factor	Pre-college classrooms	College classrooms
Student capacity	Typically 15–35 students	Often between 15–50 students, though some schools may use larger lecture halls
Use & layout of chalkboard or whiteboard	Chalkboards more common in middle school; typically the boards are at the front of the room only; some science classroom boards are vertically moveable;	Some classrooms may have chalkboards, but most have whiteboards; Boards are in front of room and often on at least one side, though use of front boards most common; In science class or large lecture halls, some boards are vertically moveable
Place of projector or other technology	Usually present in more affluent schools, LCD Projector may be on a cart or mounted to ceiling, Smartboards more common in affluent schools, ELMO's may be present	LCD projector is often present, usually mounted in middle; Smartboards and ELMO's usually not present
Types of desks	Typically full desks or half desks; some science classes have table seating	Often depends on size of room or age of school; lecture halls often have stadium like seating with half-desks or tables; traditional classrooms often have half desks
Place of instructor desk	Front of room, to one side; usually a desk, often has an instructor computer; the room is generally the instructor's room	Front of room, typically to one side; often has a table setup where the instructor connects laptop, other equipment; the room is typically shared with other classes
Location of electrical outlets	Varies greatly, but usually at front of the room and on some side walls	Varies greatly, at least at the front of the room; sometimes student tables may have their own outlets
Duration of class meeting	Depends on course scheduling; most often 1 h every day or 1.5–2 h 3 times per week	Depends on course scheduling; most often either 1 h 3–4 times per week or 2 h for 2 times per week
Availability of wireless for students	Usually at more affluent schools, though many schools can at least accommodate wireless needs for assistive technology	Usually at least associated with specific buildings, often the science and technology department buildings; many schools are either entirely wireless or increasing coverage

The common use of chalkboards in pre-college courses was a surprise to the author, but the student researchers were not as surprised given their own experiences.

4.2 Classroom Presentation

In addition to the structure of the learning environment, there are constraints and factors that impact the students' learning experience in the classroom. The factors were selected in terms of those that would impact the design and use of the AccessLecture/Math system. They include:

- Extent and Manner to Which Chalkboard or Whiteboard is Used
- Use of a projector, Smartboard, or related technology
- Style of Instruction
- What Type of Material is Written
- Type of Information Written on the Board
- Classroom Activities, including Teamwork
- Use of PowerPoint, and If Whether Slides are Shared

Table 2. Classroom presentation interview results.

Factor	Pre-college students	College students
Use of chalkboard or whiteboard	The common means of conveying class information	
Use of technology	Some teachers use overhead projectors and document projectors, but most write on the board; Some science classes project diagrams; Use of interactive whiteboards is not common in most schools	LCD projects are the most common in order to display any PowerPoint slides or diagrams. Most material is still written on the board. Some Math classes do use PowerPoint slides, but that is not common.
Style of instruction	Lecture is common; science labs are at designated times	Primary Lecture, labs/recitation are separate meetings; Some instructors have group activities during lecture
Type of written material	Textual material and drawn diagrams; Science courses contain more elaborate diagrams, including annotating projected diagrams	
Type of written information on board	Course material, announcements, quiz/lab questions	
Classroom activities, including teamwork	When conducted, often integrated in class rather than a separate meeting; the exception of some science class labs	Some instructors have short in-class activities with partners or small teams during class, but many of the group-based activities are kept for special class recitation or lab meetings
Use of powerpoint and extent of slide sharing	When used, the slides generally not shared with students though instructors were will do share them with low vision students	When used, instructors often shared the slides on class websites; may be before or after class depending on teacher but they were willing to share with low vision students

Instructors were asked specifically about their teaching style while students were asked about the presentation of class material. Both perspectives were needed as part of user and task analysis, in order capture classroom instructor diversity across the many courses that instructors teach and that students are enrolled in over time.

The results of the interviews are presented in Table 2.

The classroom presentation of material is often dependent on the individual instructor's teaching style.

5   User Analysis

With the student surveys and additional research on visual impairments as input, the need to construct the potential users' profile is needed to better meet the needs of prospective users. While some overlap exists, specific needs and characteristics do separate pre-college and university students. The primary focus is on the students, as they will be interacting with the AccessLecture/Math system on the iPad as the primary user. Educators are analyzed separately given that they will be writing on the board using the same process that they would otherwise (the whiteboard marker and eraser will have sensors attached).

Table 3. Student user analysis.

Factor	Pre-college students	College students
Age	In general, typical age for grade – Middle School: 11–14, High School: 14–18	Typically 18 and older
Cognitive development	Generally able to complete grade level work or greater, though some remediation may exist	High enough to enroll in university, even though some remedial classes may be needed
Visual acuity	Visual acuity of 20/200-20/800	
Experience with own visual impairment	Visual impairment may be from birth or very recent; may be stale or progressive	
Experience with tablets, laptops, or smartphones	More experience with laptops is likely, many in college have experience with smartphones (iPhone in particular)	
Accommodations in class	Longer test time, use of aids to view class material are most common	
Use of assistive technology	CCTV, handheld magnifier, laptop, enlarged/large print and electronic course materials are most common	CCTV, handheld magnifier, laptop, large print and electronic course materials, in class note takers are most common
Common difficulties in class	Not able to discern material on the board,	Not able to discern material on the board,
Preferences for system	Is portable, fits in backpack, accessibility features can be selected, can be used at home, does not make student stand out with peers.	Is portable, fits in backpack, lightweight, long battery life, customized accessibility feature (fonts, substitute colors)
Frequency of use of AL/M in class	Nearly every class meeting; sees possible use in other courses as well.	

The general user analysis characteristics are based on those presented in [14]. Additional characteristics were selected based on the needs of visually impaired students. User profiles were not used due to the differences in visual impairment, but the categorization of characteristics is similar. Table 3 presents the user analysis.

The ranges of skills and characteristics present in the student's user profile reflect those collected in the student surveys. Subsequent user interface design feedback sessions will provide follow-up opportunities for more detailed student visual characteristics and accessibility preferences for the tablet-based/multitouch system. Beyond the user profiles themselves, several nonfunctional requirements are derived, including:

- Students with visual acuity of 20/200 to 20/800 must be able to read content and navigate the user interface independently.
- The text within the user interface must be understandable by a user who reads at the sixth grade level.
- The icons used within the user interface must be high contrast and flat (rather than 3D or realistically styled).
- The user must be able to choose between high contrast, color icons or black and white icons.
- The user must be able to adjust the visual display to their preferences and those preferences must be persistent across sessions.
- Notes taken by the student must be in a font size that is readable and adjustable.
- The system software must be able to be used independently by the student, assuming no other disabilities.
- The system (hardware) must be portable in terms of weight (less than 6 lb) and footprint so that a typical user can carry the system from class to class if needed either in their backpack or similar case.
- The system (hardware) must be usable throughout the day with no more than 1 charging period.
- The system software must be compatible with iOS accessibility features.

6   Task Analysis

Upon analysis of the student user class and the elicitation, a workflow of the tasks of conducting a class lecture is needed in order to target specific aspects of instruction where AccessLecture/Math fits. The details and flow of the Conveying Material (Educator) task and the Attending Lecture (Student) tasks were elaborated using the Hierarchical Task Analysis (HTA) approach shown below.

0. Conveying Material (Educator)
   1. Before Class
      1.1. Preparing Lecture Notes with Text, Formulae, Diagrams
         1.1.1. Lecture Material
         1.1.2. Course Announcements
         1.1.3. Quiz or Activity Questions
      1.2. Preparing PowerPoint slides or Diagram

    1.3. Prepare Class Handouts
    1.4. Post Slides or Notes to Course Webpage
2. During Class
    2.1. Make class announcements or reminders
    2.2. Go over questions from homework
    2.3. Present course material, while speaking
        2.3.1. Writing on board
            2.3.1.1. Left to right, top to bottom across all contiguous boards
            2.3.1.2. Left to right, top to bottom on each board, before moving across to the next one
            2.3.1.3. Erase material.
        2.3.2. Projecting diagram and writing on it
        2.3.3. Drawing diagram
    2.4. Conduct a quiz or in-class activity
    2.5. Answer questions from students
3. After Class, post slides or notes to course webpage

Plan 0: Do steps 1, 2, and 3 in that order

Plan 1: At minimum, complete step 1.1. Steps 1.2 through 1.4 are optional, where steps 1.2 and 1.3 can be completed in any order. If step 1.4 is completed, it is last.

Plan 1.1: Step 1.1.1 is required to whatever depth the instructor wishes. Steps 1.1.2 and 1.1.3 are optional. If the multiple steps are completed, order is not important.

Plan 2: Step 2.1 is usually completed first and often repeated at the end of class. Steps 2.2 is optional, but if completed is usually completed next. Step 2.3 is next, optionally interrupted by the optional steps 2.4 and 2.5.

Plan 2.3: Steps 2.3.1, 2.3.2, and 2.3.3 are completed in any order and to the degree needed by the instructor for a given class meeting.

Plan 2.3.1: Style can be any combination of 2.3.1.1 or 2.3.1.2, though it is usually one or the other. Do step 2.3.1.3 as needed to correct mistakes or for space needs.

The counterpart to the teacher's perspective is the student perspective, shown below:

0. Attend Lecture (Student)
  1. Setup
    1.1. Place course text on desk
    1.2. Place note taking materials on desk
    1.3. Setup assistive technology (e.g. CCTV, magnifier, etc.)
  2. Listen to lecture and write down notes, mark information that is particularly important (for review)
  3. View lecture and write down notes, mark information that is particularly important (for review)
  4. Ask questions
  5. Take quiz
  6. Work with partner/team on in-class activity
  7. Pick up notes from note taker

Plan 0: Complete 1.1 first. Complete steps 2 and 3 where possible. Steps 4–6 are optional, and are completed depending on how class is conducted (step 5 and 6) and if student feels comfortable asking a question (step 4). If a note taker is used, complete step 7 after class (most likely). If an in-class aide is writing down the lecture material in front of the student in a large font, step 3 will be easier.

Plan 1: Steps 1.1 and 1.3 are optional. Complete step 1.2.

The focus of the task analysis is the in-class activities, excluding preparation and grading activities due to the proposed system integration into the lecture itself. The educator's task is more complicated than the student's task in terms in terms of the time needed to complete. However the student's task has different nuances depending on the assistive technology used that are not cleanly captured in the HTA. This demonstrates the need to use the student user profile as a compliment to the HTA. Both have implications on the design of AccessLecture/Math.

7   Implications on Requirements and Design

In addition to understanding the prospective users, their needs and tasks, the elicited information has direct implications on the system features and the system design. The user interface and the system architecture must meet the student needs in order to be successful.

AccessLecture/Math's high-level features are focused on the student's (iPad) interface. The features for the instructor are out of scope for this paper. Student features include:

- The student shall zoom in and out of the displayed material as desired using a pinch and zoom gesture.
- The student shall navigate the view of the board while zoomed in or out using a finger or stylus.
- The student shall center their view on the currently active part of the written material, when desired.
- The system shall snap to the current place where the instructor is writing/erasing on the whiteboard by default.
- The recorded lecture session shall include the video of the strokes/erasure and audio of the instructor.
- The system shall provide time shifting during the recording, to enable the student to rewind the material (including notes) during a lecture or after a lecture.
- The student shall flag parts of the lecture to denote the presence of notes.
- The student shall be able to bookmark spots in the lecture for later reference.

Features focus on the real-time access to content in class and to the related note taking/studying tasks. These features are mostly stated in a user-focused manner,

The features must be complemented by nonfunctional requirements, including usability and accessibility requirements. Other requirements such as performance and security requirements are also documented. Several of the usability requirements are derived from the student surveys and instructor interviews, as reflected in the user profile and HTA's.

The detailed usability requirements follow additional best practices for requirement specification in terms of stating relevant benchmarks. The list above presents demonstrates the scope of the usability needs in terms of accessibility, productivity, ease of learning, ease of recall, understandability, and user satisfaction. Each of these requirements will be tested to the same level of rigor as the features, given that the lack of usability will result in a system that will not be used or could possibly impact student performance in a class.

The analysis and resulting requirements have direct implications on the design of AccessLecture/Math. This work is ongoing as the team also becomes familiar with the technologies. Some implications directly involve the iOS libraries to be used, with architectural implications. The most notable aspects of the system design are modularity, adherence to standards, and the separation of concerns (specifically the user interface from the underlying processing and storage). AccessLecture/Math will be evolving over time, with multiple rounds of user testing and with trials of the feasibility of various hardware. As such flexibility and maintainability are critical, where the modularity and separations of concerns will be appreciated. The adherence to Apple's iPad/iPhone Human Interface Guidelines will aid in the user experience. As the design activities move forward, the mapping of the usability and accessibility features are a driver for the system's architecture.

8   Conclusions and Future Work

The information gathered during domain exploration and requirement elicitation has kept the team grounded in the students' needs. Since each student's classroom experience can vary due to prior history, visual characteristics, and the style of instruction, the study of this variety has been helpful in acquiring a big picture view. Some members have personal experience in such accommodations, but the activities completed gave the team a wide view of the student diversity, the needs of the educators, and the constraints of the classroom environment. The data gathering will give a benchmark for comparison later with the usability test participants.

The user profiles and task analysis will be revisited throughout the design and testing activities to ensure that the needs of the students are met while unobtrusively integrating the AccessLecture/Math system. Testing will be conducted for both students and educators. The status of the system is currently design and initial usability testing to determine the preferred interaction schemes. The tasks of text entry for note taking and screen navigation with multitouch are being evaluated before the overall iPad system design is completed.

Acknowledgment. Thank you to the CRA (Computing Research Association) for supporting Alex Canter and Lindsey Ellis' efforts as part of the CREU (Collaborative Research Experiences for Undergraduates) program. This project also receives support from the National Science Foundation (Award # IIS-1218801)

References

1. Abner, G., Lahm, E.: Implementation of assistive technology with students who are visually impaired: teachers' readiness. J. Visually Impairment Blindness **92**(2), 98–105 (2005)
2. American Foundation for the Blind: statistics and sources for professionals. http://www.afb.org/section.asp?SectionID=15&DocumentID=1367
3. Bureau of Labor Statistics: tomorrow's jobs. http://www.bls.gov/oco/oco2003.htm
4. Davison, B., Walker, B.N.: Sonification sandbox overhaul: software standard for auditory graphs. In: Proceedings of the International Conference on Auditory Display (ICAD 2007), pp. 386–390 (2007)
5. Fraser, W.J., Maguvhe, M.O.: Teaching life sciences to blind and visually impaired learners. J. Biol. Educ. **42**(2), 84–89 (2008)
6. Gardner, J.A.: The accessible graphing calculator: a self-voicing graphing scientific calculator for windows (1999). http://dots.physics.orst.edu/calculator/
7. National Science Foundation: Land of plenty diversity as america's competitive edge in science, engineering and technology: report of the congressional commission on the advancement of women and minorities in science, engineering and technology development, September 2000. http://www.nsf.gov/pubs/2000/cawmset0409/cawmset_0409.pdf
8. National Eye Institute: Statistics on blindness in the model reporting area, (Publication No. [NIH] 73-427) (1969–1970)
9. National Federation of the Blind. http://www.nfb.org/nfbrti/programs.htm
10. Rughooputh, S., Santally, M.: Integrating text-to-speech software into pedagogically sound teaching and learning scenarios. J. Educ. Technol. Res. Dev. **57**(1), 131–145 (2009). Springer, Boston
11. Smith, A.C., Francioni, J.M., Matzek, S.D.: A java programming tool for Students with visual disabilities. In: proceedings of Assets 2000, Washington D.C., November 2000
12. Stanley, P.B.: Assessing the mathematics related communication requirements of the blind in education and career. In: Miesenberger, K., Klaus, J., Zagler, W.L., Karshmer, A.I. (eds.) ICCHP 2008. LNCS, vol. 5105, pp. 888–891. Springer, Heidelberg (2008)
13. Walkter, B., Mauney, L.M.: Universal design of auditory graphs: a comparison of sonification mappings for visually impaired and sighted listeners. ACM Trans. Accessible Comput. (TACCESS) **2**(3), 1–16 (2010)
14. Heim, S.: The Resonant Interface: HCI Foundations For Interaction Design. Addison Wesley, New York (2007)
15. Brunet, P., Feigenbaum, B.A., Harris, K., Laws, C., Schwerdtfeger, R., Weiss, L.: Accessibility requirements for systems design to accommodate users with vision impairments. IBM Syst. J. **44**(3), 445–465 (2005)
16. AlKhanifer, A., Ludi., S.: Towards a situation awareness design to improve visually impaired orientation in unfamiliar buildings: requirements elicitation study. In: 22nd International Requirements Engineering Conference (RE), Karlskrona, Sweden, August 2014

Applications

Interplay of Requirements Engineering and Human Computer Interaction Approaches in the Evolution of a Mobile Agriculture Information System

Lasanthi De Silva[1], Tamara Ginige[3], Pasquale Di Giovanni[4],
Maneesh Mathai[2], Jeevani Goonetillake[1], Gihan Wikramanayake[1],
Monica Sebillo[4], Giuliana Vitiello[4], Genoveffa Tortora[4],
Maurizio Tucci[4], and Athula Ginige[2(✉)]

[1] University of Colombo School of Computing, Colombo, Sri Lanka
{lnc,jsg,gnw}@ucsc.cmb.ac.lk
[2] Western Sydney University, Sydney, Australia
{A.Ginige,M.Mathai}@westernsydney.edu.au
[3] School of Business, Australian Catholic University, Sydney, Australia
Tamara.Ginige@acu.edu.au
[4] University of Salerno, Fisciano, Italy
{msebillo,gvitiello,tortora,
mtucci,pdigiovanni}@unisa.it

Abstract. Very high adoption of mobile phones in developing countries can be used to empower people engaged in various sectors such as agriculture, fisheries and healthcare by providing timely information in right context, thus facilitating them to make informed decisions. Having identified lack of such information is badly affecting farmers in Sri Lanka we embarked on a project to develop a mobile based agriculture information system. We had to combine different theories and methods both from Requirements Engineering (RE) and Human Computer Interaction (HCI) on a need basis to successfully gather the requirements. When we retraced the process we saw a definitive systematic pattern as to how RE and HCI can be used to enrich such an artefact; highlighting the strong interplay between RE and HCI. Discovery of this pattern enabled us to generalise the process.

Keywords: Requirement Engineering · Human Computer Interaction · Mobile agriculture information system · ICT for development

1 Introduction

Timely access to necessary information is essential to make informed decisions. With mobiles the ability to access information without being limited in terms of time of the day and location has vastly improved. The myriads of in-build sensors in mobiles such as GPS, Camera, microphone etc. open-up new possibilities to develop next generation of social networks known as Social Life Networks [1]. These not only connect people to people, but also have the capability of providing real-time, context-sensitive local

© IFIP International Federation for Information Processing 2016
Published by Springer International Publishing Switzerland 2016. All Rights Reserved
A. Ebert et al. (Eds.): UsARE 2012/2014, LNCS 9312, pp. 135–159, 2016.
DOI: 10.1007/978-3-319-45916-5_9

information by aggregating information from a variety of sources including SMS messages, sensor data and data from public sources [2, 3].

Today the mobile has become the most popular and common way of communication among people worldwide [4, 5]. According to International Telecommunication Union (ITU) by end of 2015 there were nearly 7 billion mobile-cellular subscriptions worldwide. In terms of users there were 3.2 billion people using the Internet which is around, 51 % of the total world population. For every Internet user in the developed world there were 2 in the developing world [6]. Mobile broadband is the most dynamic market segment; globally, mobile broadband penetration is expected to reach 47 % in 2015, a value that increased 12 times since 2007 [6]. Thus, the significant growth of mobiles and use of the internet, especially in developing countries have opened up new possibilities to find effective ways to provide information related to livelihood activities of these people.

Yet there are not that many applications to support information needs related to livelihood activities of people working in sectors such as agriculture, fisheries, health-care and education in developing countries. Due to lack of such information they face difficulties in their livelihood activities as they are unable to make informed decisions. It is now technically possible to develop mobile based information systems to aggregate real time information on evolving situations such as demand, current levels of production, spread of pests and diseases in crops and natural disasters to provide just-in-time assistance and support for these people to make informed decisions [7].

Inspired by the potentials and capabilities of the mobile technology, we an international collaborative research team, embarked on a project to explore potential mobile based applications to assist people in the developing world. The research team consists of researchers from four countries in four continents; Sri Lanka, Australia, Italy and USA [2]. We carried out field visits, information gathering meetings, industry round table discussions, workshops and brainstorming sessions to identify the potential mobile based applications. During these discussions it came to our attention a persistent vegetable over-production problem in Sri Lanka [8–16]. The issue was almost all the farmers tend to grow the same crop at the same time creating an oversupply situation. This in return creates a drastic impact on the farmers' revenue [9, 10, 14, 16, 17].

Crop diversification can resolve this issue. At the time of selecting a crop to grow, farmers need to know the current production level of that crop. This information would help them to select a crop that is not in high production, hence avoiding a possible over production situation. This requires farmers sharing what they are planning to grow, aggregating this information and providing the aggregated production levels back to the farmers. This scenario is an example of how timely information in right context can enhance informed decision making. Thus, we selected the agriculture domain to explore how we can develop a mobile based information system to enhance flow of information to facilitate informed decision making.

The development of this mobile application requires identifying the information needs and deciding on the system functionality (Requirement Engineering-RE) to deliver the information to user in an effective way (Human Computer Interaction-HCI). The identification of the system functionalities requires better understanding of the application domain and their requirements. Usability is defined as the degree to which a product or system can be used by specified users to achieve specified goals with effectiveness, efficiency and satisfaction in a specified context of use [18]. This in turn reshapes the functionality and how it is presented to the user to interact with it highlighting the importance of interplay between both RE and HCI in system development.

The development of the mobile agriculture information system using the smartphone technology was a challenge during the initial phases of the research. User novelty to the technology and the unclear system functionalities made the development of the artefact a challenging task. Requirements were difficult to derive as researchers did not have a good understanding of activities specific to agriculture domain and users lacked knowledge about the relevant technologies and its capabilities. Further as the research team members were based in 4 continents, the location of researchers added another layer of complexity.

To develop the artefact presented in this chapter we had to find a process that can help to overcome these challenges. At the end, using a modified version of the Design Science Research (DSR) methodology the researchers succeeded in developing an artefact that met both RE and HCI requirements. Using the development of this mobile agriculture information system, we present the process that evolved and the way both RE and HCI requirements were captured at different stages of the artefact development.

2 Related Work

In recent years, a growing number of researchers have identified initially call phones and later smartphones as an ideal platform for developing applications for people in developing countries [19] as these can deliver not only voice but also information [5]. The user group that we were targeting was new to this technology and also had a low literacy level. Thus, we focused our literature review to identify available mobile based artefacts targeted at providing information for similar groups of people. We paid special attention to the approaches that were used in these artefacts to present information to the users.

Mehdi et al. have focused their attention on mobile phones as a platform for non-literate people to access financial services [20]. In particular, they focused on the design of user interfaces for non-literate and semi-literate users. They have observed that non-literate and semi-literate users were unable to make sense of text-based user interfaces (UIs). The task-completion rates were better for the rich multimedia UIs, and when spoken dialog was added to the UIs it further reduced the task completion time and required less assistance.

Danis et al. have observed that in the Sub-Saharan Africa there is on average one doctor for every 20,000 people [21]. This required new health approaches that were focused on prevention rather than treatment. Hence, they analysed two deployments of an SMS-based HIV/AIDS education system that uses a quiz format to assess people's knowledge of the disease, including its causes and methods of prevention. In particular they first focused on the challenges that the use of SMS presented as user interaction mechanism and later explored factors that influenced the participation in quiz games. The paper shows that mobile devices are suitable for this type of activities.

Putnam et al. [22] discusses a case study aimed at identifying user requirements of mobile phone users living in Kyrgyzstan. They used scenarios and personas to better capture the user requirements. They described in their study, how they had transformed these into a set of functional requirements. During the study they developed a working prototype and evaluated the usability.

An extensive study done on the existing mobile applications for agriculture and rural development has shown that countries such as India, Kenya and Uganda are the leading developing countries that use many such mobile applications for agriculture activities [4]. AvaajOtalo (voice stoop) is an interactive voice application developed for small-scale farmers in Gujarat, India [23]. Upon calling a toll-free number farmers are presented an audio menu to select an activity. These activities include question and answer forum to ask questions and listen to answers for similar issues, announcements board, and radio achieve on most popular agriculture radio programs in Gujarat.

eSagu is another advisory service developed for Indian farmers to seek agriculture advice from agriculture experts for different pests and disease found in their farms [24]. Farmer or a coordinator is given the provision to capture images of crop diseases and send these with a corresponding text description seeking advice. They were also required to enter the details about the current status of the soil and weather conditions to provide the farm context. This is a complex task for the farmers and they mostly depend on the agriculture coordinator to enter these values. If there is an error in the provided parameters that then will affect the advice they receive, thus restricting the usefulness of the application.

mKrishi is an agro advisory system designed for rural farmer communities in India to get access to experts living in cities. Farmers can use voice queries and images of insects and disease affected plants to ask for advice from agriculture experts. In this system the farm context is obtained by using sensors to measure parameters such as canopy and ground temperatures as well as data from small weather stations installed in the farms [25].

In Sri Lanka there are two mobile-based applications designed for farmers to obtain agriculture market information; Dialog trade net [26] and 6666 Agri-price index [27]. Both applications are based on voice and SMS. 6666 Agri Price service provide current prices at different markets in collaboration with Hector Kobbakaduwa Agrarian Research and Technology Institute (HARTI). HARTI is the main operating body in Sri Lanka to gather price related information in leading markets. However, the popularity of these services is relatively low among the farmers in Sri Lanka, when compared to similar services in other developing countries.

Table 1 shows the modality, functionalities and the HCI aspects found in the above agriculture related artefacts.

From the above reviews it is evident that the modality of the existing mobile based artefacts in the agriculture domain is based on basic voice, SMS and image uploading facilities. This presentation mechanism reduces the amount of information provided for the end users. Further, none of the reviewed artefacts has catered for the entire crop life cycle. Most of these artefacts have covered only a sub set of information required by the users. In contrast our main aim was to identify an effective way to provide information for the whole farming life cycle by addressing the above limitations.

We also reviewed ICT4D and HCI4D literature especially in relation to development process, specific methods and techniques that have been successfully used to develop similar applications. Peter [28] has reported lack of user-centred design due to

Table 1. Modality, functionalities and HCI aspects; agriculture artefacts

Application	Modality	Functionalities (Information)	HCI Aspects
Dialog trade net	Voice and SMS	Market Prices	No Specific Interface
Mobitel 6666	Voice and SMS	Market Prices	No Specific Interface
mKrishi	Voice and SMS Image uploading facility	Agro Advisory on crops, weather, prices, pest & diseases	A standard interface for SMS and image uploading
eSagu	Voice and SMS Image uploading facility	Agro Advisory on crops, weather, prices, pest & diseases	A standard interface for SMS and image uploading
AvaajOtalo	Voice and text input	Question answering on agri issues, announcements and radio archive	A menu based interface for voice and text inputs

resource constraints as major cause for high rate of ICTD project failure. He has introduced user persona from UX design as a powerful tool for considering the user's perspective within resource-constrained ICTD projects. Human-computer interaction for development (HCI4D) requires considerable time in the field interacting with users. While this is true for most HCI work, fieldwork in developing regions presents unique challenges due to differences in culture, language, ethnicity, and socioeconomic status. A group of 9 researchers having reflected on their experiences have suggested a mix of qualitative and quantitative instruments to elicit and synthesize individual experiences [29]. Above review indicated the importance of blending multiple approaches to successfully develop applications to support livelihood activities of people in developing countries.

3   Research Approach

The main aim of this research project was to design a mobile artefact that will assist farmers in decision making. Artefacts are "innovations that define ideas, practices, technical capabilities, products through which the analysis, design, implementation, and use of information systems can be effectively and efficiently accomplished" [30]. The Design Science Research (DSR) methodology is capable of designing an innovative artefact to solve real world problems [30, 31]. DSR is a matured growing field which is increasingly used in designing information systems [32–35]. DSR method is capable of making a significant impact on developing information systems as it seeks innovation and creativeness in designing the artefacts. DSR further conducts "applicable, yet rigorous research" [34] to design innovative artefacts. DSR can effectively guide the design of this innovative artefact by facilitating active participation of both researchers and end users. The research process captures the knowledge to guide the researchers to meet the desired outcomes [32]. The development of the artefact aims at achieving the utility of a solution. Thus, in turn it will enhance both efficiency and effectiveness of the artefact.

In 2004, Hevner proposed a generic DSR framework for the researchers who conduct DSR in information systems design [30]. Later in 2007 [33] it was presented as consisting of three cycles; Relevance, Design and Rigor. The relevance cycle identifies the requirements from the contextual environment and input into the research activities. It further introduces artefacts produced as a result of the research activities to the environment for field testing. The rigor cycle provides grounding knowledge to conduct the research activities and adds new knowledge generated as a result of these activities. The design cycle operates within research activities of artefact construction and evaluation. Therefore, these three cycles operate within the contextual environment, design science research activities and knowledgebase as illustrated in Fig. 1. Environment or the application domain is composed of people, organizational systems, technical systems, potential problems and opportunities. Design Science Research activities include building and designing of artefacts to meet the user requirements. The knowledgebase provides the fundamental knowledge using different modalities to ensure design rigor in DSR [33]. Scientific theories and methods, experience and expertise, meta-artefacts are some of the fundamental knowledge sources referred to in designing the artefact.

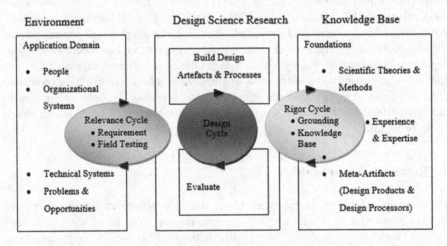

Fig. 1. Traditional DSR cycles presented in [33]

To meet the practical aspects of this project we had to modify the traditional DSR cycles. Each DSR cycle is further divided into two sub parts. Splitting of these cycles were required, in order to manage the complexity of the problem domain and also to enable international collaboration as some activities were carried out at different times in different locations. The resultant cycles can be visualised with respect to the three original cycles as explained below.

- **Relevance Cycle:** The Relevance Cycle bridges the actual environment and the research activities in a DSR project. As stated by Hevner [30] a "good design science research project often begins by identifying and representing opportunities and problems in an actual application environment". Problems and opportunities of the actual application domain could arise from its environment or from outside the environment. Identification of such problems and opportunities is essential to provide a new and innovative artefact [33]. Based on the observations Relevance Cycle was divided into two sub cycles. These were named as Relevance -Problem Understanding (*RePU*) and Relevance - Suitability Validation (*ReSV*). While RePU gathers requirements to understand the problem, ReSV check the suitability of the artefact using field validation. This split was needed as these activities happened at two different times.

- **Design Cycle:** The Design Cycle is the "heart" of any design science research project [33]. It iterates within the design, construction of the artefacts and its functional validation until a satisfactory design is achieved. Most of the hard work is carried out within this cycle before producing an artefact for field testing. Design cycle performs two main activities in relation to producing a good, efficient artefact. Two main sub parts in Design Cycle are Heuristic search (*DeHS*) and Functional validation (*DeFV*). In DeHS a design that can meet immediate goals is identified, designed and constructed. DeHS applies various heuristic search methods to create a good artefact. The constructed artefact is evaluated to ensure its functional correctness in DeFV. The designer iterates between DeHS and DeFV until the artefact is free of functional errors. This split was needed as these activities happened at different times and took place in different locations.

- **Rigor Cycle:** The Rigor Cycle provides grounding theories and methods along with domain experience and expertise from the foundations knowledge base into the research and adds the new knowledge generated by the research to the growing knowledge base [33]. First the relevant prior knowledge is identified to ground the design of the new artefact as well as to identify any gaps that may exist in relation to the requirements that the new artefact should satisfy. This ensures that the research is conducted in a rigorous manner and assists to clearly identify the innovation aspects of the solution. The new knowledge generated in this process is contributed back to the knowledge base for use of future researchers. The rigor cycle can be represented as learning's from the existing or grounding knowledge and contributions as new knowledge. Thus, Rigor Cycle can be divided into two sub cycles; Learning from the grounding knowledge (RiLe) and Contributions back to the knowledge base (RiCo). This split was needed as these activities happened at different times in different locations.

Figure 2 shows the split DSR model overlaid on the original 3 cycle model. Naming convention of the new cycles is given in Table 2.

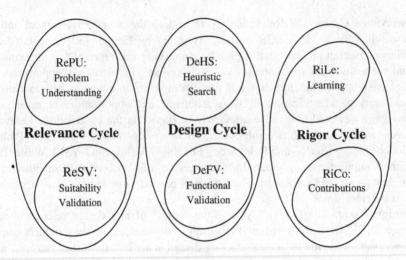

Fig. 2. Split DSR model

Table 2. Naming convention of the cycles in the split DSR model

Abbreviation	Corresponding DSR cycle naming
RePU	**Relevance - Problem Understanding** Cycle
ReSV	**Relevance - Suitability Validation** Cycle
DeHS	**Design - Heuristic Search** Cycle
DeFV	**Design - Functional Validation** Cycle
RiLe	**Rigor - Learning** Cycle
RiCo	**Rigor - Contributions** Cycle

4   Evolution of the Agriculture Mobile Information System

To develop the agriculture mobile information system we iterated through these six (06) sub cycles of the Split DSR model shown in Fig. 2. As we have used these sub cycles multiple times we assigned a number for each to clearly distinguish the sub cycles; i.e. RePU1, DeHS1 etc., The initial discussion described in the introduction triggered the Relevance - Problem Understanding sub cycle (RePU1) to gather domain knowledge relevant to vegetable over production issues faced by the farming communities in Sri Lanka. We needed to develop an understanding of the problem domain to be able to identify the required system functionalities. For this we investigated the problem domain using interviews and survey questionnaires involving farmers and agriculture officers. Initial surveys were designed to find out what farmers thought of the cause for over production and actions that they take to mitigate this issue. We discovered that some farmers were estimating current production levels by talking to seed suppliers to find out quantities of seeds that have been purchased so far. We identified that this was not an effective approach because there were many seed suppliers. Also some farmers were producing seeds for their own use as well as to sell to others. This made it difficult to get a realistic aggregated value for current production level of a crop based on amount of seeds being sold. This led us to explore the possibility of sharing production quantities via the mobile technology to derive an aggregated value.

Even with these findings and domain understanding the researchers only had a vague idea on the exact user requirements to design the artefact. Therefore, using the data collected we decided to create personas and scenarios to better understand the domain and derive user requirements [22].

4.1 Scenarios for the User Domain

The knowledge gained from RePU1cycle led us to create a scenario of truck farming (or large scale commercial farming) practices that triggered a Design - Heuristic Search sub cycle (DeHS1). The scenario formed a base for brainstorming and discussion of initial requirements. Based on information gathered so far, we defined two personas, representing possible stakeholders as shown below.

Actors
1. Sirisena is a 45 years old farmer with long experience in truck farming. Sirisena is part of Sinhalese ethnic group. He has a basic education level; he attended the primary school, he can read and write Sinhalese and he has a basic knowledge of English. Sirisena does not have advanced technical skills, the only technological instrument is his mobile phone that he uses every day. Moreover he is pretty distrustful of the technological support and, during his work, is accustomed to rely on his farmer experience. Sirisena lives in Sigiriya, a village in the central Matale District of Sri Lanka, where he owns four acres of farm land. Since the property is quite large, Sirisena in his work is supported by eight collaborators. Since Sirisena has a long experience in truck farming he manages the crop production of his family farm. His role is to make decisions on critical aspects of the production. He takes decisions on the kind of production and the time to start it. Moreover he establishes an indicative selling price.   2. Premasiri is a 40 years old low price fertilizers seller. Like Sirisena, Premasiri is part of the Sinhalese ethnic group and lives near Sigiriya. In order to raise his revenues he also acts as market middle man. Since he can speak English as good as Sinhalese and has a basic knowledge of Tamil, his intermediary role is well recognized by the farmers of the area. During the market activities his responsibility is to negotiate the best selling price of the product trying to match the expectations of his clients.

Scenarios
Sirisena manages the crop production of the farm
Sirisena is planning the new crop production. The decision will be made on the basis of three factors. He takes in to account:

1.	*the period of the year*
2.	*the crop producing high yield within a short time*
3.	*The crop selling prices of the last year*

Since the period of the year is suitable for potatoes cultivation and it gives the highest yield in a short time, Sirisena decides to produce mainly potatoes. Anyway, Sirisena makes his decision without interacting with his neighbors because he does not trust them.

Three months later the crop is ready to be harvested, he establishes an indicative price of fifty rupees for one kilogram of potatoes, on the basis of the last year selling price and the expenses incurred during the cultivation period.

Sirisena does not have means to take the harvest to the market and moreover he could not well communicate with potential Tamil buyers because of his language limitations. He decides to call Premasiri asking him to mediate during the market activities.

Premasiri acts as middle man to get the harvest sold

Premasiri agrees to sell Sirisena's harvest to the local market. Before starting the market activities all the farmers decide to raise or reduce the estimated harvest prices considering the presence of competitors. Premasiri notices that many farmers have cultivated large amount of potatoes. He is forced by the local market-law to reduce the estimated price cutting his profit. Moreover he notices that just a few farmers are selling onions so that the onions prices are noticeably higher than the last year prices.

User scenarios were then transformed to identify the design claims of the artefact. The scenarios, design claims and application requirements were used to derive a list of interface requirements for the end users considering literacy, familiarity in using a mobile device, users' cultural background and language beliefs. Further information on the scenarios, design claims and requirements can be found in [36]. These led us in identifying some core system functionalities and initial guidelines for designing the interfaces. Based on the findings we developed the first set of mobile interfaces.

4.2   The First Set of Mobile Interfaces

The first set of mobile interfaces is shown in Fig. 3. The first screen (on the left) represented a crop catalogue. We used icons to describe crops and a coloured background to indicate the approximate quantity of each crop already in production.

We used 3 colours; white yellow and red, indicating zero, moderate and intensive production respectively. After selecting a crop, users can navigate to the interface shown in the 2nd screen (on the right) to obtain a more detailed description of the product. We provided radio buttons to insert quantity of crop(s) that they want to cultivate. This minimised typing errors. This input information can be aggregated to derive the current production levels in real time.

As can be seen from rest of the paper these interfaces started to act as a focal point for the whole research team to coordinate their individual research efforts towards the overall goal. It also gave the whole research team initial glimpse of how information can be communicated via colours on a mobile interface to make best use of available screen area and effectively capture user input.

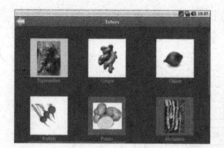

Fig. 3. First mobile sketches of the interfaces

These mock-ups triggered a Relevance -Suitability Validation sub cycle (ReSV1). The mock-ups were shown to group of farmers and Agriculture extension officers to obtain their feedback. We needed to find out their reactions to our design and whether the information is sufficient for them to make an informed decision on selecting crops (s) for a new season.

This iteration through ReSV1 cycle highlighted some HCI issues and triggered a Design- Heuristic Search cycle (DeHS2) to make changes to the interfaces. One such refinement was to change the colour coding scheme to reflect the traffic light colour scheme (green, yellow and red). Users were familiar with traffic light colour scheme and able to interpret overproduction data with this visual message better. We also modified the user interfaces to present many crops under different categories on the mobile interface as shown in Fig. 4.

In the ReSV1 cycle we also identified that in addition to the aggregated information on production levels, there were other factors that influenced farmers' decision when selecting crop(s) to grow in the next season. This triggered RePU2; a Relevance - Problem Understanding cycle, where we analysed information received from the agriculture officers and collected from newspaper articles in addition to information already collected to create the initial scenarios to identify factors that influence farmer's decision making. As a result, we developed the causal map shown in Fig. 5. From the causal map we were able to identify that the farmers' decision making depends on

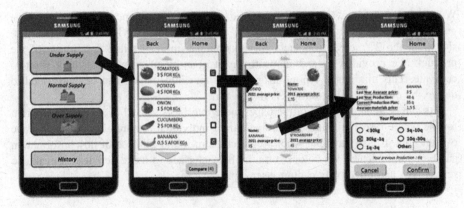

Fig. 4. Modified user interfaces to better visualise the crop catalogue

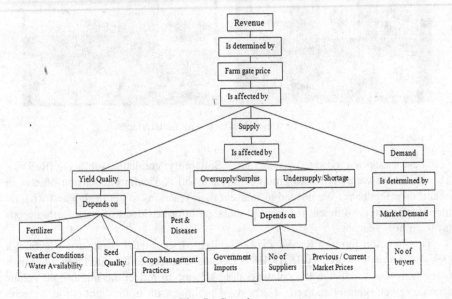

Fig. 5. Causal map

various factors depending on the stage of the farming life cycle [37]. These insights led the researchers to further learn about information needs of farmers and ways to organize the information.

At this point we conducted a Rigor - Learning (RiLe1) sub cycle to learn about agriculture related information. We identified the possibility of categorising different information needs of farmers to different stages of the farming life cycle. We further identified the need for personalised information to suit different farmers. This led us to think about user context and a farmer registration system to be able to provide contextualised information. Thus, we identified the need for a farmer registration function as shown in Fig. 6.

Fig. 6. New user interface mock-ups to provide farmers with contextualised information

4.3 Paper Prototype Design

The farming life cycle composes of 6 main stages: Crop planning, seeding, planting, growing, harvesting and selling [38]. Initially, we targeted one stage of the farming life cycle to design the artefact; crop planning. By now we have realised trying to provide information to support all stages of the farming life cycle is a complex task and a practical way to manage this complexity was to design one stage at a time.

Based on the requirements derived via iterations through RePU2, DeHS2 and RiLe1, we refined the interfaces of the mobile artefact for the crop planning stage using a Design – Heuristic Search (DeHS3) sub cycle. We identified six main tasks in the crop planning stage. Next, these tasks were further divided into more manageable parts comprised of user actions and system responses as listed in Table 3.

Table 3. Tasks, user actions and system response for 'Crop Selection'

Task	User action	System REsponse
(A) Suitable crops for the location	Location Check	List the suitable crops based on the location of the farmer.
	Crop category (Vegetables, Fruits or other)	List crops based on the crop category (Vegetables, Fruits or other)
(B) Relevant crop varieties	Crop Selection	Select a crop form the crop list
	Variety List	Display varieties of the selected crop
	Check variety specific characteristic	Display additional information on the selected variety.
	Check for seed distributors	Display available seed distributors
(C) Market price	Crop Selection	Select a crop form the crop list
	Check Price	Display last month/week price

(*Continued*)

Table 3. (*Continued*)

Task	User action	System REsponse
(D) Seed suppliers	Crop Selection	Select a crop form the crop list
	Check for seed distributors	Display available seed distributors
(E) Crop management techniques	Crop Selection	Select a crop form the crop list
	View additional information	Display additional information on nursery management, field establishment techniques, pest and disease issues etc.
(F) Crop plan	Crop Selection	Select a crop form the crop list
	Crop Planned extent	Enter the number of acres to be cultivated

Fig. 7. Designed mobile interfaces for the crop planning stage

During the paper prototype evaluation, farmers were able to see the proposed model (Fig. 7) on paper and it was easier for them to envisage a possible solution. They started to explain their information needs better. In addition they provided us with their feedback on some HCI aspects. Figure 8 shows some instances when farmers used paper prototypes during this study.

An important observation was the enthusiasm of the farmers in using a smart phone to obtain their daily information needs. Once farmers started see the proposed model on paper, they too started to get involved in the design of the artefact. This was evident from the responses and observations made during the interviews. They mentioned that they could see the potential of the proposed solution and expressed the benefits of having this information.

Fig. 8. Farmers evaluating the paper prototype

We analysed the importance of the provided information based on the farmer feedback and rankings. In Table 4 we have highlighted the most important information for the crop selection stage. The results of this study triggered another Design - Heuristic Search sub cycle (DeHS4) to refine the interfaces. Refined interfaces are shown in Fig. 9.

In order to satisfy the new information needs of the farmers, it became necessary to find potential sources for this information. Currently, this information is scattered within the agriculture domain. Different stakeholders create this information as a result of their routine activities. This made us realise the importance of developing a properly structured agriculture information repository [39]. Until that was implemented, we decided to use test information to continue designing the mobile prototype.

4.4 First Physical Implementation of the Mobile Artefact

We implemented a mobile prototype having following functionalities derived from combining insights gained so far, using a Design – Heuristic Search (DeHS5) sub cycle.

- Basic Login Facility: This was used to identify the farmer to provide contextualised information.
- Crop Planner: After a successful login farmer is directed to the crop planner interface, where crops and varieties were categorised in to three main tabs; Vegetables, Fruits and other. A colour coding scheme is used to visually represent the current production level of a crop as shown in Fig. 10. Specific colours are used

Table 4. Farmer information needs for crop selection

Farmer information need		1	2	3	4	5
1	Crop Types	100%	0%	0%	0%	0%
2	Last Year Price	33%	40%	7%	20%	0%
3	Last Week Price	33%	53%	0%	13%	0%
4	Current Production	80%	13%	0%	0%	7%
Seed/Crop Varieties						
5	Seed Varieties	93%	7%	0%	0%	0%
6	Market Price per variety	93%	7%	0%	0%	0%
7	Places to Buy Seeds	100%	0%	0%	0%	0%
8	Seed Prices	93%	0%	7%	0%	0%
9	Estimated Yield	7%	67%	27%	0%	0%
10	Seed Requirement	7%	80%	13%	0%	0%
Information regarding seed varieties						
11	Colour	100%	0%	0%	0%	0%
12	Weight/Harvest	100%	0%	0%	0%	0%
13	Quantity	100%	0%	0%	0%	0%
14	Special Qualities	100%	0%	0%	0%	0%
15	Transportation	100%	0%	0%	0%	0%
16	Pest & Diseases outbreak	100%	0%	0%	0%	0%
17	Market Demand	100%	0%	0%	0%	0%
More Information regarding crops						
18	Field Establishment	27%	60%	13%	0%	0%
19	Possible Pest & Diseases	93%	7%	0%	0%	0%
20	Climate Requirement	13%	60%	20%	0%	7%
21	Nursery Management	20%	80%	0%	0%	0%

to represent different thresholds. For example, the colour red is used to specify a threshold that will lead to an oversupply. Once the farmer selects a specific crop variety, it shows special characteristics of that variety such as yield colour, weight, length/size etc. Moreover, it also displays useful statistics such as current production and last year production for the selected crop variety. The application also provides a function for the farmer to view the history of their past activities and a mechanism to compare details of two or more crops.

Fig. 9. Refined interfaces based on the comments received from the farmers

- Profit Calculator: Profit calculator is designed to help farmers to calculate their farming expenses.

This was immediately followed by a Design – Functional Validation DeFV1 sub cycle to perform an internal validation of the implemented functions. This was done by all members of the research team. They tested the functions and any errors that were found were reported to the developers to rectify these.

Next we tested this mobile prototype to validate the suitability of the artefact using a Relevance – Suitability Validation (ReSV3) sub cycle. For this validation a sample of 32 farmers was used. The research instruments used in this validation were the working mobile prototype and a questionnaire to record the feedback from the farmers. This was the first hands-on experience of the farmers using the mobile artefact. Out of the 32 farmers, 94 % of them were new to smart phones. However, almost all the farmers got used to the technology within 5–10 min. They were asked to perform some tasks related to the farming using the developed application. Figure 11 shows how the farmers interacted using the mobile application during the field validation. Details of

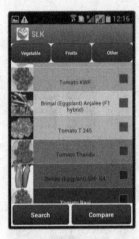
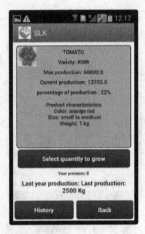

Fig. 10. First Physical Implementation of the Mobile Artefact

this field trial and findings were reported in [40] which is an example of a Rigor – Contribution (RiCo) sub cycle. In this chapter Rigor – Contribution sub cycles are not numbered as these don't form part of the main process but take place from time to time when there are new insights to be contributed back to the scientific knowledge base.

Fig. 11. The farmers using the mobile application during the field validation

The field validation of the first working mobile prototype highlighted the following aspects in three key areas.

- User reaction towards technology: Farmers adapted to the smart phone in few minutes even though they did not have much previous experience with the technology. After the training period they all got used to the application and performed set of tasks defined by the researchers. Farmer reaction towards the technology was positive and all agreed the importance of having such a system to obtain required information. They also mentioned the significance of identifying innovative solutions towards educating young farmers.
- Usability Evaluation: We observed some interface issues when farmers started using the application. Some farmers experienced difficulties in touch due to the size

of their fingers and roughness. Some experienced difficulties in touching the buttons due to small space between the buttons. Further, some found it difficult to navigate from one screen to another due to inadequate wordings and onscreen instructions.

- Information correctness: Farmers stressed the need to have accurate, complete and up to date information if they were to rely on the system for better decision making. Further, when they started using the system they felt the usefulness and started to request more functionality.

The ReSV3 sub cycle again demonstrated the potential to obtaining more complete user requirements using user centred iterative process. Though we started with unclear functional requirements, through this iterative process we were able to obtain a complete set of user requirements for the artefact. Moreover, at the initial stages we followed very few HCI guidelines in our design. However, at this stage we have become very aware of the HCI aspects of the users based on our observations during field trials. Though not much HCI requirements came to light during the initial stages of the DSR, latter interactions using the actual working artefact, HCI requirements started to dominate the artefact design.

The findings highlighted the need to concentrate more on the HCI side of the artefact at this stage of the development and provide more complete, accurate information to the farmers. This triggered a Rigor – Learning (RiLe2) sub cycle in which researchers reviewed the relevant literature to identify potential solutions to observed HCI issues.

4.5 Second Physical Implementation of the Mobile Artefact

As explained above we identified the importance of accurate, complete and up to date information. This triggered another round of Design – Heuristics Search (DeHS6) and Design – Functional Validation (DeFV2) sub cycles. In DeHS6 sub cycle, an ontology was developed to populate agriculture data to provide complete and accurate information to the farmers [39]. We also modified the user interfaces to display the additional information farmers needed.

In DeFV2 sub cycle, the research team tested the functional validation of the implemented system. At this stage GitHub was used to record the identified issues for the development team to rectify these.

The set of interfaces shown in Fig. 12 was designed and partially implemented as a mobile web application. With the development of the Ontology we were able to provide information in context for the users. One example of this is to select the crops, based on the agro-zone corresponding to farm location. The main aim of these interfaces is to provide all required information to the farmers to make decisions at the crop planning stage of the farming life cycle.

We conducted a Relevance - Validation Cycle (ReSV4) using the partially implanted web version and rest of the design as paper prototype. Using a sample of 50 farmers from two agro-zones in Sri Lanka, we tested the artefact for its suitability and usability. We observed the following during this validation.

Fig. 12. Refined interfaces based on farmer feedback

- Functional requirements: We observed that farmers were able to provide their user requirements more easily and a meaningful way. As in the ReSV3 cycle in Sect. 4.4, they continued to provide specific functional requirements that were not identified before.
- Usability issues: We observed several difficulties in using the mobile artefact by the farmers. Even with this new design, farmers face difficulties due to small button, image and font sizes. Sometimes, it took a while for a page to load and some had difficulties in understanding what was happening.

The feedback and observations generated enabled the research team to prioritise the findings. We choose usability as the first priority to increase the efficiency, effectiveness and the user satisfaction as now we have derived almost all the requirements for the crop planning stage.

4.6   Deployed Version of the Mobile Artefact

Prior to making any changes we went through a Rigour - Learning Cycle (RiLe3) to review HCI literature relating to identified issues. This led us to consider following aspects in refining the interfaces.

- Organisation of the functionalities in the Main Menu: We grouped the similar functions together while maintaining the important functions at the top of the menu.
- Navigation: We analysed the purpose of the *back* button. We minimised the use of *back* button to reduce the complexity of the design. We also considered ways to provide required information in minimum number of steps.
- Use of Colours: We used Itten colour theory; dark background and light font colours to visualise information efficiently. We used maximum of 6 colours to represent the menu items of the interface. We used same colour and/or similar shades when grouping the similar functionalities as shown in Fig. 13.
- Understand the user: most importantly since we are dealing with users new to the smart phone technology, we identified that it is very important to cater to the needs of these users. When analysing their capabilities based on the several field

validations we identified the importance of leaving substantial amount of space between the touch items. From the experience we have gained from the validation of the mobile prototype, we have left a substantial amount of space between two buttons. When designing user input widgets we tried to minimize text inputs and provided many text boxes or drop down boxes instead. As shown in Fig. 14, when designing the login module, we used a separate cage for each digit and the cursor was moved to next cage automatically at the end of previous entry. This helped farmers to enter and delete the values with ease.

Next we performed another Design Cycle; both Heuristic Search (DeHS7) and Functional Validation (DeFV3) to implement above mentioned changes and validate the new functionality by the research team. The interface design of the deployed version is shown in Fig. 15. This version is now deployed in two agro-regions in Sri Lanka. After we address the initial deployment issues, this application will become available to all farmers.

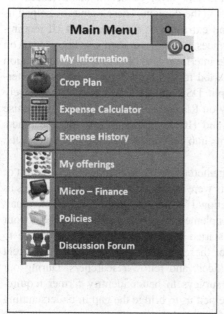

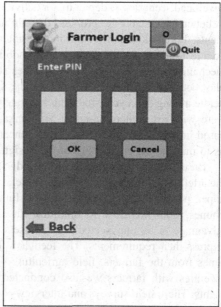

Fig. 13. Grouping of functionalities in the main menu using Itten colour theory

Fig. 14. One cage per digit in user inputs

5 Conclusion

In this project we designed a mobile based Information system to meet information needs of farmers at all stages of the farming life cycle. The design of the artefact was a challenge at the beginning due to several domain characteristics. ICT literacy of the farmers was very low. At the beginning they could not grasp the idea and specify their requirements.

Researchers were unfamiliar with the complex agriculture domain. This added further barriers in identifying the important requirements. As a result, the system functionalities were not well defined at the beginning but they evolved over time. Secondly, farmers were new to the smart phones. Majority of them use basic feature mobile phones for communication purposes. Therefore, it was essential to present the information on smart phones in a way that is easy to find and use. As a result, the usability of the artefact was identified as an important aspect of this design.

Our research approach was guided by DSR methodology. Nature of the project made us to split the traditional 3 cycle model in to 6 cycles. Starting from a RePU1 we iterated among different sub cycles of DSR. The DSR Split model greatly assisted us in this project and we strongly recommend this model for any large and complex research project aiming to develop an artefact.

We started the project with some functional requirements derived from the initial surveys. At that stage we had very little knowledge about the user requirements. Even though the users were very familiar with the activities in their domain, they were not able to articulate the requirements at a sufficient level of detail. As a result, we developed scenarios to depict major activities in the domain. These scenarios helped us to better understand the problem domain and extract both functional and UI requirements. Initial sketching of the mobile interfaces further increased our knowledge on how to visualise the information on a mobile interface. Use of colour and presentation mechanisms derived from these sketches started to highlight the advantages of interplay between RE and HCI aspects. The split DSR model assisted us to effectively iterate among sub cycles focusing separately on RE and HCI aspects. As RE expertise were with researchers based in Sri Lanka and HCI expertise were with researchers based in Italy, this ability to separate concerns into different sub cycles greatly assisted us to manage the complexity of the design.

Based on feedback and new knowledge gathered, we made changes to the design of the artefact on an iterative basis. The artefacts were presented to the users sometimes as paper prototypes and other times as functional prototypes implemented on smart phones. This was done to minimize the implementation effort. This worked to our advantage in an unexpected way as users started to annotate the paper prototype to express their requirements. The feedback for these artefacts was obtained at different times from the farmers, field agriculture officers and fellow researchers. During our meetings with farmers we also conducted surveys to better identify farmer requirements. These field surveys and interviews helped us to bridge the gap in understanding the domain activities between the researchers and the users of the targeted domain. This led us to increase user participation and obtain better feedback about their needs. This further resulted in designing models such as causal map to better understand the behaviours that can be observed among stakeholders.

The methods such as paper prototyping enabled the researchers to collaborate more closely with the end users. This technique helped the farmers to feel and envisage the real artefact and be more specific on their needs. The physical implementation of the actual artefact was carried out by incorporating the feedback received from the users. As such, at the time of field validations using the actual mobile prototype, we observed that the farmers were familiar with the way we have implemented the basic requirements. This made farmers confident to specify more requirements in details.

Gradually the knowledge gained through these initial artefacts started to speed up the requirements identification process. At the initial stages we captured more of RE aspects, but in latter stages we started to identify more and more HCI needs. Through the approach that evolved we successfully overcame barriers that were encountered at the initial stages of the research. This experience highlights the need for blending both RE and HCI to better capture needs of the user and the usability issues.

Therefore, the process we used in creating these artefacts enabled the researchers to enrich both RE and HCI aspects; highlighting the importance of interplay between both RE and HCI when designing systems for masses especially if the technology as well as the system going to be new to them.

Fig. 15. Deployed version of the mobile artefact

References

1. Jain, R., Sonnen, D.: Social life networks. IT Prof. **13**, 8–11 (2011)
2. Ginige, A.: Social Life Networks for the Middle of the Pyramid (2011, 25 March 2012). http://www.sln4mop.org//index.php/sln/articles/index/1/3
3. Singh, V.K., Gao, M., Jain, R.: Social pixels: genesis and evaluation. In: Presented at the Proceedings of the international conference on Multimedia, Firenze, Italy (2010)
4. Qiang, C.Z., Kuek, S.C., Dymond, A., Esselaar, S.: Mobile Applications for Agriculture and Rural Development (2011)

5. Standage, T.: Mobile Marvels. The Economist - a special report on telecoms in emerging markets (2009)
6. Sanou, B.: ICT Facts and Figurs. In: International Telecommunication Union (2015)
7. Dao, M.-S., Pongpaichet, S., Jalali, L., Kim, K., Jain, R., Zettsu, K.: A real-time complex event discovery platform for cyber-physical-social systems. In: Proceedings of International Conference on Multimedia Retrieval, p. 201 (2014)
8. Bandara, H.: Produce from the North creates surplus in veggies. The Sunday Times edition, Sri Lanka, 11 March 2012
9. Hettiarachchi, S.: N'Eliya carrot farmers in the dumps: bumper harvest, but prices low. The Sunday Times edition, Sri Lanka, 22 April 2012
10. Hettiarachchi, S.: Leeks Cultivators Desperate as Price Drops to Record Low. Sunday Times, ed., Sri Lanka (2011)
11. Business Times: Sri Lanka's vegetable supply exceeds demand. Sunday Times, ed. Sri Lanka, 22 April 2012
12. Weerakkody, C.: Potato farmers mashed by imports. The Sunday Times, ed. The Sunday Times, Sri Lanka, 17 August 2014
13. Hettiarachchi, S.: N. Eliya veggie farmers in dire straits. The Sunday Times, ed. The Sunday Times, Sri Lanka, 04 September 2011
14. Rodrigo, M.: Desperate farmers seek help. The Sunday Times, ed. The Sunday Times, Sri Lanka, 16 September 2012
15. Warushamana, G.: Oversupply hits big onion market. Sunday Observer, ed., Sri Lanka (2012)
16. Kumara, B.P.: Goviyagen ganne thuttuwatalu eith appita ko labeta elavalu. Divayina, ed., Lake House (2011)
17. Berenger, L.: Farmers strike veggie mafia. The Sunday Times, ed., Sri Lanka (2009)
18. ISO: ISO/IEC 25010:2011-Systems and Software Engineering—Systems and Software Quality Requirements and Evaluation (Square)—System and Software Quality Models (2011)
19. Ginige, T., Ginige, A.: Towards next generation mobile applications for MOPS: investigating emerging patterns to derive future requirements. In: Presented at the International Conference on Advances in ICT for Emerging Regions (ICTer). IEEE, Sri Lanka (2011)
20. Medhi, I., Patnaik, S., Brunskill, E., Gautama, S.N.N., Thies, W., Toyama, K.: Designing mobile interfaces for novice and low-literacy users. ACM Trans. Comput. Hum. Interact 18, 28 (2011)
21. Danis, C., Ellis, J., Kellog, W., Hoefman, B., van Beijima, H., Daniels, S., et al.: Mobile phones for health education in the developing world: SMS as a user interface. In: Presented at the ACM DEV, London (2010)
22. Putnam, C., Rose, E., Walton, R., Kolko, B.: Mobile phone users in Kyrgyzstan: a case study of identifying user requirements for diverse users. In: Presented at the Professional Communication Conference (IPCC). IEEE (2009)
23. Patel, N., Agarwal, S., Rajput, N., Nanavati, A., Dave, P., Parikh, T.S.: Avaaj Otalo: a field study of an interactive voice forum for small farmers in rural India. In: Human factors in computing systems, USA, pp. 733–742 (2010)
24. Ratnam, B.V., Reddy, P.K., Reddy, G.S.: eSagu 1: an IT based personalized agricultural extension system prototype–analysis of 51 Farmers' case studies. In: International Journal of Education and Development using Information and Communication Technology (IJEDICT), vol. 2, pp. 79–94 (2006)
25. Pande, A.K., Jagyasi, B.G., Jain, R.: mKRISHI: A Mobile Multimedia Agro Advisory System for Remote Rural Farmers

26. Dialog Sri Lanka: Dialog Trade Net, 19 November 2010. http://www.tradenet.lk/

27. Hector Kobbekaduwa Agrarian Research and Training Institute: Mobitel Agri Price Information Index, 19 November 2014. http://www.harti.gov.lk/index.php?option=com_content&view=article&id=192%3Amobitel-agri-price-information-index&catid=1%3Alatest-from-harti&lang=en

28. Peter, H.A.S.S.: Communicating user experience: "Wicked" problems, patchwork personas, and the ICTD project lifecycle. Int. J. Sociotechnology Knowl. Dev. **7**, 14–26 (2015)

29. Anokwa, Y., Smyth, T.N., Ramachandran, D., Sherwani, J., Schwartzman, Y., Luk, R., et al.: Stories from the field: reflections on HCI4D experiences. Inf. Technol. Int. Dev. **5**, 101–116 (2009)

30. Hevner, A.R., March, S.T., Park, J., Ram, S.: Design science in information systems research. MIS Q. **28**, 75–105 (2004)

31. March, S.T., Storey, V.C.: Design science in the information systems discipline: an introduction to the special issue on design science research. MIS Q. **32**, 725–730 (2008)

32. Hevner, A., Chatterjee, S.: Design science research in information systems. Design Research in Information Systems. ISIS, vol. 22, pp. 9–22. Springer, US (2010)

33. Hevner, A.R.: A three cycle view of design science research. Scand. J. Inf. Syst. **19**, 87–92 (2007)

34. Peffers, K., Tuunanen, T., Gengler, C.E., Rossi, M., Hui, W., Virtanen, V., et al.: The design science research process: a model for producing and presenting information systems research. In: DESRIST (2006)

35. Vaishnavi, V., Kuechler, W.: Design Science Reserach in Information Systems (2004). http://www.desrist.org/design-research-in-information-systems/

36. Giovanni, P.D., Romano, M., Sebillo, M., Tortora, G., Vitiello, G., Silva, L.D., et al.: User centered scenario based approach for developing mobile interfaces for social life networks. In: presented at the 34th International Conference on Software Engineering (ICSE 2012). UsARE Workshops, Zurich (2012)

37. De Silva, L., Goonethilake, J.S., Wickramanayake, G.N., Ginige, A.: Towards using ICT to enhance flow of information to aid farmer sustainability in Sri Lanka. In: Presented at the Australasian Conference on Information Systems (ACIS), Geelong Australia (2012)

38. Lokanathan, S., Kapugama, N.: Smallholders and Micro-enterprises in Agriculture: Information needs & communication patterns, pp. 1–48 (2012). http://lirneasia.net/projects/agriculture/

39. Walisadeera, A.I., Ginige, A., Wikramanayake, G.N.: User centered ontology for Sri Lankan farmers Part 2. Ecol. Inform. **26**, 140–150 (2015)

40. De Silva, L.N., Goonetillake, J.S., Wikramanayake, G.N., Ginige, A.: Farmer response towards the initial agriculture information dissemination mobile prototype. In: Murgante, B., Misra, S., Carlini, M., Torre, C.M., Nguyen, H.-Q., Taniar, D., Apduhan, B.O., Gervasi, O. (eds.) ICCSA 2013, Part I. LNCS, vol. 7971, pp. 264–278. Springer, Heidelberg (2013)

Differentiating Conscious and Unconscious Eyeblinks for Development of Eyeblink Computer Input System

Shogo Matsuno[1(✉)], Minoru Ohyama[2], Kiyohiko Abe[3], Shoichi Ohi[2],
and Naoaki Itakura[1]

[1] Graduate School of Informatics and Engineering,
The University of Electro-Communications,
1-5-1 Chofugaoka, Chofu, Tokyo 182-8585, Japan
m1440004@edu.cc.uec.ac.jp
[2] Department of Information Environment, Tokyo Denki University, 2-1200
Muzai Gakuendai, Inzai, Chiba 270-1382, Japan
{ohyama,ohi}@mail.dendai.ac.jp
[3] College of Science and Engineering, Kanto Gakuin University, 1-50-1
Mutsuurahigashi Kanazawa-Ku, Yokohama, Kanagawa 236-8501, Japan
abe@kanto-gakuin.ac.jp

Abstract. In this paper, we propose and evaluate a new conscious eyeblink differentiation method, comprising an algorithm that takes into account differences in individuals, for use in a prospective eyeblink user interface. The proposed method uses a frame-splitting technique that improves the time resolution by splitting a single interlaced image into two fields—even and odd. Measuring eyeblinks with sufficient accuracy using a conventional NTSC video camera (30 fps) is difficult. However, the proposed method uses eyeblink amplitude as well as eyeblink duration as distinction thresholds. Further, the algorithm automatically differentiates eyeblinks by considering individual differences and selecting a large parameter of significance in each user. The results of evaluation experiments conducted using 30 subjects indicate that the proposed method automatically differentiates conscious eyeblinks with an accuracy rate of 83.6 % on average. These results indicate that automatic differentiation of conscious eyeblinks using a conventional video camera incorporated with our proposed method is feasible.

Keywords: Eyeblink · Eye gaze input · Voluntary eyeblink · Eyeblink waveform · Input interface

1 Introduction

In general, eyeblinks can be classified as voluntary, reflex, or spontaneous. A voluntary eyeblink occurs consciously, a reflex eyeblink occurs as a result of external factors such as sound and/or light stimuli, and a spontaneous eyeblink is one that occurs unconsciously [1]. If a system was able to distinguish when a user has blinked with a conscious desire to enter information, then we would be able to control a computer device. In other

© IFIP International Federation for Information Processing 2016
Published by Springer International Publishing Switzerland 2016. All Rights Reserved
A. Ebert et al. (Eds.): UsARE 2012/2014, LNCS 9312, pp. 160–174, 2016.
DOI: 10.1007/978-3-319-45916-5_10

words, computer control using eyeblinks could be realized if a method that automatically distinguishes conscious eyeblinks from unconscious eyeblinks was available.

The results of psychology experiments have shown that the occurrence of eyeblinks is associated with cognitive status. Using this knowledge, a system that measures the state of exhaustion of drivers has been developed [2]. Further, studies have been conducted in an effort to determine whether it can be used as a communication support and assistance system for severely crippled persons such as amyotrophic lateral sclerosis (ALS) patients [3–5]. Systems using eyeblink as an input switch and otherwise combining it with eye gaze in an input interface to operate equipment have also been proposed [6–11]. However, in most systems, because eyeblinks occur at high speeds, accurate and dedicated equipment is required to measure them. In addition, these systems usually employ a fixed threshold or special operations.

Our aim is to develop an eyeblink input system that can be installed on conventional information devices, such as smartphones and smart glasses [12–14]. Using image analysis [10, 11], we previously obtained and examined shape feature parameters in an eyeblink waveform (i.e., the waveform representing the time evolution of the eyeblink process) and observed differences between conscious and unconscious eyeblinks among subjects [15]. In this paper, we propose a new automatic conscious eyeblinks differentiation method, and report on the results of evaluation experiments conducted using the proposed method and algorithm with 30 subjects.

2 Related Work

Conventional eyeblink input systems are classified into two basic types. The first type uses input based on pre-established time values (for example, when a user closes his/her eyes for more than 200 ms) [16, 17]. In this case, a dynamic threshold value is used for each type of eyeblink because eyeblinks show wide individual differences. A false input may occur if the threshold is fixed because the input time is user-dependent; a user might unconsciously produce considerably short or long eye movements. The second type of input system examines special eye movements, such as double eyeblinks and winks [18, 19]. However, these systems require the user to perform conscious, and occasionally complex, actions; therefore, users have to practice in order to be proficient at using these systems. In addition, the unusual eyeblinks required can cause user stress, especially when the systems are used over a long period [1, 9].

In an effort to overcome these problems, eyeblink input interfaces that incorporate more natural eyeblinks are being studied. However, a user who does not display a noticeable difference in shape feature parameters between voluntary and spontaneous eyeblinks must be conditioned and encouraged by such a system for it to accurately measure voluntary eyeblinks [7–10]. Conversely, the system proposed in this paper uses a messaging system—for example, it announces to a user, "you blinked correctly at the perceived signal"—to decrease user stress and to amplify the difference in the shape feature parameters. This system most closely approximates an actual eyeblink interface because it is expected that the user is conscious of the input when blinking, even if no user training has been conducted.

Table 1. Strengths and weaknesses of previous works.

Fixed-length threshold [16, 17]	Concepts	Special eye movements [18, 19]
Easy	Inputting	Have to practice
Necessary	Calibration	May be necessary
A bit too much	Get exhausted	Much
High	Requisite measuring accuracy	Low
Difficult	Estimate of intention	Easy

3 Characteristics of Eyeblinks Waveforms

We distinguish between conscious and unconscious eyeblinks by considering the fact that the duration of a conscious eyeblink is longer than that of an unconscious eyeblink [11, 16]. However, an eyeblink is a rapid motion that completes a series of operations on the order of a few hundred milliseconds; over and above that, individual differences are substantial. Consequently, because the time resolution of conventional video cameras is low, when measured with these cameras, significant differences in the eyeblink duration are not observed. Eyeblinks vary widely by individual, but in most cases, during a consious eyeblink, the eyelids close completely. In addition, variation in terms of the eyeblink waveform is relatively small in each individual. Therefore, we focused on the following parameters: closing-phase amplitude, opening-phase amplitude, and eyeblink duration, as discussed in a previous study [9]. Figure 1 shows a model of an eyeblink waveform in which the closing-phase amplitude Acl is defined as the height of the closing-phase starting point Ps to the minimum point $Pmin$. $Pmin$ is defined as the point where the eye-opening area is smallest; that is, from the closing-phase end point Psb to the opening-phase starting point Peb. Similarly, the opening-phase amplitude Aop is defined as the height of the minimum point $Pmin$ to the opening-phase end point Pe. Finally, the eyeblink duration Dur is defined as the field count from Ps to Pe.

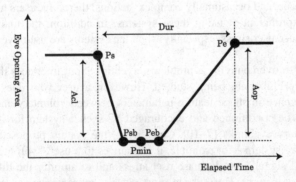

Fig. 1. Model of eyeblink waveform.

4 Automatic Measurement of an Eyeblink Waveform

If the time evolution of the eyeblink process could be accurately measured, it would be possible to express an eyeblink as a waveform. Individual eyeblinks must be measured and then analyzed for automatic differentiation of eyeblink types. The typical techniques used to sample eyeblink waveforms are electrooculogram (EOG) and image analysis. The EOG method involves placing an electrode on the skin near the eyeball. Eyeblink waveforms are then collected by recording changes in the cornea-retina potential. This technique was proposed for automatic detection of conscious eyeblinks until recently [20]. However, the EOG method requires a unique apparatus to process ocular potential, and the user must have an electrode attached to his/her skin. Therefore, the EOG method is unsuitable for a simple interface. Moreover, extraneous noise from a living body can cause interference. By contrast, image analysis examines pictures of eyeblinks captured by a video recorder. It has become popular because it requires no bodily contact and is manageable and adaptable. However, eye movements are difficult to capture with a video camera that has a standard aspect ratio (NTSC) because an eyeblink is a high-speed operation. Therefore, in this paper, we incorporate an algorithm used in previous research [10] that detects changes in eye aperture. The algorithm samples at 1/60 s using interlaced NTSC video images further divided into field images. Figure 2 shows the processing flow for detecting changes in the eye-aperture area.

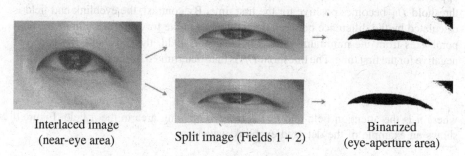

Interlaced image
(near-eye area)   Split image (Fields 1 + 2)   Binarized
(eye-aperture area)

Fig. 2. Overview of frame-splitting method and binarization.

When image analysis is used, the first step is to analyze video images of the area surrounding the eye in order to assess changes in eye aperture using binarization based on flesh color. Figure 3 shows an example of changes that occur in the eye-aperture area. The data shown in Fig. 3 include changes in the eyeblink waveform. The next step applies smoothing differentiation between the split field area and the next split field. Coordinates that reveal the maximum area difference value and the minimum area difference value are then determined using a second differentiation.

However, this step in the analysis involves excessive noise resulting from small movements in the vicinity of the eye, such as from an eyelid. Therefore, we remove three coordinate classes of extreme value (maximum, minimum, and few-moving) using the k-means method. We determine the start and end of an eyeblink waveform using its

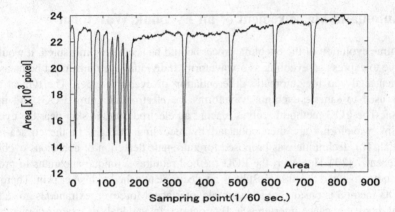

Fig. 3. Changes in eye-opening area.

maximum and minimum values because one eyeblink waveform contains only one maximum and one minimum value. Minimum values exist in the opening phase and maximum values exist in the closing phase. Data are obtained from one eyeblink waveform according to these factors. If the obtained maximum and minimum values are observed in succession as two points, the point closer to the field of temporal axes is used. An eyeblink start field is calculated by differentiating between field areas in the direction opposite to that of the temporal axes from the maximum value's field. In this field, the threshold Th_1 becomes positive for the first time. By contrast, the eyeblink end field is calculated by the difference between the field areas in the forward direction of the temporal axes from the minimum value's field. In this field, the threshold Th_1 becomes negative for the first time. The threshold Th_1 is then determined by the following equation:

$$Th_1 = f(n) - f(n+1)$$

where n is the attention field and $f(n)$ is the eye-opening area in the n field. Figure 4 shows an example of the detected eyeblink waveform.

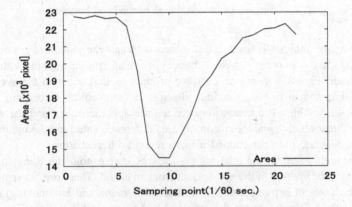

Fig. 4. Example of an eyeblink waveform.

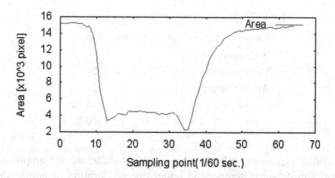

Fig. 5. Example of a difficult-to-decide minimum point.

An eyeblink waveform measured by means of image analysis can be applied to the model in Fig. 4. The eyeblink duration is represented as field numbers from the eyeblink starting point to the eyeblink end point. The eyeblink amplitude is represented as changes in the eye-aperture area. The point *Pmin,* at which an area is minimized, is determined based on the model (Fig. 1) in theory. However, it might not be determined by an actual measurement (Fig. 5). Therefore, *Pmin* is defined as the average of the eye-aperture field areas that are less than threshold Th_2 in one eyeblink waveform. Threshold Th_2 is determined from the following equation:

$$Th_2 = \frac{Amax - Amin}{10} + Amin$$

where *Amax* and *Amin* are the maximum and minimum, respectively, of the eye-opening area of the eyeblink waveform. In addition, the closing-phase amplitude is calculated based on the difference between the area of the eyeblink starting field and point *Pmin*. Similarly, the opening-phase amplitude is calculated based on the difference between the area of the eyeblink end field and point *Pmin*.

5 Automatically Differentiating Conscious and Unconscious Eyeblinks

In this section, we examine the differentiation of eyeblinks on the basis of the parameters of the extracted eyeblink waveform using the method outlined in Sect. 4. It has been reported that the duration of a conscious eyeblink is longer than that of an unconscious eyeblink [21]. However, in many cases, distinguishing between the two types of eyeblinks using this information is difficult because the difference in the duration of eyeblinks cannot be measured if the time resolution of the moving image is low. Therefore, the proposed method improves the distinction accuracy by combining the duration and amplitude. There are many cases in which differences between eyeblinks are not found because amplitude values are more sensitive to individual differences than duration values. However, we have already confirmed the following in preliminary experiments. Specifically, approximately one-half of all subjects in our

Table 2. Results of preliminary experiment [21].

Parameter type	Subject number	Rate
Both parameters	23	46 %
Duration only	12	24 %
Amplitude only	11	22 %
No difference	4	8 %
Total	50	100 %

experiment had a significant difference in both the duration and amplitude, and the other half had significant differences in either one of duration or amplitude. We also administered a t-test to the subjects using a 1 % standard deviation between conscious and unconscious parameters. And Table 2 shows the details of the results obtained.

A significant difference of 24 % (12 subjects) is evident in eyeblink duration. For eyeblink amplitude, the difference is 22 % (11 subjects). For both parameters, the significant difference is 46 % (23 subjects). Finally, no significant difference is apparent in 8 % of the subjects (4 subjects). In other words, a significant difference in shape feature parameters between voluntary and spontaneous eyeblinks is seen in a minimum of 92 % of the subjects. Moreover, the results of examination of individual parameters reveal the following. The total percentage of subjects who show a significant difference in eyeblink duration is 70 %. The total percentage of subjects who display significant differences in eyeblink amplitude is 68 %. Finally, the total percentage of subjects who show significant differences in both parameters is 46 %.

Figure 6 shows a histogram that summarizes the distribution of the average value of the eyeblink duration of the 50 subjects by eyeblink type. Conversely, the histogram in Fig. 7 summarizes the distribution of the average value of the eyeblink amplitudes of the 50 subjects by eyeblink type.

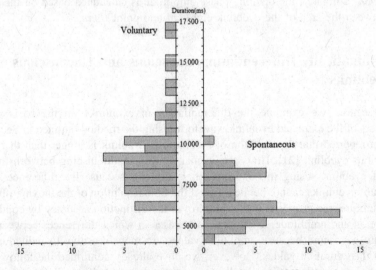

Fig. 6. Duration difference in each group [21].

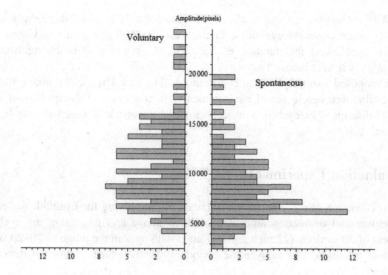

Fig. 7. Amplitude difference in each group [21].

We perform automatic differentiation using a threshold to distinguish the larger differences among the measured feature parameters between conscious and unconscious eyeblinks in every subject. In the proposed method, a normalization process is first applied to each feature parameter based on the average value of conscious eyeblinks to decide the differentiation threshold of each subject. As shown in Table 1, the trends in the parameters of subjects can be classified into three groups: Groups A, B, and C. Group A comprises subjects who exhibit significant differences in eyeblink duration only. Group B comprises subjects who exhibit significant differences in eyeblink amplitude only. Group C comprises subjects who exhibit significant differences in both parameters. The method then selects the parameter difference of the larger side among the duration and amplitude after normalization. For instance, in a scenario where there is a particular difference in duration, the threshold, Th_3, used to distinguish conscious eyeblinks, is determined from the following equation:

$$Th_3 = \frac{Tdv - Tds}{2} + Tds$$

where Tdv is the average duration of conscious eyeblinks and Tds is the average duration of unconscious eyeblinks. In this instance, an eyeblink is distinguished as a conscious eyeblink if the duration exceeds Th_3. Further, an eyeblink is distinguished as unconscious if it falls below Th_3.

On the other hand, in the case where there is a particular difference in amplitude, the threshold, Th_4, used to distinguish conscious eyeblinks is determined from the following equation:

$$Th_4 = \frac{Adv - Ads}{2} + Ads$$

where Adv is the average amplitude of conscious eyeblinks and Ads is the average amplitude of unconscious eyeblinks. In this case, an eyeblink is distinguished as a conscious eyeblink if the duration exceeds Th_4. Conversely, it is distinguished as unconscious if it falls below Th_4.

The proposed method determines thresholds Th_3 and Th_4 via the above method during calibration, before actual measurements are conducted. Subsequently, it automatically distinguishes eyeblinks as conscious or unconscious based on the feature parameter.

6 Evaluation Experiments

In this section, we discuss the results obtained on employing the eyeblink waveform measurement and distinction algorithm outlined above and measuring the eyeblink waveform of 30 subjects (22 men and 8 women with ages in the range of 20–29 years; all without disabilities) to analyze the periodicity of the shape feature parameters of eyeblinks.

6.1 System Outline

The hardware comprising our experimental system included a Sony HDR-HC9 digital camcorder for obtaining eye images, and a personal computer for image and eyeblink waveform analysis. Although the camera could capture high-definition (HD) pictures, standard-definition (SD) pictures were used in the experiments. The system is intended to be mounted on wearable and smart devices. Furthermore, an experimental system was developed as a prototype.

Ordinary indoor lighting (incandescent lighting) was used when capturing moving images. A pair of light-emitting diodes (LEDs) was placed symmetrically on both sides of the camera and at a distance of approximately 60 cm directly in front of the face of the subject. The back of the subject's head was lightly supported with a stabilizing device to prevent it from shaking. The video camera was placed in front of and below the subject's head at a distance of approximately 20 cm. The camera was then used to magnify and obtain pictures of the area surrounding the subject's left eye. Because the image format was set for SD video, the resolution was 720 × 480 pixels with a 16:9 aspect ratio and refresh rate of 30 fps (NTSC). These experiments were performed on the naked eye; therefore, eyeglasses were not allowed during filming.

6.2 Experimental Method

The subjects were given the following instructions during filming:

- Pay attention to the silver dot mark located on the upper part of the camcorder. (The mark was placed at this location by us.)
- When you hear the signal, "blink well" always.
- You do not have to resist any unconscious urge to blink.

The "blink well" instruction was meant to increase the difference in the shape of the feature parameters between conscious and unconscious eyeblinks. In other words, the signal was a means of encouraging subjects to be strongly conscious of their voluntary blinks. The signal was sounded randomly at intervals of 4 to 10 s using a digital timer. Images were captured for an overall total of 90 s during the course of the experiment. The first 20 s was used for calibration. This experiment does not use a control group because it was a conscious property the eyeblink immediately after sounding.

After measuring the eyeblink video image, we measured and analyzed the individual eyeblink waveform using moving images. The calibration determined the distinction threshold by using 20 s at the beginning of the moving image based on the method described in Sect. 4 to decide the feature parameter to use as the distinction threshold by normalization and comparison in each subject. Differentiation of conscious and the unconscious eyeblinks was then performed in the subsequent 70 s of moving images, using the obtained Th_3 and Th_4 thresholds. At this point, the system distinguished only eyeblink waveforms that had been successfully detected automatically.

At the conclusion of the experiment, the subjects were asked to complete questionnaires and/or comment about their experiences during the experiment. The items in question were age, gender, sleep time during the previous night, health condition (five levels: one (bad) through five (good)), task difficulty (five levels: one (easy) through five (difficult)), confidence in achieving the task (five levels: one (low) through five (high)), and personal interpretation of "blink well."

6.3 Real-Time Measurement Experiment

Table 3 provides data on the subjects that show a significant difference in the measurements between conscious and unconscious blinks. Representative results of the experiment in relation to measured conscious and unconscious blinks, including the average values of the durations of blinks, the closing-phase amplitude, and the opening-phase amplitude, are shown. The right side of the table shows the results after normalization and the selected feature parameter.

Using the amplitude ratio of the closing phase to the opening phase for parameters is complicated because the ratio of the closing-phase to the opening-phase amplitude was, in all cases, found to contain a minimum of one large parameter. Therefore, we redefined the average value of two amplitudes as the eyeblink amplitude. In Table 3, the tendency for variation in individual differences between conscious and unconscious eyeblinks is as follows.

Let us now analyze those subjects who either did not show significant differences or exhibited only some differences in shape feature parameters. The number of unconscious eyeblinks was found to be limited. Two reasons explain this. The first is the fact that few eyeblinks actually occurred, which may be because the subjects were under stress during the experiment. The second is that eyeblinks registered movements that were too small to be accurately detected. Therefore, this study might promote future research in eyeblink detection accuracy.

Table 3. Results of the extracted parameters.

Subjects	Conscious eyeblinks			Unconscious eyeblinks			Normalization
	Counts	Duration (ms)	Amplitude (pixel)	Counts	Duration (ms)	Amplitude (pixel)	Selected
1	4	841	6799	7	650	6789	Duration
2	5	590	7906	6	335	4875	Duration
3	5	580	7054	16	338	5725	Duration
4	3	755	14111	5	393	12195	Duration
5	5	706	13009	4	511	10558	Duration
6	2	325	18785	3	288	11858	Amplitude
7	5	1053	19852	4	450	17100	Duration
8	5	660	16718	3	553	14435	Duration
9	5	560	15216	5	256	10850	Duration
10	5	553	15552	4	316	11326	Duration
11	5	400	9370	4	278	6620	Duration
12	5	463	7829	4	341	6918	Duration
13	5	686	5883	9	445	3763	Amplitude
14	5	733	10139	2	308	6817	Duration
15	5	576	9919	3	288	7077	Duration
16	5	390	11880	6	350	10942	Duration
17	5	623	11268	1	366	11213	Duration
18	4	400	14121	3	376	8291	Amplitude
19	4	625	9160	14	331	7166	Duration
20	4	595	12904	19	263	7481	Duration
21	5	530	13494	17	336	10860	Duration
22	5	376	11559	18	345	10951	Duration
23	5	553	5644	5	486	5631	Duration
24	5	386	7059	21	256	6553	Duration
25	5	606	5564	20	400	5095	Duration
26	5	686	9257	13	385	7822	Duration
27	5	856	8673	15	436	7948	Duration
28	5	530	7122	8	279	5119	Duration
29	5	500	8699	6	435	6885	Amplitude
30	4	436	6418	3	216	3385	Duration

Table 4 provides the results of automatic distinction rate. Representative results of the experiment are displayed in relation to measured conscious and unconscious blinks. The table shows counts of detected conscious eyeblinks Vi and unconscious eyeblinks Si, distinction error of conscious eyeblinks Ev, and unconscious eyeblinks Es, distinction accuracy rate of conscious eyeblinks Cv and unconscious eyeblinks Cs, and total accuracy rate Ct. The accuracy rate values Cv, Cs, and Ct are determined from the following equations:

$$C_v = \frac{Vi - Ev}{Vi} \times 100$$

$$C_s = \frac{Si - Es}{Si} \times 100$$

$$C_t = \frac{(Vi + Si) - (Ev + Es)}{Vi + Si} \times 100$$

These equations for accuracy rate are adopted from [11].

Using our proposed method, the average rate of successful differentiating of conscious eyeblink is approximately 72.7 % for the experimental sample of 30 subjects. While, the average rate of successful differentiating of unconscious eyeblink is approximately 90.3 %. Thus, the average accuracy rate of total is 83.6 %. In unconscious eyeblinks are high identification rate, however in conscious eyeblinks are lower as compared to the unconscious rate. At this point, we believe that this passed differentiating of conscious blink is not a major problem. If these passed differentiating occur, the input can be attempted again through an intentional repetition of the conscious eyeblink. Therefore, we think the accuracy rate of unconscious is more important than conscious rate. In addition, there are often subjects of only a low accuracy rate of either conscious or unconscious. Because we used a simple algorithm in this experiment (e.g. subject 1, 3, 5, and more...) intend to improve the accuracy of differentiating by using a combination of two parameters.

Following the experiments, we interviewed the subjects and discovered that some subjects did not perform eyeblinks consciously when signals were given because their unconsious eyeblinks occurred at the same rate. On the basis of the results of these interviews, we plan to revise future instructions to promote more clarity. In addition, the classification of eyeblink types can be improved based on those subjects who did not show significant differences.

Table 4. Results of automatic distinction rate of conscious eyeblinks.

Subjects	Counts of eyeblink		Distinction error		Distinction rate (%)		
	Conscious	Unconscious	Conscious	Unconscious	Conscious	Unconscious	All
1	11	12	4	1	63.6	91.7	78.3
2	10	11	0	0	100.0	100.0	100.0
3	10	39	8	4	20.0	89.7	75.5
4	10	12	0	0	100.0	100.0	100.0
5	10	10	7	0	30.0	100.0	65.0
6	10	15	0	5	100.0	66.7	80.0
7	10	12	0	3	100.0	75.0	86.4
8	10	7	5	0	50.0	100.0	70.6
9	9	11	1	0	88.8	100.0	95.0
10	10	10	0	0	100.0	100.0	100.0
11	9	15	2	3	77.7	80.0	79.2
12	10	13	2	3	80.0	76.9	78.3

(*Continued*)

Table 4. (*Continued*)

Subjects	Counts of eyeblink		Distinction error		Distinction rate (%)		
	Conscious	Unconscious	Conscious	Unconscious	Conscious	Unconscious	All
13	10	17	1	0	90.0	100.0	96.3
14	10	12	0	0	100.0	100.0	100.0
15	9	6	5	0	44.4	100.0	66.7
16	10	12	7	0	30.0	100.0	68.2
17	10	7	4	0	60.0	100.0	76.5
18	10	3	1	0	90.0	100.0	92.3
19	7	29	3	0	57.1	100.0	91.7
20	10	43	1	12	90.0	72.1	75.5
21	10	49	3	4	70.0	91.8	88.1
22	10	23	1	8	90.0	65.2	72.7
23	10	17	5	0	50.0	100.0	81.5
24	7	58	3	5	57.1	91.4	87.7
25	9	47	7	5	22.2	89.4	78.6
26	10	35	2	7	80.0	80.0	80.0
27	10	21	4	3	60.0	85.7	77.4
28	10	16	2	1	80.0	93.8	88.5
29	10	15	0	3	100.0	80.0	88.0
30	11	10	0	2	100.0	80.0	90.5
Average					72.7	90.3	83.6

7 Conclusion

In this paper, we proposed a method for automatic differentiation of conscious eyeblinks. A method that can automatically differentiate between conscious and unconscious eyeblinks is an important prerequisite for developing an input interface for eyeblinks. The results of the evaluation experiment conducted using the proposed method show that it is possible to automatically distinguish eyeblinks with higher accuracy than in previous studies if there is a small difference in the eyeblink duration. The proposed method shows that it is possible using a frame-splitting method even in environments that use a low time resolution video camera. The results of our evaluation experiment conducted with 30 different subjects indicate that the average accuracy is 83.6 %. We required to fix head lightly and to detach glasses from subjects. This is a problem at actual use. We believe that this problem can be solve by image processing using motion vector. Consequently, typical information devices will able to control using eyeblinks, only installing software based on proposed method.

In the future, we plan to develop a real-time computer input system based on proposed measuring system. We also plan to improve this method to increase the detection accuracy and investigate methods by which this system can be incorporated into mobile devices. And we want to validate racial and cultural difference influence to eyeblinks.

Acknowledgment. We thank Mr. Hironobu Sato of the Kanto Gakuin University College of Science and Engineering for his advice, comments and help in this study. This work was supported by JSPS KAKENHI Grant Number 24700598.

References

1. Matteo, B., Rocco, A., Gregori, B., Belvisi, D., Ottaviani, D., et al.: Voluntary, spontaneous and reflex blinking in patients with clinically probable progressive supranuclear palsy. Brain **132**(2), 502–510 (2009)
2. Majaranta, P., Raiha, K.-J.: Twenty years of eye typing: systems and design issues. In: Proceedings of Symposium on ETRA 2002, pp. 15–22. ACM (2002)
3. Richard, C,S., Heidi, H,K.: Adaptive one-switch row-column scanning. In: IEEE Transactions on Rehabilitation Engineering, vol.7, no.4, pp. 464–473 (1999)
4. Melanie, B., Andrew, T.: Indirect text entry using one or two keys. In: Proceedings of 8th International ACM SIGACCESS Conference on Computer and Accessibility, pp. 18–25 (2006)
5. Kiyohiko, A., Shoichi, O., Minoru, O.: An eye-gaze input system using information on eye movement history. In: Proceedings of the 4th International Conference on Universal Access in Human-Computer Interaction: Ambient Interaction, pp. 721–729 (2007)
6. Diogo, P., Maria, D.G.P., Amy, W., Khai, N.T.: Filteryedping: design challenges and user performance of dwell-free eye typing. ACM Trans. Accessible Comput. **6**(1), 3:1–3:37 (2015). Article 3
7. Naoaki, I., Takumi, O., Kazutaka, S.: Investigation for calculation method of eye-gaze shift from electro-oculograph amplified by AC coupling with using eye-gaze input interface. IEICE Trans. Inf. Syst. **J90-D**(10), 2903–2913 (2007)
8. Dekun, G., Naoaki, I., Tota, M., Kazuyuki, M.: Improvement of eye gesture interface system. In: Proceedings of the 16th Asia Pacific Symposium of Intelligent and Evolutionary Systems, no. 3, pp. 1–3 (2012)
9. Tanabe, K.: Eyeblink activity during identification of Katakana characters viewed through a restricted visual field. IEICE Trans. Fundam. Electron. Commun. Comput. Sci. **E87-A**(8), 2189–2191 (2004)
10. Abe, K., Ohi, S., Ohyama, M.: Automatic method for measuring eye blinks using split-interlaced images. In: Jacko, J.A. (ed.) HCI International 2009, Part I. LNCS, vol. 5610, pp. 3–11. Springer, Heidelberg (2009)
11. Abe, K., Sato, H., Matsuno, S., Ohi, S., Ohyama, M.: Automatic classification of eye blink types using a frame-splitting method. In: Harris, D. (ed.) EPCE 2013, Part I. LNCS, vol. 8019, pp. 117–124. Springer, Heidelberg (2013)
12. Miluzzo, E., Wang, T., Campbell, A.T.: EyePhone: activating mobile phones with your eyes. In: Proceedings of the Second ACM SIGCOMM Workshop on Networking, Systems and Applications on Mobile Handhelds, pp. 15–20 (2010)
13. Mayberry, A., Hu, P., Marlin, B., Salthouse, C., Ganesan, D.: iShadow: design of a wearable, real-time mobile gaze tracker. In: Proceedings of the 12th Annual International Conference on Mobile Systems, Applications, and Services, pp. 82–94. ACM (2014)
14. Matsuno, S., Akehi, K., Itakura, N., Mizuno, T., Mito, K.: Computer input system using eye glances. In: Yamamoto, S., Abbott, A.A. (eds.) HIMI 2015. LNCS, vol. 9172, pp. 425–432. Springer, Heidelberg (2015). doi:10.1007/978-3-319-20612-7_41

15. Matsuno, S., Ohyama, M., Abe, K., Sato, H., Ohi, S.: Automatic discrimination of voluntary and spontaneous eyeblinks. Use of the blink as a switch interface. In: The Sixth International Conference on Advances in Computer-Human Interactions, pp. 433–439 (2013)
16. Grauman, K., Betke, M, Gips, J., Bradski, G.R.: Communication via eye blinks—detection and duration analysis in real time. In: Proceedings of IEEE CS Conference on Computer Vision and Pattern Recognition (CVPR 2001), vol. 1, pp. 1010–1017 (2001)
17. Mackenzie, I.S., Ashtiani, B.: BlinkWrite: efficient text entry using eye blinks. Univ. Access Inf. Soc. 10(1), 69–80 (2011)
18. Missimer, E., Betke, M.: Blink and wink detection for mouse pointer control. In: Proceedings of 3rd International Conference on Pervasive Technologies Related to Assistive Environments, no. 23. ACM (2010)
19. Gorodnichy, D.: Second-order change detection, and its application to blink-controlled perceptual interfaces. In: Proceedings of the International Association of Science and Technology for Development Conference on Visualization, Imaging and Image Processing, pp. 140–145 (2003)
20. Tetuya, O., Hironori, K., Masashi, K.: Development of an input operation of the communication tool using voluntary eye blink. In: Papers of Technical Meeting on Medical and Biological Engineering, vol. 6, pp. 1–4. IEE, Japan (2006)
21. Matsuno, S., Ohyama, M., Abe, K., Ohi, S., Itakura, N.: Analysis of trends in the occurrence of eyeblinks for an eyeblink input interface. In: Proceedings of IEEE Conference on UsARE2014 in Conjunction with RE 2014, pp. 25–31 (2014)

A Virtual Community Design for Home-Based Chronic Disease Healthcare

Yan Hu[1](✉), Guohua Bai[1], Jenny Lundberg[2], and Sara Eriksén[1]

[1] Department of Creative Technologies, Blekinge Institute of Technology,
37179 Karlskrona, Sweden
{yan.hu,guohua.bai,sara.eriksen}@bth.se
[2] Department of Media Technology, Linnaeus University, 35195 Vaxjo, Sweden
jenny.lundberg@lnu.se

Abstract. The internet based social network has been applied to serve many social functions, such as democratic decision making, knowledge sharing, education, and healthcare. In this paper, we provide a prototype of virtual community designed for home-based chronic diseases healthcare. We studied the concept "community" from the activity theory model in order to design the prototype with a solid theoretical base. Then we conducted a questionnaire from healthcare recipients and interviewed healthcare providers to gather the requirements for the design of the community. With some user stories we described the requirements as use cases for our design and a conceptual prototype is built based on the requirements. This virtual community servers as a shared platform for all the stakeholders who are engaged in the healthcare activity. With this shared community platform, the interoperability problems of current healthcare systems can be moderated.

Keywords: Virtual community · Self-management · Home-based chronic disease healthcare · Requirements · Activity theory

1 Introduction

Chronic diseases are increasingly becoming a main factor influencing human health and wellbeing all over the world. According to the World Health Organization (WHO) [1], chronic diseases represent 60 % of all deaths in the world, and are thus the leading cause of mortality. Chronic diseases last for a long time, and can hardly be cured [2], therefore how to provide preventive and monitoring healthcare becomes a worldwide goal. Since patients suffering from chronic diseases have to be monitored from time to time, it leads to high cost, and becomes time consuming and inconvenient for the patients. This time-to-time monitoring limits the patients' daily activities and is especially inconvenient for aged people. Since mostly chronic diseases do not need urgent medical diagnosis and treatment [3], we suggest moving the front desk of chronic diseases healthcare from hospital-based to home-based care. This shift may save a lot of patient time and medical

Published by Springer International Publishing Switzerland 2016. All Rights Reserved
A. Ebert et al. (Eds.): UsARE 2012/2014, LNCS 9312, pp. 175–189, 2016.
DOI: 10.1007/978-3-319-45916-5_11

resources, and provide a convenient environment for continued living at home despite an increasing need of monitoring of health.

Thanks to the development of information and communication technology (ICT), the above suggested home-based healthcare is now becoming highly recommended [3]. Many physiological signals can be measured by individuals in their living environments during daily activities [4]. This paper will propose one important service function for such a home-based solution, namely virtual community based web-services. With this virtual community, people with chronic diseases can quickly and directly communicate with each other (supporting peer-to-peer learning), and also with healthcare providers and family members concerning their ongoing situation. With various needed services based on this virtual community, patients can have an independent living at home with improved life quality.

This paper will start by discussing the understanding of 'community' based on social-psychological activity theory and interpreted in the concrete context of home-based healthcare for chronic diseases. In the second part, a requirement elicitation is carried out based on a survey among potential users (55+ with chronic diseases). In the third part we analyze the collected 27 answers we got concerning the most needed requirements for a virtual community. Based on the defined requirements, in the fourth part we present a prototype we have developed to demonstrate how to design a web-based virtual community to integrate those identified needs for the targeted users, especially elderly users. Finally, we discuss some weaknesses and limitations with the proposed solution, and conclude with conclusions.

2   What is a Virtual Community?

A community is broadly defined as "a group or network of persons who are connected (objectively) to each other by relatively durable social relations that extend beyond immediate genealogical ties, and who mutually define that relationship (subjectively) as important to their social identity and social practice." [5]. Since the introduction of the now widely used Internet, the concept of community today has less geographical limitation, as people can now gather virtually in an online community and share common interests regardless of physical location. This kind of community, with far less constraints due to genealogical distance and far more oriented to shared interests and objectives, is what we call a virtual community. A virtual community is a social network that people interact with through specific social media, of which there are many good examples, such as Facebook and Twitter. This virtual community allows people to communicate with each other about their common interests without considering geographical distance.

Based on the model of Activity Theory (Fig. 1), a community is generally defined as a group of people who are engaged in conducting activities to approach a shared goal or outcome. In relation to service oriented activity where the object is the recipients of the conducted service activity (not as a materialized object), the members of this community can be divided into three groups: (1) people who are actively conducting the service activities, here called a subject; (2) people who are acted on by the subject, here called an object; and (3) people who are not directly acting or being acted on, but who are associated with the ongoing activity.

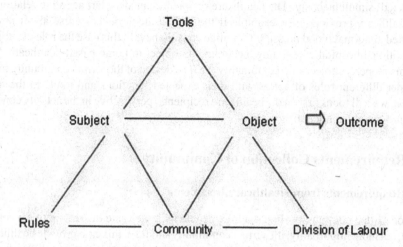

Fig. 1. Engeström's activity model [6]

The model in Fig. 1 visualizes the components that compose an activity and inter-actions in an activity. According to the model, an activity is always conducted by one or several goal-oriented actors, labeled as a subject in the model. The subject is always directed towards or acting on an object in order to produce an outcome. The community in this model is the collective of the above three groups of people involved in conducting the activity. Rules are various regulations for how to conduct activities and serve as mediating function within the community if any disagreement appears in conducting the activity. Tools are artifacts (physical, conceptual, or signs) used by the subject in the process of acting in order to produce the outcome. Division of labor specifies the responsibility within the community, i.e., which parts of the object's needs should be implemented by which members of the community.

To apply the above concept of community in the activity context of home-based healthcare, we will interpret the model in concrete terms related to the context. The outcome or goal of the activity is to improve the healthcare recipient's health. The subject is the healthcare providers such as doctors, nurses, family members. The object is the healthcare recipients, in this case they are people who are suffering from chronic diseases. Tools are all kinds of artifacts, which are used to support the activity, physical and non-physical, such as EHRs, Internet, healthcare monitor devices, as well as treat-ment-related knowledge and methods. The rules regulate the actions of the actors, and consist of for example healthcare laws, privacy and security policies and so on. Division of labor determines the responsibilities of different healthcare providers and healthcare recipients themselves. In this activity model, besides subject (actors) and object (recip-ients), the community includes also other healthcare actors, such as family members of the care recipients, other healthcare recipients who share the same interest, and research institutes that are associated with the results of the activity.

In home-based healthcare, self-management is highly encouraged, and in this self-management the healthcare recipients become the subject (actor) and the object (being self-acted) simultaneously. The healthcare recipients can also start acting in relation to the healthcare providers, for example if the patient alerts his/her nurse about newly recorded abnormal blood pressure for online consultancy. In this case the role of subject in traditional hospital care is now becoming an object in home-based healthcare. We call this property subject-object mutuality [7]. The design of the virtual community must consider different roles of actors with their expected functions and tools. In the next section, we will focus first on the healthcare recipients' perspective in the activity context of home-based healthcare.

3   Requirements Collection of Community

3.1   Requirements from Healthcare Recipients

A good virtual community should attract people with the same interests into a meeting place, but more importantly, the virtual community should in this case provide healthcare tools and services. Patient-centered self-management is the main trend for home-based chronic disease healthcare, and the virtual community in this case should first focus on the needs of the targeted patients. There are already some commercial or research-based solutions for supporting self-management. For instance, HealthVault [8], launched by Microsoft, is a web-based PHR system for storing and managing health information. A lot of specific third-party applications, such as blood pressure management tools and medical image viewers, as well as hundreds of devices such as blood glucose meters and blood pressure monitors, can cooperate with this platform to record health data.

In order to meet most users' needs when designing the online virtual community, we begin with requirements specification. There are two types of requirements in website design and software engineering, functional requirements and non-functional requirements [9]. As we mentioned above, in home-based healthcare, patients are at the center of the healthcare, as well as the main users. So we selected online questionnaires to be answered by the potential healthcare recipients as the key data-gathering technique.

Questionnaires include a series of questions designed to elicit specific information from the users. Well-designed questionnaires are a good way to get answers to specific questions from a group of people, especially for people whom it is not feasible to visit individually and interview [9]. In this case, the questions are mostly designed for functional requirements as seen from the healthcare recipients' perspective. Due to the time and resources limitation, for our questionnaires, the questions are published on surveymonkey.com as the electronic form rather than a paper form. The respondents are selected from within an age group consisting of people above 55 years of age and living with one or more chronic diseases. We send out the questionnaires through social network websites, for example, social groups of some specific chronic diseases ex. Diabetes from patientslikeme and facebook. The questionnaire contains 10 questions, and includes both simple Yes or No questions, questions allowing the respondent to choose from a set of pre-supplied answers, and open comment questions. In the end, 25 valid responses out of 27 are gathered. Most of the respondents are from US (8) and

Sweden (12). We consider that the geographical difference may effect some results, so the questions are designed to reduce this influence as possible. From the collected answers, we find that the influence is very low.

Problems in Current Healthcare.   The first open question is about the problems people face concerning their current healthcare. Almost all the respondents mentioned that the long time they spend waiting for doctors' appointments make them uncomfortable. "The resource is limited. It means I need to spend more time waiting for the healthcare service. And since I am waiting for the doctor, I really also need suggestions to keep my body stable, not get worse." "Really long queue every time when I visit some hospitals". In some countries like Sweden, the shortage of healthcare providers leads to long waiting lines for visiting primary care as well as hospitals. Sometimes the patients have to wait so long that they lose the best opportunity for diagnoses and treatments in relation to curing or sustainably managing their diseases. Another big problem the respondents highlighted is lack of information sharing among different healthcare providers. When they come to the new healthcare organizations, their historical healthcare records are difficult to find. "When I went to another hospital which I never visited before, the doctor didn't know my health history, if I am hypersensitive to some drugs, he didn't know, so this may cause some healthcare problems. If I need to have a new scratch test taken to determine what I am hypersensitive to, it wastes time and resources." "There is no shared information among the hospitals. It cannot help the care providers to communicate to each other." This causes overlap check-ups for the healthcare recipients, which is a waste of time and resources. Besides the above two quotes, some respondents also point out that the location of the healthcare center is far away from their home, and that it is inconvenient for them to go to healthcare centers frequently.

Views of Online Healthcare Community.   When asked about the time spent on Internet per day, 60 % of the respondents spend more than 6 h on-line, see Fig. 2, which means Internet has already become an essential part of their daily lives. Because of the high rate of Internet usage, the online healthcare community is acceptable. All the respondents say they would like to have an online healthcare community, where they could chat with all stakeholders related to their healthcare through one platform.

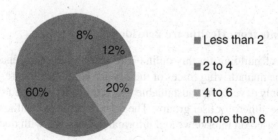

Fig. 2. Hours spent on Internet per day

The answers concerning which people they want to chat with through the online community show the following: doctors (96 %), other healthcare providers (84 %), other people with same symptoms (72 %), family members (68 %) and some healthcare research institutions (64 %).

Online Community Functions Design. In Questions 5 to 8, we ask about some specific functions of the online healthcare community. The results are shown in Fig. 3. From the figure, we can see that all functions we plan to develop are supported by most of the respondents. Question 10 is an open question about other functions they would like to have. Online simple diagnose was one of the most desirable functions. Free seminars and lectures about healthcare is another suggestion by most of the respondents. "Simple medical suggestions and brief medical diagnosis", "Diagnosis, chatting, forum, online seminar" "diagnosis online" and "Healthcare lecture" were mentioned most. In addition, fast contact and response, risk prediction, decision support systems and information about nearby healthcare centers were also suggested. In Question 9, the respondents were asked which features are important for them as the users of online community. Availability (100 %), usability (88 %), security (88 %) and privacy (84 %) all got very high support.

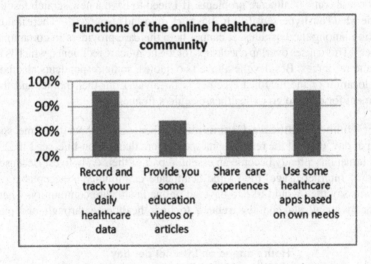

Fig. 3. Functions of the online healthcare community

3.2 Requirements from Healthcare Providers

One of the aims of building up this online care community is to encourage the care recipients to be the main driving forces of their home-based healthcare. Still, the virtual community will only develop in a sustainable way if the tools provided support and meet the needs of all the aimed-for user groups. The requirements of healthcare providers are gathered mainly based on interviews and informal discussions with doctors, nurses and homecare providers.

In the current Swedish healthcare system, most nurses are working daily with 5 to 10 different IT systems, and only a few of these systems share data with each other. Sometimes they just record the same simple data repetitively in different systems due to this lack of compatibility between systems, which is perceived as a waste of time and in some way decreases the work enthusiasm. There is a national electronic service called National Patient Overview (Nationell Patientöversikt - NPÖ), which enables healthcare providers to share patient healthcare records with other healthcare providers through computer networks. The purposes of NPÖ are to facilitate cooperation among different healthcare providers in Sweden, as well as giving healthcare recipients access to their own healthcare information [10]. NPÖ assists cooperation among different healthcare providers at the national level. However, it is predominantly a solution for hospital-based healthcare, as the direct beneficiary of this service is the healthcare providers. Even for the healthcare providers, only doctors have full access to the records. When shifting to home-based chronic disease care, NPÖ can provide few access rights for healthcare recipients. Also, as home-based healthcare involves other parties like family members and other patients with the same symptoms, how to share data with these parties is another challenge. In addition, NPÖ is only used for sharing healthcare information in Sweden; when people go abroad, it is quite difficult for them to access their healthcare data. In Europe, there are some projects aims to provide cross-border eHealth services by exchange patients' summaries between healthcare institutions such as epSOS [11], however, most of them are still in the test phases.

The basic way of communicating with care recipients now is still face-to-face. The emergence of the national digital healthcare portal 1177 [12] helps most healthcare recipients to communicate with their providers without face-to-face visiting, but there are still several issues it cannot cover. For example, it cannot provide medical suggestions because of different care duties, and communication is lagging in some cases due to technical reasons and wrong contact responsible line. Through the minavårdkontakter contact provided by 1177, care recipients can send some message to their providers, but the average response time is around 5 days. And from the care providers' view, a telephone call is better than sending an online message or email, because it is difficult to understand the text written by the care recipients.

For the management of chronic diseases such as diabetes, the normal way now is that the healthcare recipients go to the hospital, and are checked and given advice by nurses first. The nurses will teach the patients how to self-record every day's blood sugar values. Then when the patients go back home, they record the data as instructed and send their values via SMS to the nurse. There is an IT management system in hospitals for the nurses, but it does not share any information to neither other care providers nor care recipients.

4 Main Functional Requirements

In this section, we list the simple functional requirements of the online virtual community as documented through our questionnaires. Table 1 is the requirements list of the online community design. The traditional way of documenting requirements consists of contract style requirement lists [13]. This provides a high level requirements description for a large system. However such requirements descriptions usually cover hundreds of pages and are not reader-friendly. For our community design, we use the user stories style to describe the functional requirements in order to support easy and comprehensive understanding and quick changes. A user story is used with agile software development methodologies. It contains one or more sentences in everyday language to describe what an end user wants to do or needs as part of the functions [14].

Table 1. Requirements list

User types	Descriptions
All users	As a user, I want to register an account on the online healthcare community and choose my user type based on different roles
	As a user, when I log in to my account, the information page will be displayed automatically according to my user type
	As a user, I want to have an online chat with my contact persons such as care providers, care recipients, family members and so on
	As a user, I want to have alarms to remind me of my care activities
	As a user, I want to have the all contract persons' address book with detailed contact information
	As a user, I want to share some useful healthcare information with my contact persons
Care recipients	As a care recipient, I want to contact my care providers directly through the online community for simple diagnose and care suggestions
	As a care recipient, I want to have some videos for providing healthcare education
	As a care recipient, I want to record my daily health data myself in the community and share it with people whom I want to share with
	As a care recipient, I want to have some tools to trace and check my care data, as well as to print it out when necessary
	As a care recipient, I want to share my care experiences with people who have the same symptoms as I do
	As a care recipient, I want to book a doctor's appointment online
	As a care recipient, I want to integrate some healthcare relevant apps in the community based on my individual needs
	As a care recipient, I want to have the address and open hours information of the nearest healthcare centers
Care providers	As a care provider, I want to share some care information with other providers
	As a care provider, I want to have some online seminars with other providers and my care recipients
	As a care provider, I want to update the care histories of my recipients to the online community
	As a care provider, I want to have some decision support systems to help me for providing diagnoses and treatments
	As a care provider, I want to have a list of every day's work

5   Non-functional Requirement Issues

A non-functional requirement is a requirement used to measure the operation of a system, rather than specific behaviors [15]. In software systems, non-functional requirements are also considered as quality attributes. For our community design, usability, security and privacy, as well as availability are main issues of non-functional requirements [16].

Usability: Usability is defined as "the extent to which a product can be used by specified users to achieve specified goals with effectiveness, efficiency, and satisfaction in a specified context of use." [17]. According to [18] usability can be measured by five variables which are defined as learnability, efficiency, memorability, errors, and users' satisfaction. The main users of this online community are elderly people with chronic diseases, thus the designed services in the virtual community should be extremely simple to use and easy to learn. As design guidelines, we follow the "Ten usability heuristics [19]", especially principles about knowing the users' needs, special visibility for elderly, consistency with elderly's daily language, and helping them recognize previous experience (reducing recall problem for elderly).

Privacy: The patient health information includes personal information, details of medical history, symptoms, treatments, associated diseases or even the family health history. It is important to ensure that only the patients can authorize exactly who can view the shared health information and for what purposes [20]. All the information generated by a patient is not at the same sensitive level. Data segmentation may provide a method to protect specific sections of health information while giving choices to patients, and abiding requirements of legislation. Technical considerations and definition of sensitive information have to be addressed when segmenting data [21].

Security: Security is assurance that only authorized persons or entities can gain access to patients' data. Employees' illegitimate access and theft is one of the most frequent reasons of data leakage [20], as well as innocent disclosure because of system problems. Another issue is unauthorized access and malicious attacks from outside. So the encryption, identification and access control of patient health data are not optional for the online community development [20].

Availability: As an online healthcare community, being available 24/7 is very important, because some functions, such as monitoring, tracking, alarming are critical for users' lives. Availability means also that the authorized users should be able to access the community from anywhere. More and more people, even elderly with chronic diseases are traveling worldwide, and the healthcare community must be mobile in the sense that it must allow them access from anywhere in the world, just like when they are in their own home.

6   Prototype Design

With the requirements specified above, we will demonstrate a simple prototype in the following. We adopt a horizontal prototyping strategy, which means that the prototype should cover most parts of the required users' functions, without implementation of details [22]. Since it is a user-centered online community prototype, we try to keep it simple to use and easy to learn. The home page of the community is shown in Fig. 4, which is a very simple site for sign-up and sign-in with some guidance. In our prototype, the roles of users are divided into three types: healthcare recipient, healthcare provider and others like family members and researchers. The user type is selected by the users when they register in the system. After successfully registering, the information related to the role in the community will be displayed based on the user types. The role of the users decides the information and activities they can have access to in the online community.

Fig. 4. Home page of the community

When the user has finished registration and logged in to his or her account using a user name and password, the system will automatically direct the user to his or her sites according to the specified user role. As shown in Fig. 5, Anna Nilsson is a healthcare recipient, and the profile site has her basic information and the information relevant to her, such as her healthcare community, tools and rules that apply to her in her role. The contacts list in the middle has detailed information about all her care providers and other people relevant to her healthcare. In the right-bottom part, she can note her main symptoms so that people who have the same conditions can easily find her and they can share care experiences with each other. Figure 6 is the profile page of a healthcare provider, Maria Karlsson; similar to the recipient's page, it contains her basic information and contacts list. In the right-bottom part, the tasks she has to do today are listed as a reminder.

Fig. 5. Healthcare recipients' profile

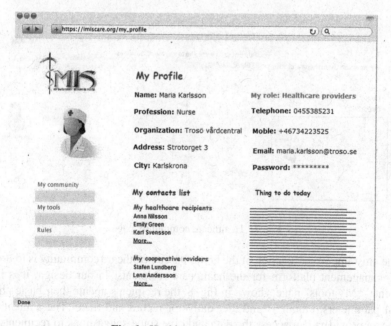

Fig. 6. Healthcare provider profile

The page "my community" is designed based on the needs of the respondents who answered the questionnaires see Fig. 7. All the contact persons are listed in the right, including healthcare providers, family members and others. They can chat with each other when they are online, so the healthcare recipients can get feedback immediately from the healthcare providers without physically having to visit any healthcare organizations. The community also provides a space for users to post discussions, videos, links to websites etc. to share with their contacts. Another important function is that the community will always show information about the nearest healthcare centers based on the gathered user geographical data. The scheduled care activities will be shown rolling in red to remind the recipients.

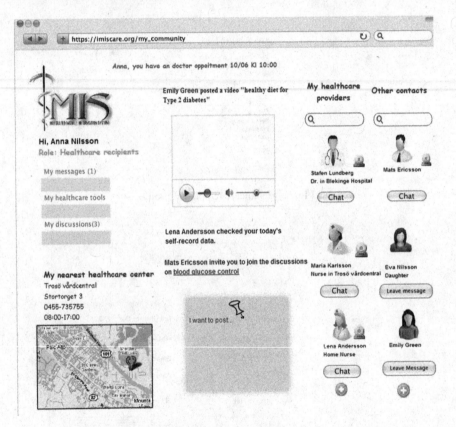

Fig. 7. Healthcare community page

The most important function of the home-based healthcare community is to provide a self-management platform for the healthcare recipients. In our design, it is in the recipients' "My tools" page, shown in Fig. 8, the recipients update their basic physiological parameters, emotions and diet daily for record and trace. The authenticated healthcare providers can access the data and give some suggestions to recipients. The recipient can print out this data covering a long period as well to show the doctors and other care providers when they have an appointment. Online appointments are also proposed to reduce the waiting time for meeting doctors. In addition, personalized tools are introduced to the users so that they can use them based on their own needs. The healthcare providers' tools page includes functions for updating care history, appointment reminders, decision support systems for diagnoses and treatments and so on.

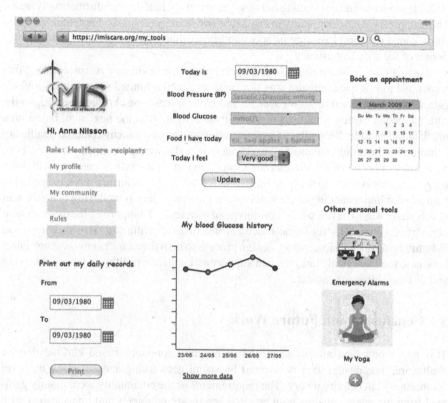

Fig. 8. Healthcare recipients' tool page

7   Discussion and Limitation

The above prototype presents a general view of the design for a virtual community for home-based healthcare of chronic diseases. The design aimed to integrate healthcare recipients, healthcare providers and other relevant stakeholders into one community. This virtual community makes it possible to share the same platform for all the stakeholders who are engaged in the healthcare activity. With this shared community platform, the interoperability problems of current healthcare systems can be moderated. There exist various ways of applying ICT in eHealth, for example cloud computing. Cloud computing is beginning to demonstrate its great potentials in our daily healthcare due to its powerful services in managing big data, accessibility, flexibility, scalability and cost-effectiveness for services. Cloud technology mitigates the need to invest in

IT infrastructure, by providing access to hardware, computing resources, applications, and services on a 'per use' model. And thus it dramatically brings down the cost and eases the adoption of technology. Besides, there are lots of existing privacy control mechanisms and security techniques in cloud computing which could help sensitive healthcare data protection. This will lead to radical new circumstances for offering eHealth services and constructing our new generation of healthcare information systems. The proposed virtual community in this paper will in the next step be implemented based on the cloud platform to ensure its accessibility, availability, and mobility, with careful design of security and privacy.

There are some limitations of this paper. Firstly, the healthcare recipient group that responded to our questionnaire was not large, due to the limited scope of our investigation and our restrictive rules (over 55 and have at least one chronic disease), so the care recipients' needs would require further investigation in the next step, based on a much larger sample. Secondly, as we are aiming to design a patient-centered healthcare community, the requirements of care providers would also require further investigation. In this case, they were gathered through interviews and informal discussions with only a few respondents, due to the time limitation for the study, so further work is needed to gain a better understanding of the needs of the care providers as well. However, the aim of this study was to develop a first prototype of a system for supporting the development of a virtual community for home-based chronic disease healthcare. This prototype can in future be used in a participatory design process to help future users envision and enact how new technological solutions can support and enhance healthy independent living and disease self-management.

8   Conclusion and Future Work

This paper proposed an online virtual community for home-based chronic disease healthcare. The design idea is inspired by social networking and based on the term "community" in activity theory. The requirements of the community were mainly gathered from the questionnaires with targeted healthcare recipients and interviewers with healthcare providers. We use "user stories" as they are used in agile software development to describe the requirements, and finally a prototype is designed based on the identified user requirements.

In the future, we will demonstrate this prototype to the potential users for evaluation. Further, more extensive interviews and surveys will be conducted with both healthcare recipients and healthcare providers to get more in-depth requirements from their respective perspectives. After this, we will develop the tools for supporting an online community based on cloud technology and test the proposed solution with future users for continued improvement and redesign. Ideally, such tools should be continuously further designed in use, together with the users, as part of quality lifecycle product and service management as well as part of the development of quality healthcare provision and self-management.

References

1. WHO | Chronic diseases and health promotion. http://www.who.int/chp/en/
2. What is Chronic Disease? | Center for Managing Chronic Disease - Putting People at the Center of Solutions. http://cmcd.sph.umich.edu/what-is-chronic-disease.html
3. Lin, C.-C., Lee, R.-G., Hsiao, C.-C.: A pervasive health monitoring service system based on ubiquitous network technology. Int. J. Med. Inf. **77**, 461–469 (2008)
4. Chen, C.-M.: Web-based remote human pulse monitoring system with intelligent data analysis for home health care. Expert Syst. Appl. **38**, 2011–2019 (2011)
5. Zimmer-Tamakoshi, L.: Sustainable communities, sustainable development: other paths for Papua New Guinea. Pac. Aff. **86**, 962–965 (2013)
6. Engeström, Y.: Learning by Expanding: An Activity-Theoretical Approach to Developmental Research. Orienta-Konsultit Oy, Helsinki (1987)
7. Bai, G., Guo, Y.: A general architecture for developing a sustainable elderly care e-health system. In: 2011 8th International Conference on Service Systems and Service Management (ICSSSM), pp. 1–6 (2011)
8. HealthVault. https://www.healthvault.com/se/en
9. Rogers, Y., Sharp, H., Preece, J.: Interaction Design: Beyond Human - Computer Interaction. Wiley, Hoboken (2011)
10. Patientjournalen – 1177 Vårdguiden - sjukdomar, undersökningar, hitta vård, e-tjänster. http://www.1177.se/Blekinge/Regler-och-rattigheter/Patientjournalen/#section-3
11. epSOS: About epSOS. http://www.epsos.eu/home/about-epsos.html
12. 1177 Vårdguiden - sjukdomar, undersökningar, hitta vård, e-tjänster. http://www.1177.se/Blekinge/
13. Berenbach, B., Paulish, D., Kazmeier, J., Rudorfer, A.: Software & Systems Requirements Engineering: In Practice. McGraw-Hill Osborne Media, New York (2009)
14. Guide to Agile Practices. http://guide.agilealliance.org/guide/user-stories.html
15. Glinz, M.: On Non-functional requirements. In: 15th IEEE International Requirements Engineering Conference, RE 2007, pp. 21–26 (2007)
16. Chung, Lawrence, do Prado Leite, Julio Cesar Sampaio: On non-functional requirements in software engineering. In: Borgida, Alexander T., Chaudhri, Vinay K., Giorgini, Paolo, Yu, Eric S. (eds.) Conceptual Modeling: Foundations and Applications. LNCS, vol. 5600, pp. 363–379. Springer, Heidelberg (2009)
17. ISO 9241-1:1992 - Ergonomic requirements for office work with visual display terminals (VDTs) – Part 1: General introduction. http://www.iso.org/iso/iso_catalogue/catalogue_ics/catalogue_detail_ics.htm?csnumber=16873
18. Nielsen, J.: Chap. 1 – What Is Usability? In: User Experience Re-Mastered, pp. 3–22 (2010)
19. Nielsen, J.: Ten usability heuristics (2005). Ten Usability Heuristics
20. Braunstein, M.L.: Health informatics in the cloud. Springer, New York (2012)
21. Goldstein, M.M., Rein, A.L., Heesters, M.M., Hughes, P.P., Williams, B., Weinstein, S.A.: Data segmentation in electronic health information exchange: Policy considerations and analysis (2010). Data Segmentation Electron. Health Inf. Exch. Policy Consid. Anal.
22. Narlikar, G.J., Blelloch, G.E.: Space-efficient scheduling of nested parallelism. ACM Trans. Program. Lang. Syst. **21**, 138–173 (2002)

Author Index